Strategy and Capability

Strategy and Capability
Sustaining Organizational Change

Graeme Salaman and David Asch

Blackwell
Publishing

350 Main Street, Malden, MA 02148-5018, USA
108 Cowley Road, Oxford OX4 1JF, UK
550 Swanston Street, Carlton South, Melbourne, Victoria 3053, Australia
Kurfürstendamm 57, 10707 Berlin, Germany

First published 2003 by Blackwell Publishing Ltd

Library of Congress Cataloging-in-Publication Data

Salaman, Graeme.
   Strategy and capability : sustaining organizational change / Graeme Salaman and David Asch.
      p. cm.—(Management, organizations, and business series)
   Includes bibliographical references and index.
   ISBN 0–631–22845–4 (hbk : alk. paper)—ISBN 0–631–22846–2 (pbk : alk. paper)
   1. Organizational change.   2. Strategic planning.   3. Organizational effectiveness.
   I. Asch, David, 1948–   II. Title.   III. Series.
   HD58.8 .S253 2003
   658.1′6—dc21

                                                                        2002010323

A catalogue record for this title is available from the British Library.

Set in 10 on 12.5 pt Palatino
by SNP Best-set Typesetter Ltd., Hong Kong
Printed and bound in the United Kingdom
by TJ International, Padstow, Cornwall

For further information on
Blackwell Publishing, visit our website:
http://www.blackwellpublishing.com

We shall not cease from exploration
And the end of all our exploring
Will be to arrive where we started
And know the place for the first time.
T. S. Eliot, *Four Quartets*

To the memory of a fellow student, colleague, co-author and loved friend,

Gavin McKenzie
1942–2001

Contents

Acknowledgements   viii
List of Figures and Tables   x
About the Authors   xi
Introduction   xiii

1 How Organizations are Changing and Why   1
2 The Model: Five Ways to Improve Organizational Performance   23
3 'Fit': Fitting Organizational Structures to Business Strategy   34
4 The Resource-Based View of Strategy   65
5 Formulating Strategy   92
6 Developing Strategy   126
7 The Adaptive Organization   149
8 Summary and Conclusion   183

References   186
Index   197

Acknowledgements

P. G. Wodehouse dedicated one of his funniest books to his beloved step-daughter Leonora, 'Without whose never-failing sympathy and encouragement', he wrote, 'this book would have been finished in half the time.' We find ourselves in similar circumstances. Without the sympathy and help of a number of people, listed below, this book too would have probably have been completed in half the time. And it would have been half as good. The suggestions, criticisms, questions, contributions of many people in many organizations over many years have delayed us, and have caused us to stop and reconsider and clarify and so to improve our argument.

This book is based on a series of workshops and seminars run by the authors separately or together over a number of years for a number of groups of managers and HR professionals in companies such as Sun Microsystems, Morgan Stanley, Pakistan Tobacco Company, Willis, Allianz Cornhill, BAT, Rolls Royce and Ernst & Young. Managers in those businesses have contributed to the ideas in the book in ways they probably did not realize or sometimes even intend. But they helped and we are grateful to them.

Friends in the government of Ethiopia – Seeye Abraha, Meles Zenawi, Teklewoini Asefa, Abadi Zeno, Arkebe Uqbuy, Tefera Waluwa and many others – not only taught us much about strategy and capability (which we were meant to teach them) but also taught us far more important lessons about the importance of loyalty, commitment and courage.

A number of colleagues and friends are of particular importance – and deserving of specific gratitude. Toby Hoskins is a staunch ally and a source of acute insights into his business and our analyses; Mike Mister is familiar with the approach of the book and has contributed to it; Graham Mole, whose commitment to the role and value of management learning is never failing even under trying circumstances, has offered analyses of his organization which are a constant source of understanding and humour; Maurice Dunster's attempts to assist his organization to design and manage change have been a source of inspiration (for it is one thing to write about organizational change, another thing to try to achieve it); Jim Butler has never ceased to try to understand the sources of organizational irrationalities, and to battle against them; Christopher Cook combines elegance of analysis with clarity of insight; with Michael Sargeant and Rosemary Arnot we have spent much time speculating happily about the complexities of organizations in general and specifically in Ethiopia, and Roger Plant has stood shoulder to shoulder with one of the authors when it mattered.

The book also builds on work on courses and collaborations in the Open University Business School. Academic colleagues, members of the Strategy and Human Resource Management course teams have contributed to the book, again probably without knowing it. John Storey at the Open Business School has been and remains a stimulating and delightful colleague and supportive friend. Paul du Gay is an exciting and energizing colleague and friend whose work with one of the authors informs much of this work. Students on the Open University Business School MBA courses Managing Human Resources and Strategic Management have also contributed to this book. Trying to get the world of Strategy and HRM clear for them helped to get it clear for us: to teach is to learn.

Colleagues outside the Open University have been a source of ideas, stimulation, support and reflection: Chris Argyris, Maurice Saias and Cliff Bowman, colleagues on seminars on organizational and management learning, and Andrew Pettigrew and Richard Whipp, associates on courses on strategy and capability. Karen Legge has been a loyal friend and unfailing source of inspiration and support over many years and in many contexts.

Cathy Playle has been an unflagging, resourceful, patient source of support with the practicalities of the book. Tricia Tierney showed her usual skill and ingenuity in managing the completion of the project. Rosemary Nixon, a friend for many years, has supported this venture from its early tentative beginnings with enthusiasm, patience, understanding and wonderful lunches: the perfect publisher.

The epigraph on page v is reproduced from *Collected Poems 1909–1962* by T.S. Eliot, published by Faber and Faber Ltd and Harcourt Brace. The epigraph to chapter 7 (p. 149) is reproduced from *Austerlitz* by W.G. Sebald, translated by Anthea Bell and published by Random House.

List of Figures and Tables

Figures

1.1	Types of restructuring within organizational boundaries	4
4.1	A resource-based approach to strategy analysis	81
4.2	Factors influencing a manager when defining strengths and weaknesses	82
6.1	Porter's generic strategies	133
6.2	Growth share matrix	143
7.1	The learning company profile	158
7.2	Moral foundations and their connections with characteristics of learning organizations	160

Tables

3.1	Critical human resource activities at different organizational or business unit stages	46
3.2	Schuler and Jackson's model of employee role behaviour and HRM policies associated with particular business strategies	48
3.3	Miles and Snow's model of business strategies and HRM systems	50
4.1	Views of resources and competences	68
4.2	Hierarchies or markets?	79
5.1	Specification of the groupthink model	107
5.2	Selected heuristics and biases	113

About the Authors

Graeme Salaman is Professor of Organization Studies, Director of Programmes and Curriculum and Director of the Business Studies programme, at the Open University Business School.

Having graduated from the University of Leicester with a first-class degree in Social Sciences he took a Ph.D. in Organizational Sociology from the University of Cambridge. After two years at the Institute of Industrial Psychology he joined the Open University. He has also taught courses at the University of Cambridge.

His current academic specialisms are the management of innovation, the management of change, management competences, strategic human resource management and performance management. He has chaired or contributed many courses in the Social Science Faculty in Industrial and Organizational Sociology and in the Business School, including courses in the BABS and MBA programmes in business strategy, decision-making, and strategic human resource management.

He has written over 60 books and articles in his areas of research interest. His most recent publications include *Strategic Human Resource Management* (Blackwell, 1996), *Organizations* (2000), *Decision-Making* (2001) and *Improving Organizational Performance* (Blackwell, 2002). He is currently working (with John Storey) on a book on the *Management of Innovation*. His most recent articles have been a critique of the Learning Organization thesis in *Human Relations* and an analysis of the Management of Innovation in the *Journal of Management Studies*, both in 2002. He edits a series entitled 'Managing Work and Organization' for the Open University Press.

He has worked as a consultant for a number of organizations. Current or recent clients include Allianz Cornhill, Willis, the John Lewis Partnership, Ernst & Young, Sun Microsystems, British Oxygen, PowerGen, Morgan Stanley, Rolls Royce, and the Post Office. He has worked for a number of years as a consultant to the government of Ethiopia. He is currently working for the prime minister's office on issues of governance and management in a major development organization, and is chairing a team restructuring the Ministry of Foreign Affairs.

His areas of consultancy and training include the management of change, the management of performance, improving strategy and organizational capability, decision-making and problem-solving. He has considerable experience, recent and current, of working with senior teams to identify and resolve issues of individual, team and corporate performance.

David Asch M.Sc., FCA, FRSA is Pro-Vice Chancellor (Strategic Planning and Resources) and Professor of Management at De Montfort University, Leicester. He has written over 50 books and articles on strategy, competition and change, including *Managing Strategy* (1996) and *New Economy – New Competition* (2001). His recent research centres on an industry-funded project examining the drivers for competition and globalization across a range of industries, including domestic appliances, electrical products, professional service firms and telecoms.

He has worked with the senior teams of a range of firms including Allianz Cornhill, Ernst & Young, Fujitsu/ICL, 3M, Rank Xerox, Siemens Computer Systems, and Sun Microsystems. In addition, he was an adviser to the Office of Fair Trading on competition policy and to the federal government of Ethiopia. He was also an adviser to the World Bank on designing technology-based distance learning in developing countries. Prior to his academic career he worked for a merchant bank and an international firm of management consultants.

Introduction

This book is the culmination and expression of many years of research and enquiry into how organizations are changing, how they should change and how various experts and advocates recommend that they should change, and the quality of that advice. It arose out of a concern to make sense of the plethora of prescription and advice which surrounds and risks swamping the modern manager. It became important in the face of the apparent confusion of much of that material. It became urgent in the face of the increasing stridency and forcefulness of much of the advice that besets managers.

Our subject is organizations, and what's happening in organizations; our role is to question and to clarify. How is the manager – or indeed the student – to find a path through the complex, contested, chaotic terrain of advice and thinking on organizations? They will need a map. We offer it.

This book seeks to address the deceptive simplicity and attractive but misleading certainty of much of the advice offered to the modern manager. We recognize that managers want answers to the problems they face and we recognize that much academic writing, however well-intentioned, and indeed valid and to the point, does not help them, at least initially, being more concerned with critique than construction.

Of course critique is essential; if proposals are ill-based, poorly researched, based on clearly invalid assumptions, this must be noted. It is the duty of academics to warn; to state these uncomfortable truths, not to join the piles of airport bookstall hucksters. But managers still need help. After critique, what? It is good to show weaknesses; but it is not enough. We remain convinced that the way for managers to find answers is for them not to look for answers, but to identify problems, including the problems in solutions, and the ability to understand and evaluate the offerings and recommendations of consultants is a critically important attribute. When reality is complex, simplicity seems attractive, and is for this reason doubly dangerous. This book, we hope, will help develop the ability to assess and evaluate, not only by offering a route map through the different prescriptions on offer, mapping, locating and assessing them, but also by helping our readers identify the snares and pitfalls of those siren voices which would entice them from these paths.

Much of the advice and prescription is associated with or part of the body of ideas, recommendations and analysis which is now known as Strategic Human Resource Management (SHRM). SHRM, in bringing two subjects – strategy and HRM – together, can be seen as an exciting new area of academic and practitioner activity; it can be seen as a worthy attempt to combine the scepticism and rigour of the academics with the down-to-earthness of the practitioner or HR professional. Or it can be seen as a bit of a mess with a number of distinctive, discrete and different, if not opposed, ideas and frameworks and types of knowledge coexisting uneasily and unhappily together.

If SHRM means anything useful or important, it is about ways in which the performance of a business or organization can be improved. But what does this mean – to improve the performance of an organization? It means in essence that the organization becomes better at developing and achieving *a* strategy. It means better strategies and better organizational capability to deliver the strategic objectives. That's obvious and quite simple, although of course difficult to achieve in practice.

And this is what this book is about. It shows that, at its best, SHRM consists of five different ways of improving the performance of an organization.

Chapter 1 sets the scene. It identifies and addresses some of the key changes currently occurring within organizations and isolates some of the key features of these changes – features which are then discussed throughout the book.

Chapter 2 presents the broad features of each of the five different approaches to improving organizational performance. It is a summary of the argument of the book as a whole.

Chapter 3 presents and discusses two approaches: the open (or 'fit') approach and the closed or absolute approach. Both argue the merits of making organizational changes to support strategies: one argues in favour of identifying the specific and different organizational requirements of different strategies; the other asserts the importance and benefit of a number of organizational measures in any strategic context.

Chapter 4 presents the resource-based approach, which essentially reverses the logic of the 'fit' approach. Whereas 'fit' argues for adjusting the organization to suit a new strategy which is based on analysis of developments in the organization's environment, the resource-based view argues for building a strategy around the basic strengths of the organization.

Chapter 5 analyses the ways in which features of an organization – its structure, cultures, systems, etc. – can have consequences for the ways in which strategy is developed. One way of improving organizational performance, then, is to reduce the scale and impact of such factors and thus to improve the ability of the organization to formulate intelligent and creative strategy.

Chapter 6 looks at the strategic options available to organizations and addresses some of the complexities and uncertainties of the notion of strategy itself. All too often strategy is seen as a rational, systematic, top-down management process which is straightforward and unproblematic. Anyone with any knowledge of organizations knows this is a dream: an attractive dream possibly, but nevertheless unrealistic.

Chapter 7 addresses the final approach to improving organizational effectiveness, and a popular and frequent element in SHRM writing: the learning organization or the adaptive organization. This too may be a dream, but it is influential and attractive since it seems to offer the possibility of an organization that is free of some of the consequences of the basic features of organization. It is a non-organizational, or even anti-organizational, organization.

Chapter 8 offers a summary and conclusion to the argument.

1

How Organizations are Changing and Why

INTRODUCTION

Modern managers are beset by two pressing, urgent and intractable problems. On the one hand life is becoming increasingly difficult: they face increasingly dynamic, complex and unpredictable environments where technology, the nature of competition, industry boundaries and the rules of the game are changing dramatically. On the other hand they are faced by an avalanche of advice and prescription about how to develop competitive strategies, how to change, how to improve efficiency, how to adopt strategic human resource practices such as business process re-engineering (BPR), downsizing, delayering, competence architectures, 360-degree feedback and many others. And at the same time business schools supply courses – and academics supply texts and consultants write management best-sellers – which set out how to manage strategically, how to design and manage change, how to design strategic HR practices, how to improve capability. But the harsh reality is that, despite all this advice, despite (maybe because of) the plethora of prescription, exhortation and critique of prescription, the end result of all this help is often confusion. Managers don't know who to listen to. This book aims to clarify this confusion, to make sense of this advice.

Firms have choices to make if they are to survive. Those which are strategic include: the selection of goals, the choice of products and services to offer; the design and configuration of policies determining how the firm positions itself to compete in product-markets (e.g. competitive strategy); the choice of an appropriate level of scope and diversity; and the design of organisation structure, administrative systems and policies used to define and co-ordinate work. (Rumelt, Schendel and Teece 1991: 6)

And making the right choices is difficult. Not because there are not suggestions on offer; not because help is not at hand. There is an enormous amount of advice available; there are precedents to follow – or avoid. There is change everywhere, advice everywhere, exhortation, insistence, promises, everywhere. There is too much help, too much advice. The problem is choosing which advice to follow, how to understand and assess this advice. This is the world of the modern manager, and it is this world of advice and exhortation that we are going to clarify, classify and review.

This chapter looks at some of the more important types of fundamental change that have been occurring recently in organizations. We do this for a number of reasons. First, because if we are to offer our own framework for understanding or designing attempts to improve organizational performance it is useful and relevant to be aware of the nature and scope of some of the more important and pervasive change projects which claim this objective. But in this introductory chapter we have another objective: to use our analysis of common forms of organizational change to unearth some common features and assumptions of such programmes – features and assumptions which frequently characterize change projects but which should ideally be treated critically and with reservations. Our concern is primarily with the ideas underpinning these projects, and their weaknesses; but we also need to show how these ideas matter, how they affect organizational structures and functioning, people's jobs, job security, careers. We shall not attempt a comprehensive coverage of all recent types of organizational change. That is not our purpose in this book; nor is it necessary for our purposes. What we will do is consider a few examples of change in order to indicate some of the key issues and contradictions that surround them and which supply the backdrop to our argument.

Recent years have seen an enormous increase in the scope and velocity of change, affecting nearly every aspect of organizations. In the early 1990s Kanter's study of 12,000 managers from 25 countries revealed widespread experience of downsizing, reorganization, mergers, acquisitions and divestitures (Kanter 1991). Change has become normal and inevitable. A recent study shows that managers are expecting more far-reaching organizational change – nearly 80 per cent of respondents said they expected more radical change by 2010. A UK study in the mid-1990s showed that 70 per cent of private and public sector managers reported that their organization had recently restructured (Thompson and Warhurst 1998: 17).

▶ Changing Structures

One of the most important and pervasive types of recent organizational change is structural change. This is popular and highly pervasive. This is change which alters the 'shape' of the organization, the number of levels of management, the nature and number of jobs, or the principles by which organizations are structured (region, product, function, client group, or some combination of two or more of these):

> Organisations in recent years have sought to enhance business and customer-oriented behaviours and priorities through the creation of Strategic Business Units (SBUs). They have sought to induce flexibility through cross-functional teams. Cost competitiveness has been pursued through slimmed corporate centres, the cutting away of 'overhead' and a cut back in service functions by requiring production units to embrace a much wider range of functions and responsibilities. (Mabey, Salaman and Storey 1998: 232)

Note how this quotation identifies some of the apparent or intended goals of these forms of restructuring – 'business and customer-oriented behaviours and priorities', 'flexibility', 'cost competitiveness'; we will return to these goals later.

Recent organizational restructuring has tended to follow a number of directions: for example, away from large organizations to smaller ones, from heavily bureaucratized systems to less rigid and rule-bound systems. Figure 1.1 suggests in general terms some of the directions of recent change. However, it is important not to be misled by this figure. It simply shows recent patterns of change. It does not indicate an inevitable and long-term historical linear progression from bottom left to top right. The direction it suggests is simply a recent tendency; it can be changed, and the pattern of organizational restructuring could well soon show a return to earlier patterns. In fact, this is beginning to happen: the recent move away from centralized control towards decentralization and autonomy is being reversed, with a move to 'shared services' and 'shared infrastructure' (to call it recentralization might be to risk public acknowledgement that decentralization was unsuccessful) as the costs and inefficiencies of decentralization of key services (HR, ICT, finance, etc.) become apparent. Organizational change is not linear; if it has any direction, it is very often cyclical. Many current forms of organizational change, although they are described as if they were the very latest in modern thinking, have been around before, often more than once and sometimes very long ago, although often under a different name.

As figure 1.1 suggests, one major recent direction of change has been away from bureaucratic forms. Bureaucracy is currently much maligned (although most large organizations still retain significant bureaucratic elements). The critique of bureaucracy focuses on the claimed inadequacies of control by regulation (rigidity, lack of responsiveness to client or particular prevailing

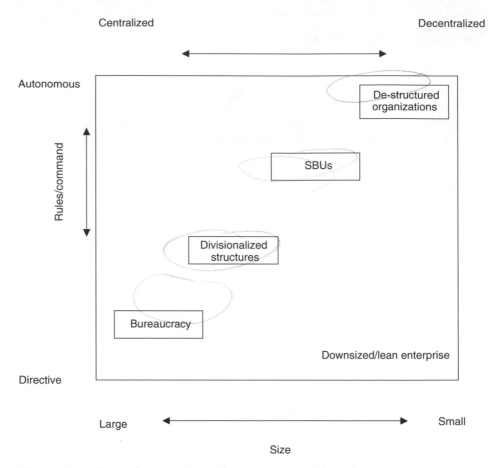

Figure 1.1 Types of restructuring within organizational boundaries
Source: Mabey et al. (1998: 235). Reproduced by permission of Blackwell Publishing Ltd.

circumstances, 'red tape', the discouragement of innovation or individuality). These charges are often well founded. However, the advantages of bureaucracy also need to be stressed. Bureaucracy encourages impersonality and discourages nepotism and arbitrary decision-making; it is highly efficient for the administration of large-scale complex but routine tasks.

The figure suggests another principle of current programmes of organizational change: the deliberate introduction, into the organization, of market-type relationships, structures and forces. Some 40 years ago Alfred Chandler, a well-known commentator on business matters, argued that the modern business enterprise of that time had replaced co-ordination by market mechanisms with co-ordination achieved through organization – by organizational structures, processes, functions and relationships. In other words, instead of buying services, the organization supplied them itself.

When he wrote, and for some time afterwards, Chandler was right; but now we are told he was wrong when he argued that, within the firm, the invisible hand of market forces was replaced by the firm hand of management (Chandler 1962). Now the hand of management is most obvious in its introduction of market forces, and organizational relationships are increasingly coterminous with, and difficult to distinguish from, managerially induced market forces.

Much recent and current organizational restructuring seeks to replace organization controls by market forces. This approach advocates the market as a purifying moral force, neutralizing the dysfunctionalities of bureaucracy: 'I urge every one of you to develop a passionate and public hatred of bureaucracy' (Peters 1989); 'Don't automate, obliterate!' (Hammer 1990).

The rigidity, impersonality and rule-focused nature of bureaucracy, it is argued, must be replaced by flexibility, passion, involvement. The new organization must be structured *for*, and most importantly *by*, the market. The best principles of organization are those that force it to respond to market forces.

The free market system is seen as providing the inherently virtuous model through which all internal organizational relationships should be restructured. Exposing the organization and its employees to the pressures of the market – and the sovereign consumer – is, however, a necessary but not a sufficient means of ensuring the radical and moral reconstruction ('reform') of the organization. It is also necessary for every member of the organization and every department and specialism to 'get close to the customer', to develop enterprise – not to rely on, or require, organizational rules, but to understand and be able and willing appropriately to respond to market requirements and customer demands. The internal world of the organization is restructured along market lines in order to ensure that the organization and its employees are focused on identifying and satisfying customers' needs.

Thus internal management hierarchical control is replaced by simulated or real market control: divisions, regions, hospitals, schools, become quasi-firms, and transactions between them become those between buyers and sellers. Corporations are decentralized into semi-autonomous, market-facing business units or profit centres required to achieve identified contribution targets. This policy is seen to remove obstructive and dysfunctional bureaucratic controls, liberate innate entrepreneurship and make local management sensitive to the need to meet market requirements in order to meet performance targets. A key element of this style of government is the crucial role it allocates to the notion of contract (or service-level) agreements in redefining social relationships. Entrepreneurial forms of government such as contractualization involve the re-imagination of the social (the organizational) as a form of the economic.

This form of organizational restructuring is not confined to private sector organizations. The defining feature of the new approach to organization and governance is that the enterprise form is generalized to all forms (public and private) and all areas of organization. Inefficiencies can only be removed by the application of a stiff dose of market forces. In such cases (the National Health Service (NHS), the UK railway system, etc.) the imposition or creation of markets and customers is either through direct privatization or, less directly, through competitive tendering, the introduction of surrogate markets, the manipulation of funding policy, service level agreements, benchmarking, and so on.

In the UK attempts to reform organizations in terms of market forces and relations have proceeded not only through the dominance of the discourse of the market and enterprise (still strongly maintained by the current Labour government) but also through legislation requiring public sector organizations to offer services to external competitive tendering, and through the progressive enlargement of the territory of the market – of the realm of private enterprises and market rationality.

Interestingly this insistence that organizations should be restructured in terms of markets and consumers in order to overcome the dysfunctionalities of bureaucracy not only often entails an enormous expansion of bureaucratic regulation in itself (the completion of paperwork by police, teachers, academics, doctors, etc., all of which is then reviewed by an inspection body or process) but is frequently the result of centralized and bureaucratic compulsion.

The application of market forces as principles of organizational restructuring does not stop with relations between organizational units and their marketplaces. It also applies internally through a variety of initiatives – for example just-in-time (JIT) or total quality management (TQM) systems, both of which require the redefinition of the relationship between units or workers in terms of a customer model: workers become each other's customers. Teamworking is built on the same mechanism.

Thus the customer – as agent of the market – enforces the necessary organizational, and crucially, personal, discipline. By changing the rules, organization and behaviour will change too: 'the focus on the outside, the external perspective, the attention to the customer is one of the tightest properties of all . . . It is perhaps the most stringent means of self-discipline. If one is really paying attention to what the customer is saying, being blown in the wind by the customers' demands, one may be sure he is sailing a tight ship' (Peters and Waterman 1982: 32). Or: 'Total customer responsiveness inaugurates a new form of control – self-control born of the involvement and ownership that follows . . . Being responsible for results will concentrate the mind more effectively' (Peters 1987: 363).

The moralized notion of the market – that is, the idea that, by introducing market forces and relationships, the organization, its processes, relationships and employees will be cleansed of their adherence to old-fashioned, rule-bound ways of behaviour and liberated to seek the interests of the customer – assumes semi-mystical qualities as a force which acts as a relay between organization, internal structures and processes and the individual, reconstituting the individual and the manager in terms of the qualities required for organizational success, and as individualized businesses. Firms, it is claimed, get the most out of their employees by harnessing the

> psychological strivings of individuals for autonomy and creativity and by chan-
> neling them into the search for customer satisfaction. Enterprising, market-
> focused customers make meaning for people by encouraging them to believe that
> they have control over their lives, that they have chosen to make a personal and
> vital contribution to personally shared organisational goals. Quite simply these
> companies are simultaneously externally focused and internally focused – exter-
> nally in that they are driven by the desire to provide service, quality and innov-
> ative problem-solving in support of their customers, internally in that quality
> control for example, is put on the back of the individual line worker, not primar-
> ily in the lap of the quality control department. (Peters and Waterman 1982: 321)

The application of the principles of the market to organizations occurs at a number of levels.

It affects where organizational boundaries are drawn and how they are conceptualized. Typically, boundaries are drawn more tightly. Activities are, whenever possible, located outside the organization: this transfers risk, in-vestment, costs, warehousing, logistics, etc. It also means that the organization can concentrate core skills. Nike, for example, the biggest supplier of trainers in the world, doesn't itself manufacture a single trainer.

The nature of the boundary – wherever it is – is also now seen differently. It is now the focus of intense activity and analysis. Supply-chain management as a new(ish) discipline is an example of this. The expansion of marketing, the emergence of the role of the account or client executive, the focus on client man-agement skills, BPR, the move to market-facing structures – all reveal attempts to address and manage the interface between organization and supplier or client.

Within the organization and between SBUs and other departments – or other SBUs – relationships and processes are increasingly designed *as if* they were contractual, buyer–seller relationships.

The recent critique of bureaucracy in the name of market forces and the associated qualities of flexibility, customer focus and enterprise reveals some contradictory themes which merit particular attention, and they are themes to which we will return in this analysis. The flight from bureaucracy and the rush towards market forces and relationships within organizations suggests that a major driver of organizational change may be as much fashion and prevailing ideology as rational analysis of the advantages and disadvantages of different principles of organization.

But fashionable ideas may not always be good ideas, and fashion-based enthusiasm may mask complexity and contradiction. For example, although in its day the move to decentralized SBUs was regarded as so obvious, so neces-sary as to be beyond debate – an act of faith, a testament to modernity in the face of stick-in-the-mud indefensible bureaucratic rigidity – in the fullness of time this approach to restructuring began to reveal its problems. Decentralized organizations, as one would expect, tend to lose across-the-board synergies; corporate benefits can be sacrificed to local business advantage, long-term strategies to short-term results, necessary investments to immediate harvesting. SBUs can breed 'silo' thinking, can reduce the possibility of knowledge management and transfer, and can produce other disbenefits.

Furthermore, despite the fact that, in recent years, the market has assumed considerable significance both as an ideological shibboleth and as a principle of organization (and government), bureaucracy still continues to be enormously significant: 'it has been frequently pointed out that throughout the world the largest organisations are essentially still bureaucracies. They remain so despite the competing ideas because they meet their goals through this type of structure' (Mabey et al. 1998: 238). So despite the popularity and acceptability of the critique of bureaucracy and the assumptions it carries, it seems there are definite limits of the practicality and value of these ideas. This too is a theme to which we will return.

Another issue raised by the recent history of bureaucracy and attempts to 'reform' it also concerns the limitations of the critique and the model that is offered as a superior basis for organization. The market model may seem attractive: flexible organizations focused not on rule-books but on client needs, with employees rewarded and promoted for performance, and the relationship between employer and employee being a market relationship: a performance, or client-focused, organization. But such types of organization, however apparently attractive and consistent with current thinking, may carry unexpected and unforeseen problems. One of the features of maligned bureaucracy was an emphasis on internal labour markets, with extensive and clear career ladders, explicit development and succession systems, with investment in training and development, and frequently welfare provision of some sort. These encouraged a certain sort of 'psychological contract' which may not have been explicitly performance-focused but which encouraged commitment, co-operation, and the development and sharing of knowledge and expertise. To the extent that the critique of bureaucracy has encouraged the destruction or erosion of this psychological contract, organizations may experience – and learn to regret – the passing of the characteristic consequences of this for employee attitudes and relationships, particularly when increasingly employee commitment and knowledge development and sharing are recognized as critical features of successful organizations.

Furthermore, although much organizational restructuring is justified in terms of a new model of organization, the reality of much organizational change is a familiar one. As noted earlier, 70 per cent of UK managers in the mid-1990s reported organizational restructuring. But they didn't report that this heralded in a new type of organization; on the contrary, they reported that their organizations had 'recently restructured with staff cutbacks and cost reduction initiatives, resulting in greater workloads, increased and often unpaid responsibilities, longer hours and less job security' (Thompson and Warhurst 1998: 17).

This third issue illustrates another theme of this book: that, however superficially appealing the 'theory' or ideas which underpin programmes of organizational change may seem, closer inspection reveals that they can have contradictory, or short-term, results. Indeed it is possible to argue that fashion or ideologically driven change which fails to identify and address the nature, origins and implications of organizational difficulties or which operates on a simplistic view of organizational structure and functioning can oversell its promises and exchange one set of problems for another. All the more reason to try to identify and understand the different bases on which claims to improve organizational performance can persuasively be made.

▶ Changing Processes

Another common form of recent and current organizational change focuses on the stages involved in the production of the key outputs of the organization: the ways in which the tasks and functions that are divided and differentiated by organizational structures must actually combine in sequences of operations or tasks, which must add value to what is particular to a customer. 'Organizational processes' refers to the activities that occur within an organization, in contrast to the location of these activities, which is structurally determined. A process is:

> a structured, measured set of activities designed to produce a specified output for a particular customer or market. It implies a strong emphasis on *how* work is done within an organization in contrast to a product's focus on *what*. A process is thus a specific ordering of work activities across time and place with a beginning, and end, and clearly identified inputs and outputs: a structure for action. (Davenport 1993: 5)

A process can extend through a number of organizational departments and across organizational boundaries. A number of management writers have recently advocated not only that organizations should focus less on structures and more on processes, but also on the transformation of these key business processes. This is what is called business process re-engineering (BPR).

The elements of BPR need not concern us here. They have been described by the original authors, Hammer and Champy (1993), Hammer (1996) and Davenport (1993). BPR, it is claimed, requires a 'fresh start'. It requires a total redesign of business processes, not the normal tinkering with historical processes: 'Don't automate, obliterate!' demands Hammer, one of the movement's champions, in a seminal and characteristic statement of the case.

Once again there are aspects of the BPR movement that are important to our concerns in this book. First, the BPR movement shares with other recent types of organizational change a remarkable popularity with senior management. It is calculated that as many of 70 per cent of UK companies have re-engineered (Mabey et al. 1998: 259). The appeal of BPR may well be due in some measure to the way the merits of this approach are described by its proponents. Their language is remarkable, often evangelical, messianic, or eschatological: BPR alone offers salvation, refusal to install BPR will signal the end of the organization, denial of the merits of BPR will bring down terrible punishment. Like a religion, acceptance of BPR is all or nothing: total conversion is demanded. Like a religion, it changes everything. The sinful past must be rejected: we – or our organizations – must be reborn; everything we thought we knew about organizations is now rejected; it's all wrong. Everything must be learned anew, everything changed, under the guidance of the BPR expert:

> everything must be rethought: the kinds of work people do, the jobs they hold, the skills they need, the ways in which their performance is measured and rewarded, the careers they follow, the roles managers play, the principles of strategy that enterprises follow. Process-centred organisations demand the complete reinvention of the systems and disciplines of management. (Hammer 1996: 259)

BPR is thus a good example of the difficulty facing the modern manager: not how to install BPR, but how to understand and assess the merits of the advice and exhortation with which they are bombarded. As usual the authors are not prepared to offer any dispassionate analysis of the strengths and weaknesses of their cause: they are convinced, their cause is unassailable, there is no alternative, they offer redemption and salvation. There is only one possible response from the manager: total and instant acceptance and commitment.

> In the face of intense competition and other business pressures on large organisations . . . Objectives of 5% or 10% improvement in all business processes each year must give way to efforts to achieve 50%, 100% or even higher improvement levels in a few key processes. Today firms must seek not fractional, but multiplicative levels of improvement – 10 x rather than 10%. (Davenport 1993: 1)

Yet the results of BPR are far less convincing than its proponents promised. And, as with other much-hyped modern organizational panaceas, BPR advocates are coy about its assumptions, particularly those that might be untenable or insecure. BPR adopts a highly formal approach to the organization. It assumes that there are no conflicts or sources of dissension or difference. Purposes are clear, and shared, staff are committed: the only source of difficulty is the possible survival of old-fashioned and obstructive organizational structures. But this approach assumes what is known as a unitary view of the firm – that is, that all members of the organization share, and are equally committed to, the same organizational values and goals, namely customer focus. Hammer admits that 'No matter how well designed a process is, it's the people who make it work' (Hammer 1996: 117). This admission is strangely redolent of the admission by Henry Ford decades ago at the beginning of the modern industrial period that 'Machines alone do not give us mass production. Mass production is achieved by both machines and men. And while we have gone a long way towards perfecting our mechanical operations, we have not successfully written into our equations whatever complex factors represent Man, the human element' (quoted in Littler and Salaman 1984: 91).

In other words, Hammer recognizes that the success of BPR depends on the solution to an age-old problem: how to manage employees so as simultaneously to achieve maximum efficiency and to attract their commitment.

Yet, although they acknowledge the significance of this issue for the success of BPR, not only do Hammer and BPR's other proponents have no solution to a problem on which the success of their approach depends, but the application of BPR, which is frequently associated with downsizing and the intensification of work effort, may very well exacerbate the problem by increasing resistance, alienation, and conflict. This is potentially a fatal weakness in his approach.

The interesting and important point about BPR for our purposes is that once again this type of change is more concerned with prescription – implement BPR as the answer to all or most organizational performance issues – than it is with analysis and understanding. Once again BPR as an approach is predicated on a view of the nature of organizations which is seriously problematic.

Changing Cultures

The question of employees' attitudes is the key focus of our third type of prevalent and pervasive current organizational change: culture change. This deserves attention not only because of its pervasiveness but because many of its key propositions have been too readily accepted and incorporated into management thinking with little impact on organizational performance and little impact on the ability of managers to understand why their well-meaning attempts to improve performance have failed.

Recent organizational change has focused not only on changed structures, or the critique of bureaucracy, or the advocacy of process re-engineering, but on the heart and mind of the employee. Indeed one of the key features of recent change has been the argument that structural change in itself is limited in effect since it does not engage with or generate change in a key performance-related factor: employee attitudes. The attempt to change organizational cultures is extremely common. Nearly all current programmes of organizational change, whatever their primary focus and content – 360-degree feedback, competence systems, performance appraisal, TQM, BPR, the move to SBUs, etc. – have one common element: the attempt to change the way employees think and feel about their work and its purposes and priorities. Central to the successful creation of the new, non-, or anti-bureaucratic organization is the transformation of the employee, from someone who, at best, did as they were told, to someone who does what is necessary because they want to do it. Restructuring organizational life in this sense involves 'making up new ways for people to be': it refers to the importance of individuals acquiring and exhibiting particular 'enterprising' capacities and dispositions. Corporate culture projects seek to achieve corporate success by creating individuals who reflect, represent and implement organizational priorities in their attitudes and behaviour. As Thompson and McHugh point out, it consists of management attempts to manipulate and mobilize values, language, ritual and symbols in an effort to 'unlock the commitment and enthusiasm of employees' (Thompson and McHugh 1995: 198).

It is based on the claim that organizations have cultures (shared systems of meaning and values) and that these can be manipulated by management to make staff hold and be committed to shared goals and values concerning the purposes of the organization and their contribution to these. When employees are committed to their organization and its purposes, the performance of the firm, the argument goes, will be positively affected. When a company's culture is 'right' and 'strong' and 'positive', staff want to do what they need to do, they energetically and enthusiastically carry out their work because they identify with it, see it as 'theirs', share the purposes to which it is directed. They don't have to be told what to do or when to do it because they see what needs to be done and want it done well: 'The guiding aim and abiding concern of Corporate Culture . . . is to win the "hearts and minds" of employees, to define their purposes by managing what they think and feel, and not just how they behave'. The strengthening of corporate culture , Peters and Waterman claim, ensures 'unusual effort on the part of apparently ordinary employees' (Peters and Waterman 1982: p. xvii).

Since the beginning of industrialization and certainly since the development of the large-scale organization, employers have tried to find a solution to the central problem of management: how to get people to do what managers want them to do. One solution is to control them tightly by the assembly line, by rules and procedures, by technology. This is tempting, and it works – up to a point. But soon it begins to achieve diminishing or even negative returns: tight control destroys commitment, it may achieve obedience and compliance when it is vigorously policed, but it is likely to generate resistance and to destroy commitment. Tight control often produces poor quality, poor industrial relations, high absenteeism, and other indicators of alienated, low-commitment workers.

Allowing workers a greater degree of autonomy, allowing them to use their own judgement and skills, does generate the sort of commitment managers want. But allowing workers autonomy often puts management control at risk. If employees can decide what needs to be done, how can managers ensure the workers do the right thing? The history of the changing philosophies of management, organization and work-design systems is the history of different managements' efforts to 'solve' this dilemma. And as a result 'all forms of control contain, in different degree, two dimensions of control: the specification of levels of performance . . . and some effort to develop some level of content or acceptance of the legitimacy of the employment relationship' (Littler and Salaman 1984: 57).

Recent interest in management's manipulation of organizational cultures is a further attempt to 'solve' this dilemma. So ensuring staff share a positive company culture becomes the essence of management according to the culture gurus: 'symbols are the very stuff of management behaviour. Executives after all do not synthesise chemicals or operate fork lift trucks: they deal in symbols' (Peters 1978: 10). The results: 'Symbolic action may serve to motivate individuals within the organisation and to mobilise persons . . . to take action . . . Symbolic actions may serve to mollify groups that are dissatisfied with the organisation thereby ensuring their continued support of the organisation and the lessening of opposition and conflict' (Pfeffer 1981: 34–5).

However, if it is easy to see the appeal of culture change – and once again the language of its proponents is extravagant in its claims and promises – it is far less certain that these promises are fulfilled. When the excitement dies down and calm analysis replaces febrile over-excitement, doubts have been expressed both about the grounds of the gurus' claims and about their efficacy. As with the other change regimes discussed earlier, we need to understand the origins and robustness of the theory on which the corporate culture is based.

Close analysis of the claims made by the best-selling texts which initiated recent interest in changing organizational cultures, such as Peters and Waterman's *In Search of Excellence*, has revealed a host of methodological weaknesses which seriously undermine its claims to truth. Drucker, for example, described the book as 'a book for juveniles' and predicted interest wouldn't last a year (Silver 1987: 106; Thompson and McHugh 1995: 209). Indeed, some critics have argued that the success of *In Search of Excellence* was due not to the book's actual merits or the strength of its argument, but to US managers' need for reassurance in the face of Japanese competitive success: '*In Search of Excellence* succeeded because it brought welcome balm for America's battered self-image. Here was a better wholly indigenous solution to declining productivity and industrial decline, and Peters and Waterman's argument is put in terms that most people could immediately grasp' (Keisling 1984: 40).

For some commentators the deficiencies of the culture change literature are so numerous and so obvious that its appeal to managers can only be explained in terms of the psychological vulnerability of US (and in due course UK) managers: 'Corporate culture is positive. It appeals to American pride. It says Americans – at least some Americans – know how to manage. The secret Japanese potion is available at the corner drugstore, not just in Kyoto. The message is just what the doctor ordered for a nation which is questioning its ability to compete in an economically restructured world' (Maidique 1983: 155).

Other critics have questioned the claimed connection between 'excellent' companies and strong cultures, noting that this linkage was weakened by the subsequent poor performance of many of the identified companies (*Business*

Week 1983), and by the fact that the performance of some of these excellent companies was the result of factors other than the existence of strong cultures (Delamarter 1988).

Commentators have also taken issue with the way in which the corporate culture authors use (or misuse and simplify) the concept culture itself (Smircich 1983; Meek 1992), assuming – once again – an excessively consensual and unitary organization. Finally, researchers have demonstrated mixed evidence as to whether cultures actually have been changed. There are empirical and theoretical reasons for this. Much of the practitioner literature recounts tales of heroic cultural transformation (often short-lived if it happened at all) at Jaguar, British Airways, etc. This literature is aimed to enthuse and to advance the reputation of the author or consultant, but its empirical validity is questionable.

Much of the more empirically based research evidence tells a mixed story. Some research suggests the management programmes of culture change do not succeed in radically transforming employees' values and beliefs. But even here a change of behaviour is conceded. Ogbonna, for example, makes the point that culture change messages are 'heard' and 'interpreted' in the light of existing values and beliefs. But he ends his assessment with the conclusion that culture change programmes can only produce *surface* behavioural change: 'management was only able to generate behavioural compliance from an indifferent workforce – changes in the visible manifestation of culture were observable while values and assumptions remained intact' (Ogbonna 1992: 94).

The case of culture change programmes and their proponents then confirms the assessment of the two other types of prevalent organizational change discussed earlier. There is no need to consider other types of change: competences, TQM, or whatever new projects have risen to popularity by the time you read this book. The characteristics will be the same: tremendous hype and exhortation, allied with an apparently totally convincing case, extraordinary promises of organizational salvation – the end to organizational problems, the beginning of the new, golden age – all that was past is condemned, here lies the way ahead! All based, however, on some questionable assumptions, poor research, and a simplified view of organizational processes and dynamics and decision-making. It may well be that the appeal of such programmes and the texts on which they are based lies in their 'capacity to transport readers symbolically from the world of everyday experience to a mythical realm' (Conrad 1985), but this simply makes the need to understand and classify the different sorts of *theories* of organizational change and restructuring that underlie current (and presumably future) organizational change all the more pressing.

▶ Using Consultants

However, if the management writers and consultants, with their powerful and passionate advocacy of organizational solutions, can be charged with oversimplifying the nature of organizational structures and processes and over-selling flawed or ill-based panaceas, academic writers, though using a different style and approach to the problem of organizational change, do not always escape criticism. The criticism of academics is not that they simplify but, possibly, that they make matters excessively complex and obscure, focusing on conceptual matters or on issues of definition or on the provenance of key ideas. And it is probably true that academic attempts to analyse, assess, or comment on recent programmes of organizational change sometimes seem to obscure rather than illuminate, at least from the point of view of the thoughtful, curious manager. There are reasons for this: academics are not naturally or deliberately obfuscatory, but they have their own agendas, their own points of interest, their own styles of analysis, which are not necessarily those of immediate priority to a manager faced with a bewildering array of recommendations and prescriptions.

But in fact academic commentators have made a significant contribution to the analysis of recent changes, not only by analyses of particular programmes of change but in two other ways: first, by a critique of the sort of consultancy ideas or 'theories' that underlie many recent change programmes; second, by seeking to clarify, identify and analyse exactly what is involved in the claimed new approaches to organization and management.

The first approach analyses the nature and appeal of recent consultancy proposals; the second draws attention to and analyses the key elements of the emergence in recent years of a new, distinctive and significant approach to the design and management of organizations which is called strategic human resource management (SHRM). We shall briefly consider the contribution of each of these.

Academic analysis of consultancy knowledge or theory – the ideas which underpin consultancy packages – recognizes the extraordinary success and appeal of these writings and the programmes they inspire. We have already discussed some of these ideas – for example, the *In Search of Excellence* phenomenon, which not only sold millions of copies of the original book but spawned numerous examples of culture change programmes which were inspired by it. Faced with the evident inadequacy of many consultancy projects and the ideas on which they are based – poor (if any) research, inadequate analysis and conceptualization, flawed understanding of the complexity of organizations, poor results of projects – many academics identified a key issue that required analysis: 'How . . . are we to explain its popularity and its apparent success in capturing the imagination of academics and industrialists alike?' (Guest 1990: 378).

One feature of these ideas which may supply a clue to their appeal is their cyclical quality. Although the proponents of recommendations and prescriptions claim, as we would expect, that their solution is entirely new and uniquely useful, in fact many consultancy ideas are old ideas that have been repackaged and resold. The appeal of these consultancy packages in the face of the failure of earlier packages needs to take into account the transitory nature of much managerial activity, which seems to proceed from deep disillusionment with one panacea that has run its course to high enthusiasm for the next (Gill and Whittle 1993).

It may also need to recognize that some organizational problems cannot be solved: that organizations involve a number of basic tensions (for example between centralization and decentralization, between organizational control and market forms of control, between managing employees in ways which encourage commitment and managing them too tightly), and that any 'solution' to these tensions will reduce some difficulties but exacerbate others, or will only work for a short time under certain conditions.

Another explanation of the power and appeal of consultancy ideas centres on their fashionable quality. If the appeal of consultancy is defined in terms of their status as 'fads and fashions' then the explanation of the appeal of these fads explains the appeal of consultancy. 'Today's management fashions hold much in common with the early ones: bold promises, bustling consultants, magic, and sporadic references to strict academic science' (Keiser 1997: 50). So the question arises: 'Since the Second World War, personnel management and human resource management have been exposed to a plethora of new and constantly changing ideas and approaches . . . Why do these different fads come in and go out of fashion?' (Huczynski 1993b: 443–4).

This is an important question. The life-cycle of many key consultancy ideas shows a strikingly similar pattern: an early phase of gathering excitement and popularity, at the zenith of which the idea or package in question is so dominant as virtually to overrule and make ridiculous any critique or questioning, followed by a rapid decline into obscurity. Not only this, but new reforms are frequently very similar to older reforms (if under new names), and the original reforms had failed to achieve all that was promised for them. But managers forget and forgive their earlier enthusiasm and are no less prepared to embrace the next panacea. 'How is it that managers seem to be insatiably keen on the next wave of management fashionable thinking when they have hardly got over the last?' (Clark and Salaman 1998: 138).

One answer to this question has been offered by Brunnson and Olsen (1993). They point out that consultancy theories and associated projects inevitable offer highly inflated claims. These inevitably fail – to some extent – to deliver what is promised. The solution is then to offer something new. Brunnson and Olsen argue that there are a number of features of organizational reforms which make them attractive even in the face of a pervasive experience of earlier reform failure. One of these features is that reforms are simple and straightforward, reducing messy reality to a few simple principles, offering generalized promises in the face of confused and often unsatisfactory organizational practices (Brunnson and Olsen 1993: 33).

Clark and Salaman (1998) also identify a number of explanations: management anxiety and need for reassurance; managers' distinctive styles of thinking and learning which could make them vulnerable to the way consultancy ideas are packaged and presented; the force and impact of gurus' performance.

Sometimes consultancy ideas just 'seem' right. Commentators have suggested that one reason for the appeal of particular approaches to organizational redesign might lie in the resonance between the consultancy approach and ideas popular in the wider society – cultural ideological forces which make certain ideas in certain epochs seem natural and obvious. Guest, for example, argues that the success of many US consultancy ideas – for example the corporate culture approach of Peters and Waterman – is due to their close links and resonances with core US values: optimism, simplicity, the American dream, the idealized notion of possibility, the focus on individualism and enterprise. More than this, accepting the package itself is American. This applies particularly to the pervasiveness and appeal of the application of market forces and relationships to organizations.

Hammer and Champy are good examples of this attempt to align consultancy ideas with patriotism:

> The alternative is for corporate America to close its doors . . . Reengineering isn't another imported idea from Japan . . . reengineering capitalises on the same characteristics that made Americans such great business innovators: individualism, self-reliance, a willingness to accept risk and a propensity for change. Business Process Reengineering, unlike management philosophies that would have 'us' like 'them', doesn't try to change the behaviour of American workers and managers. Instead it takes advantage of American talents and unleashes American ingenuity. (Hammer and Champy 1993: 1–3)

However, despite serious misgivings about the quality and validity of much consultancy thinking; despite the fact that the appeal of such thinking – and its associated practices – may lie not in its inherent validity and truth but in its resonance with current ways of thinking, with received values, or with management fashion, or its inflated claims – it is still important because these ideas are significant in their impact. These ideas still need to be taken very seriously because they are serious in their implications, for organizations and their employees.

Developing Strategic Human Resources

As well as the sort of highly prescriptive, consultancy-driven change packages discussed above, recent years have also seen the emergence and growing acceptance (to varying degrees, admittedly) of the body of ideas mentioned above called strategic human resource management (SHRM). This approach is fundamental to this book. SHRM claims to offer a way of analysing and improving organizational performance. In many ways this book could be seen as an analysis and clarification of what this claim could – or should – mean in practice. Essentially this book is an analysis of the different ways in which organizational performance could be improved and therefore, if this is the aspiration of SHRM, the different ways in which SHRM could be understood and applied.

Many academic commentators, mirroring managers and their professional HR advisers and consultants, are convinced that the last 20 years have seen a significant and fundamental change in the ways in which organizations and employees are structured and managed, although some see this development as more rhetorical than real. This change subsumes the various specific projects discussed earlier – decentralization, BPR, culture change projects, etc. – but it goes much further. It is not simply a specific project; it is a fundamental change of approach: 'a major and qualitative change in the design of work and the structuring of work organisations, and the design of key personnel processes, which signifies a comprehensive programme of radical, strategically-driven organisational change' (Mabey et al. 1998: 55).

This raises a crucial question: what, then, is SHRM? And this is where complexity comes back in: because academic commentators do not agree on what SHRM is, or indeed on whether or not it is actually occurring. We need to consider some overviews of this approach and its elements offered by influential academic commentators.

A number of authors have stressed a critical feature of SHRM: that it involves integration or alignment of key aspects of organizational functioning with organizational strategies. Hence the reference to *strategic* human resource management. For many this is key:

> just as firms will be faced with inefficiencies when they try to implement new strategies with outmoded structures, so they will also face problems of implementation when they attempt to effect new strategies with inappropriate HR systems. The critical management task is to align the formal structure and the HR systems (selection, appraisal, rewards and development) so that they can drive the strategic objectives of the organisation. (Fombrun, Tichy and Devanna 1984: 37)

Other authors stress another key element: the *commitment* of employees:

> The new HRM model is composed of policies that promote mutuality – mutual goals, mutual influence, mutual respect, mutual rewards, mutual responsibility. The theory is that policies of mutuality will elicit commitment which in turn will yield both better economic performance and greater human development. (Walton 1986, quoted in Legge 1995: 64)

Definitions thus stress two features: integration (the alignment or fit of structures and strategies) and commitment. Some authors stress both. Hendry and Pettigrew, for example, list two factors among others: 'Matching HRM activities and policies to some explicit business strategy and seeing the people of the organization as a "strategic resource" for achieving "competitive advantage"' (Hendry and Pettigrew 1986, quoted in Legge 1995: 65).

This emphasis on commitment is crucial. It is a feature of a number of approaches to SHRM. It clearly resonates with the emphasis placed on employee commitment in the corporate culture literature discussed earlier. However, this emphasis on both alignment and commitment raises two related problems. While these may seem to be merely academic problems of definition, they are in fact, like many such issues, also extremely practical. The issue in essence is: can both these goals – alignment and commitment – always coexist, or does the pursuit of one inevitably mean that, sooner or later, the other must be sacrificed?

The emphasis on employee commitment might seem attractive; it may seem good sense. It is certainly a frequent element in company annual reports ('Our people are our most precious asset', etc.). But there are difficulties in combining the alignment of HR strategy with business strategy (sometimes called 'integration') and the importance of employee commitment. If 'mutuality' and commitment are to be pursued at all costs in every situation then sooner or later one is going to give.

For example, there may be occasions when the achievement of a strategy – say of a low-cost volume producer – means that it is simply not possible to treat the workforce in ways which encourage their commitment. The key priority is the cost of labour, not the commitment of labour, unless commitment can be achieved without cost (which it cannot).

The third definition of SHRM (Walton and others) seems to argue that mutuality, and its consequence, commitment, is important and necessary on every occasion. It is an absolute. The first two definitions, on the other hand, seem to suggest that there are no absolutes: what works best will depend on the business strategy being pursued; the most appropriate form of HRM strategy is *relative* to the business strategy. So academic (and possibly practitioner) definitions of SHRM reveal an underlying distinction (or confusion) between what we can call 'closed' or absolute versions of SHRM, which claim that some measures always work in all circumstances, and 'open' or contingent versions, which argue that what works will depend on the strategy being pursued.

The definitions reveal the possibility of another distinction or confusion, between what Legge calls 'hard' and 'soft' forms of SHRM. Some approaches to SHRM, for example Walton's, argue that the new approach to organization and management involves treating employees in ways which earn their commitment, and that this commitment will yield better organizational performance. This is the 'soft' view. However, the emphasis on achieving a 'fit' between HR strategy and business strategy may mean treating staff in ways which reduce their commitment: redundancy, intensification of work, reduced salaries, changed employment contracts, etc. Downsizing, a common type of organizational change, is a good example of this 'hard' approach.

Clearly both soft and hard approaches are possible; but they are in opposition. This distinction is very important in practice. If firms use the hard approach they are likely to achieve cost savings and efficiencies, but they may also damage the commitment of staff. If commitment is important this could be a serious cost. Despite the frequent references in consultants' texts and CEOs' statements to the crucial importance of companies' precious human resources, and the importance of treating employees in ways that encourage commitment and creativity, studies show that the actual reality of recent organizational changes is frequently more 'hard' than 'soft'. One recent researcher has concluded that most companies in the US remain traditionally managed, wedded to a low-trust, low-skill, authoritarian route to competitiveness.

This distinction between hard and soft approaches is important because it allows us to identify when actual organizational change contributes to or reduces employee commitment. Often the language is soft but the reality hard. The result can be that, where there is simultaneous use of hard forms (for example downsizing) and soft projects which rely on or seek to generate employee commitment (such as TQM, continuous improvement, customer care programmes, etc.), the hard approaches negate the benefits of the soft projects and reduce commitment.

Stephen Reich, the 'downsizing guru', has reportedly recanted, and has argued that corporations have taken his strategy too far. How compatible are downsizing or delayering with flexibility and teamwork? When insecurity prevails and redundancy threatens, people may be less inclined to train others, and where people have been encouraged to behave as independent, competitive operators they may be less inclined to share knowledge, information and ways of working.

So if there is a new and distinctive approach to organization and management it seems it can be of two different and even opposed sorts: either it is relative (i.e. open and variable) or absolute (i.e. closed and fixed) in its elements; hard on staff if necessary, or committed to their development and involvement.

But there are further internal contradictions and problems surrounding the nature of SHRM as a distinctive approach to organizations. When academics, consultants and managers talk about the new approach – whether or not they use the term SHRM is not terribly important – and when they describe a common set of elements which constitute this new approach (integration, a new approach to staff etc.), are they claiming that these elements are occurring with increasing frequency and that they tend to occur together, or are they advocating an approach which *should* occur? In short, are their statements *descriptive* or *prescriptive*? And are they themselves clear on the difference?

Finally, definitions of SHRM reveal a number of other difficulties. We have noted that definitions of the new, strategic approach to organizations stress the need for a link between business strategy and the internal organization of HRM strategy. This surely makes good sense (subject to the difficulties about 'open' and 'closed' types of linkage noted earlier), there is little point having a business strategy if the organization is not capable of developing it, or if existing arrangements encourage unproductive behaviour (they often do). But in fact more careful thought reveals a number of potential difficulties with this argument.

If there is to be linkage between organizational and human resource strategy, then there may be circumstances when the linkage should be reversed – when a business strategy is built on the basis of organizational strengths. To argue for the importance of 'fit' between the two key elements of organizational performance – business strategy and organizational capability – does not and should not necessarily assume that the latter always has to fit the former. The reverse can also occur, with benefit. As Hendry and Pettigrew note:

> HRM [has] a role in creating competitive advantage, in which the skills and motivation of a company's people and the way they are deployed can be a major source of competitive advantage. A company can methodically identify wherein its HR strengths lie and gear its HRM policies and business strategies towards utilising and developing these advantages. The HR skills that will be crucial for the future in the industry can be identified, and [the company] can take steps to acquire these. (Hendry and Pettigrew 1986: 7)

The final problem with the assumed linkage between business strategy and the organization – or the HR strategy – concerns the nature of the process that produces the business strategy and indeed the quality of this strategy. Many SHRM models, such as those quoted earlier, assume that business strategy exists, that it is sensible, and rational, well based on data and analysis, detached, objective, thorough, clear and agreed. In short the models assume a rationalistic, simplistic, top-down view of strategy: that there is a rational process of strategy formulation; that this process has taken place and produced a strategy that is worth pursuing and worth using as a basis for significant organizational change and restructuring.

This model of strategy formulation, and this assumption of the existence and quality of an organization's strategy, may differ sharply from the actual reality in many organizations. The models of SHRM discussed above tend to assume that strategies emerge from 'a conscious, rationalistic, decision-making process, fully formulated, explicit and articulated' (Legge 1995: 98). Furthermore, they tend to assume that the resulting strategies are intelligent, alert, well-based, offering an appropriate and firm foundation for any necessary organizational (SHRM) adjustment.

But this is only one view of how strategies are developed. Whittington, in a useful review, has called it the classical view of strategy formulation. An alternative method of strategy development, which (although they may *aspire* to the classical approach) may be nearer the truth in most organizations, is what Whittington calls the processual method. This acknowledges the uncertainties and confusion surrounding both the business environment and the internal processes of strategy development: 'both organizations and markets are often sticky, messy phenomena, from which strategies emerge with much confusion and in small steps' (Whittington 1993: 22). Environmental assessment and analysis, the identification of strategy options, and the processes of choice and decision-making are, crucially, not only limited by the complexity of the

environmental data and analysis, they are also limited by the nature of the organization itself (i.e. its existing structures, cultures, history, etc.), which can establish political barriers, distort and block key data, encourage sectional priorities,
limit cognitive processes, and discourage frank and radical debate or risk-
taking. Thus the processes of strategy development also need to be addressed
if organizational performance is to improved.

Conclusion

Organizations are changing, possibly radically. Senior managers know
that their organizations are under pressure from all directions. They are
aware that they need to change – to make some key decisions – in order
to ensure that their organizations are capable of achieving the goals set
for them. They are flooded with advice from all directions on how to
change. Consultants try to sell them packages, beautifully presented,
forcefully marketed, clearly stated in persuasive language, which promise
radical, dramatic organizational transformation. Many of these seem to
make sense. The consultants seem to know their business (and the
managers').

On the other hand academic commentators – Cassandra-like – warn
against too easy acceptance, noting numerous problems with the advice
and recommendations on offer, pointing out inconsistencies, contradictions and simplifications. Our view is that very often these criticisms
are well founded. Managers need to be warned against glib prescription
or ill-founded assumption and poorly based organizational analysis.
Organizations are complex phenomena; no one is well served by simplify-
ing them. The recent record of consultancy packages is poor.

The result of this situation for the thoughtful manager is confusion and
uncertainty: recognition that new times, new market and competitive
pressures, and new technologies and other changes demand new types of
organization; recognition also that many new models of organization are
on offer, and that some of these new models seem strangely familiar, or
almost too glib – too good to be true. This is the situation this book seeks
to clarify; we will organize, classify, unpack the key ideas underlying the
plethora of advice, offering a map of this terrain to enable the reader to
locate the ideas and suggestions on offer, and to find a route through it.
If managers wish to improve their organization's performance this is
possible. It can be done in a number of different ways through focusing
on a number of different features of the organization or by using a number
of different approaches. This is what this book is about.

2

The Model:
Five Ways to Improve
Organizational Performance

INTRODUCTION

We have seen that the literature on organizational change divides into two camps. On the one hand there is the literature which is broadly and sometimes glibly prescriptive – the 'how to' books, the airport bookstall texts which tell us to transform our companies, ourselves, even our families in minutes, half-minutes, seconds. Much of this is clever, much is cleverly wrong, some is half-right. On the other hand, there is the more academic literature which snipes at the prescriptive stuff, finding fault (with reason), showing the dubious background, the suspicious provenance, the misplaced concepts, the poor research base (when there is one), the confused, untenable and contradictory assumptions and definitions. As we have seen, much of this is right: the criticisms are deserved. But the consequences are wrong: the consequences are often confusing. We – and managers – need critique: we need to assess the quality and coherence of advice. But we need more: we need help and clarity. That's what this book supplies.

However, it is possible to make sense of this disparate, confused, contradictory and contested field: to rescue what is worthy and useful and interesting. This involves identifying and analysing and classifying the different sorts of theories that underpin the different and disparate approaches to organizational change and transformation. Within all the differences there are some patterns, some broad similarities; behind all the contradictions and confusions there are some coherent and tenable regularities; behind the excitement and exhortation, the critique and disappointment, we can discern some sustainable, defensible, and indeed useful and sensible arguments. However, these vary; they may even be opposed to each other. There are a number of basic but different ways in which organizational performance can be improved.

Identifying the broad positions underlying the prescriptions and recommendations on organizational change means uncovering the theories underlying these approaches – whatever they are. It means identifying the often implicit approach to organizational structure, functioning and change inherent in the recommendation. This may seem odd. People who advocate a particular type of organizational change – BPR, culture change, decentralization, downsizing – often seek actively and vigorously to distance themselves from matters of theory. Theory, they say, is for academics, while their approach is unashamedly practical; they are down-to-earth people whose approach, they like to claim, is not based on books or ivory-tower theorizing, but on the realities of organizational life, to which they have unique and privileged access. They have seen organizations as they are really are; they have seen the truth. But this disparagement of theory is misplaced. As has frequently been noted, there is nothing as practical as a good theory, and nothing as impractical as bad theory. The only thing more dangerous than poor theory is invisible theory – people who try to insist that their recommendations are not based on theory at all, but are mere common sense. This is incorrect because it is impossible. Any set of recommendations is based on some theory – some conviction that changing one variable will have an impact on another factor. Often, when people insist that their recommendations are not based on theory, they may be deluding themselves, but they certainly shouldn't be allowed to delude anyone else. Maynard Keynes identified this situation long ago: 'Practical men, who believe themselves to be quite exempt from any intellectual influences, are usually the slaves of some defunct economist. Madmen in authority, who hear voices in the air, are distilling their frenzy from some academic scribbler of a few years back' (Keynes 1936: 383).

What, then, of the theory that underlies current approaches to organizational change and transformation? What form does this take and how is it distinctive? These are the questions this book will address.

First, it is possible to say something about the concerns, the focus (or actually the focuses) of this literature. Secondly, it is possible to say something about five different and distinct approaches to these issues.

▶ Understanding Strategy

What in essence are the change, strategy and HR literatures about? In essence recent and current approaches to organizational change and transformation are in various ways concerned with improving the performance of organizations. Strategy itself has been defined as 'the match an organisation makes between its internal resources and skills ... and the opportunities and risks created by its external environment' (Hofer and Schendel 1978: 12). In other words, there is little point in developing strategies that cannot be implemented due to deficient organizational capability. Attempts to change organizations must therefore be concerned with the links between strategy and capability. They must be: what else could they sensibly be about? But what does this mean? How can performance be improved? It means in essence *improving organizational capability – improving the capability of the organization to design, generate, support or deliver strategy*. Regardless of whether or not they know it, or state it, they all seek to achieve this improvement by advocating some adjustments and manipulation to the relationships between three absolutely central variables. These variables are:

- E: organizational or business environment
- S: business strategy
- C: organizational capability.

The consultancy books, the 'how to' books, the exhortatory texts, and the associated change projects may not state this clearly or even at all. But in essence any proposal for improving the performance of an organization is a proposal for improving one or more elements of the E–S–C model. That is, for example, they are proposing ways in which environments can be scanned, measured, monitored, analysed, understood. Or they are suggesting ways in which environmental information can be used to develop intelligent, alert, sensible strategies. Or they are proposing ways in which these strategies can be supported by appropriate organizational structures, systems, processes and cultures. Or they are identifying ways in which organizational capabilities can be the basis for distinctive business strategies. Or, finally, they are proposing that certain changes to organizational structures, cultures and systems are in themselves useful and beneficial – for example by improving efficiencies.

Anyone who offers recommendations for the improvement of organizational performance is implicitly using this simple model. This is what they are all about – at least if they are worth taking seriously. Improving organizational performance is an attractive proposition. But we need to be clear about what it means to improve organizational performance and to be clear about, and able to assess, the different propositions that have been advanced for how performance can be achieved.

The three core elements in organizational performance are clear and obvious.

Organizational environment

Environment includes pressures from competitors (current, possible, would-be); it refers to the requirements and expectations of clients and other key parties (staff, suppliers, citizens); it refers to the nature and impact of regulation, from whatever source, government, international agency, trading partners, external licensing or quality assurance agencies, etc. It refers to the changing nature and implications of technology and many other factors.

However, when we talk about organizational environments in this book we are not focusing on the actual, objective nature of these environments and how they are changing. Our concern is primarily organizational, so our interest in environments is less in the environments themselves and more in how – how well, how often and how thoroughly – managers within a business monitor, analyse and understand their business environments: that is, how well the organization understands and monitors its environment.

This raises the important and somewhat complex issue of the relationship between organizations and their environments. Most people see these environments as objective realities which supply pressure, opportunity, or constraint on organizations, and which managers 'see' 'recognize', 'understand' and 'analyse'. The environment in this view exists as an objective fact: the issue is how well managers perceive and respond to these objective developments. There is obviously a lot in this view: business environments are changing whether individual organizations and their managers like it – and see it – or not.

But there is another way of understanding the relationship between environments and organizations – this is one which points out that, however real environments and environmental change may be, from the point of view of any particular set of managers the environment they face and to which they respond is the one they *think* they see. Managers' reactions to, or attempts to manage and anticipate, environmental developments are determined not by 'real' or actual environmental developments but by the developments they identify or emphasize. To this extent it is possible to say that a business's environment is to some extent defined, or even enacted by, the managers in the organization – in other words, to draw attention to the distinctive and different ways in which managers in different organizations in different sectors at different times hold particular notions of what their business environment is and how it is (or is not) changing. Indeed one of the most striking variables in the way in which managers 'see' their business's environment lies in how – and where – they define the environment itself. We will return to this point later, because it helps us understand how managers can sometimes fail to see what everyone else sees – because they share a particular way of seeing and understanding the world.

Business strategy

Business strategy is a multifaceted concept which can be seen in a number of ways. Some of the issues surrounding this concept have been touched on in the previous chapter, where a contrast was noted between a very simple, formal, rationalistic view of what strategies are and how they are developed and a more processual view which stresses the complex and messy negotiations and iterations which underlie attempts by managers with different and incomplete data and differing priorities to identify and agree a satisfactory conception of the preferred direction of the business. However, despite the complexity of the concept – or rather the complexity of the processes that produce strategy within organizations – the concept itself is pretty clear and as easy to describe as it is difficult to achieve. Strategy is simply the identification of the ends the organization intends to pursue and the means chosen to achieve these ends.

Organizational capability

Organizational capability refers to the ability of an organization to achieve the goals that have been set for it. The goals, whatever they are and whatever the process that identified them, are what we mean by strategy. Capability refers to the degree to which the organization is structured to ensure achievement of the goals: the extent to which the culture is appropriate for their achievement, the degree to which there are the right sorts of people with the right attitudes and skills and attributes in the right numbers, motivated, rewarded, equipped, trained and managed to do the right sorts of things in the right sorts of ways. This is organizational capability. It is obviously crucial, because if the organization is not capable of achieving the strategy the strategy is an expensive waste of time.

▶ Understanding Organizational Capability

If we are concerned to improve an organization's ability to achieve its objectives this can mean five significantly different approaches, all of which are important and desirable, each of which proposes a distinct approach to organizational change: different types of change and, most importantly, different reasons and purposes for change. And all five forms concern the nature and quality of the relationship between the three factors listed above: organizations' environments, strategies, and capabilities. To explain this more fully requires some more detailed consideration of five different senses or versions of 'capability'.

1   The first and probably the most common type of capability enhancement is when organizations are exhorted (very sensibly) to change themselves (the various elements of organization include structure, cultures and systems) in order to improve the 'fit' between organization and strategy. Forty years ago, for example, Chandler argued that companies, driven

by market developments and growth and technological change, were likely to respond by increasing the diversity of their product range and to manage these strategies by adopting a particular organizational form which he called the M-form – the classic multi-divisional organizational form. How did this 'fit' between structure and strategy come about?

> The reason this structural form proved so powerful was because it defined a new set of management roles and relationships that emphasised the decentralisation of responsibility to operating divisions whose activities were planned, co-ordinated and controlled by a strong corporate management – the general office ... which also made the firm's 'entrepreneurial decisions' about resource allocation. He showed how the management process created by this organisation allowed companies to apply their resources more efficiently to opportunities created by changing markets and developing technologies. (Bartlett and Ghoshal 1993: 351)

This argument – a very sensible if possibly over-rational argument – sums up the first approach to improving organizational capability. Managers are encouraged to ask themselves: what sort of organization do we need in order to achieve what we are trying to do? Or, more negatively (but often very revealingly): what features of our current structure, culture, systems, skills, etc., get in the way of what we are trying to achieve? This is the approach to organizational improvement advanced by Fombrun, Tichy and Devanna in the quotation in the previous chapter. These authors talk about 'appropriate' HR systems. Note the importance of 'alignment' of structures, systems and strategy. Similarly Beer and Spector (1985) refer to 'fit', linking HR elements to strategic planning.

This first sort of capability starts with the strategy process and then builds (or modifies) the organization so that it can deliver the strategy. Structure follows strategy. This is important because simply to emphasize 'fit' does not inherently imply which element – strategy or structure – follows which. This type of capability enhancement starts with a process of environmental mapping. The organization must map its environments, gather data, analyse these, interpret them rationally and exhaustively, and on this basis develop a market-focused and market-facing business strategy. Once such a strategy is designed, the organization's capability often needs to be adjusted to make it better able to achieve its strategy. This sort of change is sometimes referred to as strategic HRM.

It's attractive and it makes sense. This approach stresses the relative or contingent nature of necessary organizational arrangements. What might work well for one type of strategy would work less well, might hardly work at all, for another. An organization that is strategically committed to innovation must have a very different sort of structure, culture, skill set and reward system to one geared to a value-for-money cost-control strategy. But there are difficulties, as we will see later.

This approach makes three key – and plausible – assumptions: that organizations can differ in their structure or capability (we will discuss the key elements of organizations' capability shortly); that in principle it is possible for senior managers to choose which type of organization they want (although of course they may choose wrongly, or may find it hard to effect the change they desire); and finally that senior managers can choose the strategy and strategic objectives of the organization.

2   The second approach to improved organizational effectiveness stresses not relative or contingent features but absolute ones. If the first approach is open, this is closed: it asserts that there are some measures or features of organizations which are always useful, always efficient, regardless of circumstances. Obviously, as noted earlier, it is difficult to combine these open and closed approaches. We have seen some examples of this closed approach in the previous chapter. Guest offers a good example: he defines a key feature of a strategic approach to human resource management as 'Optimal employee commitment to enterprise goals and practices' (Guest 1987). Note how this quality is being recommended as beneficial – indeed possible – under all circumstances. It is an absolute. It is *always* beneficial.

3   The third approach to the improvement of organizational performance or capability is rapidly becoming a major focus of interest. Rather than trying to convert the organization – its structures, cultures, systems, etc. – to support the strategy, this approach involves building the strategy on the basis of real organizational strengths. Rather than ask 'What sort of organization do we need to support the business strategy?' this approach asks 'What sort of strategy would take advantage of and exploit our existing strengths?' In a way it is another form of 'fit', but here the relationship between strategy and structure is reversed. This is called the resource-based approach to strategy, and it is important since strategies built on an organization's core capabilities (if it has any) are a more durable and hard-to-imitate source of competitive advantage than off-the-shelf strategies which anyone can copy. Capabilities can be based on production technologies, on supply-chain management, on key processes (such as innovation), or on the recruitment, retention, motivation and development of staff.

Caution is important when assessing organizational capabilities. Senior managers have been known to delude themselves about their organization's capabilities, confusing features they admire and enjoy with capabilities that are strategically relevant. This relevance has three elements: a capability must be must be something customers perceive and value, it must be durable and hard to copy, and it must be deployable in new markets. The great strength of organizational capabilities when they occur is that they are not the result of an easily replicable consultancy package which competitors can install as easily as you, but of numerous subtle, often tacit aspects of the way the organization work: values, habits, patterns of relationship and co-operation and trust built up over time.

Change programmes associated with this form of capability (which are increasingly common) seek to identify an organization's core capabilities (if any), to cherish and nurture them, to identify new market opportunities for them, and to build the organization around their development and deployment.

4   The fourth relationship between strategy and capability takes the form of efforts to modify the organization to make it more capable of developing alert and intelligent strategies by addressing how, and how well, strategy is developed by the strategy-formulating team. In other words, rather than simply adapting the organization's structures, cultures and systems to a new strategy, the intention here is to make the strategy team better able to generate a succession of relevant strategies quickly and intelligently. This is crucially important. There is little point in painfully transforming the organization to make it capable of delivering a new strategy if the new strategy is unoriginal or misconceived or imitative, or if in a few years that strategy will clearly be obsolete so that the whole process has to be repeated. Better to address the adequacy and quality of the strategy-formulation process itself. This is sensitive and difficult, because it requires the identification and analysis of those aspects of organizational structure, culture, and functioning which can regularly and systematically disturb the rationality and reasonableness of organizational decision-making at the strategic level. It is easy to find evidence of widespread but well-intentioned irrationality on the part of committed and intelligent executives. The passion for mergers is a good example: they rarely deliver their promise but they continue to be popular. This fourth type of capability considers how well the senior strategy group thinks and analyses and develops strategies. It addresses the numerous ways in which established organizational structures, cultures, systems and people can limit the ability of the strategy group to understand the business environment, make the necessary analyses, and develop appropriate and intelligent strategies. One of the paradoxes of organizations is that, by attempting to achieve regularity, control and predictability (all desirable organizational objectives), they may also limit their ability to think beyond their history and their systems.

5   The fifth approach to the improvement of organizational performance focuses neither on organizational capabilities (structures, systems, cultures, etc.) nor on the improvement of the organizational strategy-forming processes, but on both together. This approach refuses to

separate strategy and capability; it refuses to regard change as an occasional activity which is the responsibility of a specialist group – senior management. It regards the separation of capability and strategy, thinking and doing, and of change designers and those who experience change, and indeed the distinction between change and stability, as themselves highly problematic. The unique and attractive feature of this approach is that it denies the very notion of 'fit'. For fit implies a process of adjustment – of structure to strategy or strategy to structure. But this fifth approach argues that it is precisely this process of adjustment, whichever way round it occurs – that is so time-consuming and debilitating. After all, these writers would note, change programmes frequently fail (at least to some degree); they take time and energy; they distract management attention. And when they fail they often fail precisely because they fall foul of the very organizational features they are trying to change: existing structures and politics, and existing organizational cultures.

This fifth type of capability improvement seeks to develop an organization that is alert, adaptive, quick to spot opportunities and threats, quick to respond, not weighed down by historic baggage, but alert to an unknowable future. If organizations need to change frequently (and we are told that they do and will) then their ability to design smart, intelligent, and not off-the-shelf, changes ahead of the competition and to install them more quickly and less painfully, while continuing with business as usual without confusing their staff and clients, becomes critical. This approach to organizational change aims to help the organization to change more quickly and more effectively: it avoids the traditional sequence and process of change (top-down, episodic, imposed) and enables the organization to change constantly as required and as initiated from any level. It eschews the normal pathologies of the traditional hierarchical, structured, machine-like organization.

It comes in a number of forms. Some have called it the boundaryless organization (Ashkenas et al. 1995). These authors advocate an organization where structures and boundaries (which are seen as imparting rigidity and conservatism) are replaced by permeable structures and processes. Features of traditional organizations that are well known for their propensity to establish sectional thinking, ingrained routines, organizational politics and all the other dysfunctions that organizations are heir to, will be replaced: 'behaviour patterns that are highly conditioned by boundaries between levels, functions, and other constructs will be replaced by patterns of free movement across those same boundaries. No longer will organisations use boundaries to separate tasks, processes, and places; instead, they will focus on how to permeate those boundaries – to move ideas, information, decisions, talent, rewards and actions where they are most needed' (Ashkenas et al. 1995: 2–3).

Others have called it the 'knowledge-based' company, stressing the strategic significance of an organization's being able to create, disseminate, assess and deploy knowledge and expertise quickly and effectively and noting that traditional forms of organization (for the sorts of reasons identified by Ashkenas et al. among others) is not effective in these respects. Therefore a new sort of organization is required, which is adept at identifying, recognizing, accessing, developing and sharing the knowledge of employees. This requires a number of untypical organizational features. It also assumes a high level of employee commitment.

Another statement of this approach to organizational change is 'the learning organization', which seeks to improve organizations' capability and strategies by making the organization more adaptive: better able to design and implement change effectively, quickly and painlessly. The popular, if optimistic, notion of the 'learning organization' is often used in connection with the aim of improving the adaptiveness of organizations.

If any programme of organizational change is to make sense and be coherent and sustainable, it must logically address one or more of these five relationships. If programmes of organizational change are justifiable they must in one way or another be attempts to improve the linkage between strategy and capability in one of the ways described.

This raises three issues. First, managers concerned in change programmes will not necessarily see their actions in these terms. The model proposed here may or may not be one that explicitly informs management practice. We think it should, but recognize that it often doesn't. Either way we propose it as a powerful way of understanding, analysing and thinking about – or even designing and implementing – strategy-based organizational change. The point of this book is to help those who are trying to change their organization, or who need to understand the advice and exhortations with which they are bombarded, to make sense of the advice that surrounds them by classifying it into its separate and, in many respects, opposed categories. The categories are ours.

Secondly, not all programmes of organizational change must be concerned with one or more of these relationships. This is manifestly not the case. Much organizational change is driven not by attempts to resolve organizational problems but by the availability of organizational solutions. Change is probably harder to resist than to initiate. Change is often fashion-driven. But the fact that much organizational practice differs from the framework offered here does not vitiate the model. Indeed, one of the strengths of the framework is that it enables us to assess to what extent any particular example of organizational change is concerned with improving strategic capability. The model is obviously idealized. It suggests some ideal-typical relationships between strategy and capability which can be used to assess the likely impact and relevance of change, or even to identify promising areas and forms of future change. It is not, and is not intended to be, a description of all actual programmes of orga-nizational change.

Thirdly, a key element of the model is its rational nature. It offers a model for analysing or designing organizational change that is rational, suggesting that, to be useful and productive, organizational change must be concerned with one of these capability–strategy relationships. This does not, however, imply that the model ignores or glosses over the many systemic sources of limited or distorted rationality within organizations. Indeed, one of the five types of change is explicitly devoted to the analysis of these forces, their origins within the organization and their implications. To offer an idealized framework does not imply that the world is seen solely in terms of this model. But using the model enables us to identify and assess the nature of the organizational world and the extent to which it differs and deviates from the framework.

Conclusion

Designing and implementing appropriate and timely organizational change is not only complex and difficult; it is arguably a major factor in determining an organization's success and survival. The corporate grave-yards are littered with the corpses of business that changed too little, too late, or too much or too glibly: who confused current fashion with good sense, who listened to consultants rather than to their own staff, who believed that there were easy answers to complex questions. We see around us at this very moment organizations desperately trying to undo the harm done by previous change regimes – in the UK, for example, the BBC. This book argues for a return to basics: it suggests that essentially there are five different ways in which change programmes or prescrip-tions could be useful. All are important and beneficial. All that is required is that managers should consider which is appropriate in their circum-stances and how any proposed programme of change might impact on one or more of them.

3

'Fit': Fitting Organizational Structures to Business Strategy

INTRODUCTION

A central gap in the literature to date is that the rich content of strategies has never been related to structure. It may be, for example, that strategies of differentiation through innovation would not be easy to implement within a bureaucratic or mechanistic structure . . . It also seems incongruous that bureaucratic structures could give rise to differentiation through innovation. By the same token organisations that have embraced a cost leadership strategy pursue extremely efficient, low cost production to lower prices. They might then require bureaucratic, 'mechanistic' structures that place a great deal of emphasis on sophisticated cost controls; standard, repetitive procedures; cost information systems, etc. Organic structures could be too flexible and inefficient to appropriately serve cost leaders. These conjectures are worthy of further study as the match between strategy and structure may vitally influence performance. (Miller 1986: 267)

The key idea behind the 'fit' or the contingency approach to increased organizational performance is simple – simple at least to state, although for a variety of reasons not necessarily simple to achieve. It is an appealing idea with a great deal of face validity – that the nature of an organization is (or should be) determined by the purposes it is trying to achieve.

In terms of our basic model of the three elements involved in all approaches to the improvement of organizational performance – E, S and C – the 'fit' approach argues that environmental scanning and analysis results in an accurate perception of environmental developments, threats and opportunities. In the light of this the strategic group develops an alert, intelligent set of objectives and the strategies to achieve them. The final phase – achieving organizational fit – is for the managers to assess the extent to which the organization is currently capable of achieving the strategy, and to make whatever organizational changes are necessary to build an organization that is consistent with and which can deliver – which fits – the strategy.

We recognize that there are a number of problems with this simple (and idealized) picture. And we will return to them at the end of this chapter and in chapter 5, which looks at the processes of strategy development. But for now we intend to stay with this simple but powerful – and very pervasive – approach to organizational change. Diagrammatically it can be represented as follows:

$$E—S—C$$

This simple idea needs some amplification and development.

▶ Understanding Organization

First, what do we mean by the 'nature' of an organization, or by organizational 'structure'? These expressions are used to describe the various features of an organization that determine how its employees behave. 'Fit' theorists argue that the structure and systems of organizations should encourage and require and enable members of the organization to behave in ways which support and contribute to the achievement of the goals the organization is pursuing. This seems sensible, and desirable. However, some key issues need to be clarified.

First, how is employees' behaviour determined? What features of an organization determine how people behave? To answer this fundamental question we need to distinguish between two levels of causation: the factors that directly influence employee behaviour, and the organizational features which determine the nature and content of these factors.

Employees' behaviour is determined by a combination of three interrelated factors which directly influence their behaviour:

- First, how their jobs or roles are *specified* – the content, responsibilities, targets, performance indicators, etc. associated with their work roles. Employee behaviour is influenced (but not entirely determined) by what employees are told and required to do.
- Secondly, employee behaviour is influenced by their *capacity* to do what their job roles require them to do. Capacity includes such matters as raw materials, skills, knowledge, equipment, staff, information, budgets, authority.
- Finally, employee behaviour is a consequence of their *motivation* to do what they are clear they are expected to do and what they have the capac-

ity to do. Motivation is a consequence of a number of factors, of which financial remuneration is only one. Motivation is also a consequence of cultural factors within the organization – shared systems of values and ways of thinking which define some behaviours as virtuous or admirable and others as unimpressive or worse. It is a consequence of the personal drives and aspirations of the recruits identified and selected by the organization and how organizational experience impacts on such aspirations to develop or suppress them. It is a consequence of the existence and nature of employee development systems which at best can inculcate a long-term loyalty and commitment in exchange for an expectation of career or personal development. It is a product of organizational relationships, between units, levels and functions within the organization, between managers and their reports, between colleagues and peers and, crucially, within teams.

These three factors directly influence how employees behave: what they do, how they do it, when they do it, to what standards they do it. Of course they are supported by a number of organizational systems, structures and processes: the values of the organization, the shared beliefs, the established routines and patterns of behaviour, the nature and flow of information, the processes of recruitment and development, the nature of leadership.

Each of these is an organizational matter. They are shaped by organizational choices, although these choices may be explicit and conscious or implicit and unconscious – forgotten in history, seen as 'natural'. But it is these choices which determine the 'nature' or 'structure' of an organization – and therefore its capability. The exact nature of the three factors in any organization – how jobs are defined, how capacity is developed and supported, how people are motivated – is itself determined by the interplay of three features of organization – the second-level factors mentioned earlier. These features are obvious and familiar aspects of organizations. They are:

- organizational *structures*
- organizational *systems and processes*, including those concerned with recruiting selecting, training, developing, assessing and appraising, rewarding and managing employees
- organizational *cultures*.

The combination of these factors across an organization produces the *capability* of the organization – the extent to which it is capable of achieving what those who have designed its strategy intend it should achieve.

The nature of these three factors – the nature, shape and height of an organization's structure, the relationship between organizational units and levels, the nature of organizational processes, the shared values and mindsets – impact directly on specification, capacity and motivation and thus powerfully influence how people behave. And the nature of these three factors determines the extent to which people's behaviour is appropriate to, or contributes usefully to, the achievement of the purposes of the organization.

The 'fit' approach simply argues that an organization's capability should match its strategy. This is what is meant by the expression: *strategic* human resource management'; the suggestion that human resources (i.e. the capability of the organization, the way people are treated and the way they behave) should support the achievement of what the organization is trying to do: 'the key message of the literature . . . is the need to establish a close, two-way relationship between business strategy or planning and SHRM strategy or planning' (Beaumont 1992: 40). Or, 'A business enterprise has an external strategy: a chosen way of competing in the market place. It also needs an internal strategy: a strategy for how its internal resources are to be developed, deployed, motivated and controlled . . . external and internal strategies must be linked' (Beer and Spector 1985: 6); note the prescriptive tone of these comments: the use of 'need' and 'must'.

But there is another type of linkage that is also stressed, the fit *between* various human resource policies – or the various dimensions of organizational capability – so that they are consistent and mutually supportive. 'the two forms of match that were seen as conditions for competitive advantage were distinguished first as the match between SHRM policies themselves and secondly as the match between SHRM policies and the business strategy pursued by the company . . . The theme of simultaneously maximising internal and external fit has been explored by a number of authors' (Mueller 1996: 761).

Obviously both forms of 'fit' are desirable and sensible. They certainly made sense to a group of students with whom we worked in the early 1990s. They were an unusual group in that they had worked together as a group under very difficult and dangerous circumstances for some 17 years. The work they had done together was designing and conducting military opposition to the oppressive Mengistu dictatorship in Ethiopia during the 1980s and 1990s. They were ultimately successful, and after 17 years of opposition their army defeated the government army of Mengistu.

Soon after their victory they decided they wished to resume their studies – as a group – and since they thought they knew little about management and business took an MBA with the Open University Business School. We were their tutors. It was a remarkable experience. We found they knew more than they knew – and often more than we knew. And when we discussed the 'fit' approach to organizational performance they immediately recognized it because they had applied exactly this approach to their own organization.

The opposition was started in the north of the country, in a province called Tigray, by ex-students from that area. In the early period of what they call the armed struggle the loose federation of guerrilla bands managed to liberate much of the Tigrean countryside and gradually took over the administration of the liberated areas. But they were poorly armed initially (they had no outside military support) and they were not able to take major garrisons in Tigray, although they could harass and contain them. They knew to the minute how long they had with their hit and run raids before MIGs from Addis could reach the besieged government troops.

But after years of this sort of warfare they realized that they had issues of strategy to resolve: although they had become a major nuisance to the Mengistu regime, and had liberated much of the north of the country, a continuation of the current hit and run strategy was not going to win the war. If they wanted to win, they had to change what they were doing. They were faced with a major decision about their strategies and objectives.

Typically this issue was discussed at length at conferences. Apparently it was a long and painful discussion, taking place against a background of constant guerrilla warfare and of strongly held views, not about what was desirable, but what was possible. Finally, however, a decision was reached: there would be a major change of strategic objective. Now the goal was to break out of Tigray and the relative safety of the high mountains and to defeat the government army. The trouble was that the military force as then constituted was totally unable to achieve this objective or to support the strategy for its achievement. This new objective required an entirely new organization, or in our terms, new organizational capability. They realized this. That was why years later our discussion of the 'fit' approach was familiar to them. The existing organization, such as it was, an assembly of guerrilla bands, had to be replaced by a large-scale army. Specialized units (logistics, engineers, artillery, etc.) were required; greatly increased co-ordination would be needed; a new organization was necessary, with a new structure and command-and-control system. The military leader described the necessary transition as exchanging hit and run tactics for hit and stay. Now decisions about attacking or running or staying were taken by the high command. The bands now became units. They had to do – reliably and under great pressure – what they were directed to do. They had to support overall purposes regardless of the cost to the unit. Military strategy was developed which required a disciplined and trained and equipped organization. Achieving the necessary discipline, capacities, specialization – i.e. changing the organization's capability – was a major task. It took two years to build the new army. Not everyone wanted the change; not everyone was willing to change; not everyone was capable of change. It was painful. But it was done, and some five years later the tanks of the EPRDF (Ethiopian Peoples' Revolutionary Democratic Front) rolled into Addis Ababa to the surprise of the outside world, if not of the EPRDF leadership.

This is a classic case of 'fit'. New objectives and new strategies required new organizational capabilities. The EPRDF leadership realized that, if the new strategy was to be achieved, it was necessary to change or increase capability to make it compatible with new goals, and that this required the manipulation of structures, systems and cultures in turn, to redefine three factors listed above which impact directly on what people do and how they do it: specification of roles, capacity and motivation.

Consider another, less unusual, example. A UK health trust – a public sector organization required to deliver various types of health care within a state-financed system – recently initiated a management competences project. The trust was under pressure to change in order to respond to the new internal market in health-care provision. Government changes had brought devolved budgets and required a higher degree of management involvement in previously centralized planning and budgeting. At ground level, employees (nurses, social workers, health visitors) were formed into independent multi-disciplinary teams, and the new CEO aspired to change the trust into an organization where, as he put it, 'people moved faster, were more flexible and less expensive'. He wanted to use competences to 'break down traditional demarcations and destroy bureaucracy and change the culture'. Competences were developed in an attempt to achieve the organization's goals by developing a basic structure of competences which aligned the organization's objectives with individuals' behaviours.

The competences were also connected to the achievement of a basic change of focus – 'from a professionally driven service to a customer-driven service'. Competences were used to force the organization to focus on customers' needs and to satisfy these needs to develop new and more flexible ways of working, and to do this within reduced budgets. The new manager – based on the competences – was someone who understood and accepted the vision of the trust and its strategies, and who achieved these through the people they managed. The new values which were operationalized through the competences and which were radically distinct from the traditional, professional NHS values, provided the 'underlying principles for the long-term economic survival of the trust'.

Again in this case, organizational change – the competence architecture – was installed in an attempt to spearhead and disseminate change throughout the organization in order to make staff behave in ways more compatible with new organizational strategies, which in turn were seen as necessary in the light of major, government-driven, environmental change.

Exploring Organizations

The idea that different goals and strategies will require a different type of organization is, as we noted, intuitively appealing. But it hasn't always been. For a long time – and up to about 40 or 50 years ago – it was assumed that efficient organizations would look broadly the same. There was one model for every purpose, any colour as long as it's black. And the model was bureaucracy.

Bureaucracy is a much-maligned word these days. For many years proponents of organizational change have unrelentingly maligned bureaucracy and extolled instead what is defined as its virtuous opposite: the flexible, responsive, customer-facing organization. Control by bureaucratic rule is contrasted unfavourably with control by market forces. We will return to this argument in due course. There are things we want to say about it. But for now our interest is less in recent critiques of bureaucracy and more in the dominating status of this approach to organization up to the post-war period.

The first modern form of organization, which developed in the UK during the Industrial Revolution, was the bureaucracy. Nineteenth-century social commentators and theorists realized this, and realized also that this new form of organization represented a fundamental and highly significant departure from earlier types of organization. Bureaucracy represented new principles of organization: specialization, formal procedures, clearly defined roles and responsibilities, a hierarchy of authority, appointment to positions on the basis of competence, impersonality. These were in sharp contrast to previous organizations characterized by favouritism, individualism, nepotism, unpredictability, arbitrary decision-making, variability.

Not only was the new form seen as dramatically and significantly different: it was recognized as offering enormous improvements in efficiency. Max Weber, a nineteenth-century analyst of the societal changes of that period, and a major theorist of organizations, identified the key qualities, and the key implications, of the new type of organization; in a classic passage, he wrote:

> The decisive reason for the advance of bureaucratic organisation has always been its purely technical superiority over any other form of organisation. The fully developed bureaucratic mechanism compares with other organisations exactly as does the machine with the non-mechanical forms of production . . . Today it is primarily the capitalist market economy which demands the official business of the administration be discharged precisely, unambiguously, continuously and with as much speed as possible. Bureaucratisation offers above all the optimum possibility for carrying through the principle of specialising administrative functions according to purely objective considerations. Individual performances are allocated to functionaries who have specialised training and who by practice learn more and more. The 'objective' discharge of business primarily means a discharge of business according to calculable rules and without regard for persons. (Weber 1964: 214–15)

There are a number of interesting ideas in this passage. Weber sees bureaucracy as efficient in a machine-like way. He was right: it was efficient, and under the right circumstances it still is – those circumstances being where a 'machine-like' organizational response is required – i.e. stable, routine and predictable circumstances.

Weber also sees bureaucracy as *appropriate*, or necessary. It is seen as fitting the situation, and presumably the strategies these circumstances require: 'Today it is primarily the capitalist market economy which *demands* the official business of the administration be discharged precisely, unambiguously, continuously and with as much speed as possible . . .'. But if bureaucracy is necessary or required, this fit was largely a generic one: bureaucracy was well adjusted to the generic requirements of the newly developing capitalist economies.

Weber's suggestion that capitalism required one basic type of organization – bureaucracy – was taken up in the twentieth century by a number of managerialist writers who also advocated an universal form (or universal principles) of organization. Taylor advocated his principles of scientific management; Fayol his principles of management. The conviction that one unitary set of principles was appropriate for all circumstances is not these writers' only link with Weber: the nature of these principles in both cases strongly resembled the bureaucratic principles listed by Weber. Fayol, for example, emphasized division of labour, authority, discipline, centralization, unity of command, etc. Readers wishing to know more of these and other early management writers should see Clegg and Dunkerley's impressive summary: *Organizations, Class and Control* (1980).

However, during the course of the twentieth-century experience, research and reflection began to produce a growing recognition of a different reality. Two developments in thinking about organizations are central to the emergence of the 'fit' approach to enhanced organizational performance: the recognition that organizational structures and other features vary, and the argument that these variations are related to the goals of the organization.

The recognition that organizations could vary started when researchers began to notice some of the dysfunctions of bureaucracy – features such as 'red tape', suppressed individual initiative, slowness of response, over-centralized or -controlled employees, the excessive emphasis on compliance rather than on the requirements of circumstances, and others. If bureaucracy could be dysfunctional this implicitly raised the possibility that other forms or organization might, under some circumstances, be less problematic and more functional.

At the same time researchers into bureaucratic industrial organizations argued that in fact the bureaucratic model could take a number of different forms. They reported that in fact the shape, structure and approach of organizations could vary quite considerably. This was a major step towards what we now call the 'fit' approach to improving to organizational performance. There can be no improvement in fit if all organizations are the same. If they are not the same then the questions arise: how do they differ, and what causes the differences?

For example, work by Burns and Stalker (1961) discovered two different types of organization among Scottish electronics firms. One type approximated to the traditional, classical bureaucracy. But the other, which they termed the 'organic' form, was less rigid, less hierarchic, more flexible, less rule-bound, more focused on what needed to be done than on compliance with rules. This 'organic' form of organization was much better 'adjusted' to changing and unpredictable circumstances. The organic form of organization involves:

work roles which do not have precise boundaries, relationships which ignore the formal chart or status distinctions in favour of getting the job done, rules which are for the guidance of wise men but not to be equated with the laws of the Medes and Persians, a degree of 'professionalisation' of the inter-relationships and a reward system which reflects contribution on a continuing basis rather then length of service, but in fact it makes it more possible for this kind of organisation to deal with changing problems more effectively than would a more rigid bureaucracy. (Thomason 1972: 29; quoted in Clegg and Dunkerley 1980: 157)

Another important series of studies, known collectively as the Aston studies after the university where the research was based, developed our understanding of the nature – and possibly the sources – of variation in organizational structure and other features. The Aston researchers measured a number of organizations against a set of dimensions they developed. These were: specialization, standardization, formalization (the extent to which communications are written and recorded), centralization and configuration (the structure of authority as, for example, set out in an organization chart).

The subsequent research did indeed show variation against these dimensions, but also suggested that some of the dimensions could be reduced to four critical factors on which organizations varied: structuring of activities, concentration of authority, line control of workflow, relative size of the supportive (services) component. The Aston researchers found variation in structures and identified the dimensions along which variation occurred. They showed conclusively that there is not just one model: 'It is demonstrated here that bureaucracy is *not* unitary, but that organizations may be bureaucratic in any of a number of ways. The concept of the bureaucratic type is no longer useful' (Pugh and Hickson 1976: 61).

But simply to show that organizations vary (and this has by now been demonstrated quite conclusively) is not enough to support the 'fit' thesis. Two other things are necessary.

In the 'fit' approach variations in structures must be related to organizational strategy – to what the organization is trying to achieve. This idea that features of the organization should be adapted to make them consistent with, and contribute to, the purposes of the organization, derives originally from systems theory, which defines organizations as oriented and structured around the achievement of certain goals, one of which is the goal(s) of the organization itself: 'The realisation of the goals of the system as a whole is but one of several important needs to which the organization is oriented . . . The organization, according to this model, strives to survive and maintain its equilibrium' (Gouldner 1959: 405).

However, it is clear (to systems theorists among others) that this is an idealized picture: in practice organizations may not be oriented appropriately towards their overall objectives. To argue that an organization *should* be structured to support the achievement of its goals is to accept the possibility that in reality it may not be.

This leads us to the other necessary element of the fit approach: the role and possibility of human (or managerial) choice, or conscious agency. If, for example, it were argued that organizational variation as described by the Aston researchers or others followed somehow automatically from certain key determinant variables (for example, technology or size) then there would be no room for, or need for, fit, since it would occur naturally and automatically. Such a view would have to postulate that somehow causal forces (technology, size) determine organizational structures. Such an argument would be difficult to sustain. How would this causation occur: for example how could technology *cause* organizational structure? The answer could only be that choice of technology, or choices about how to use technology in production processes, have implications for organizational structures. And this is obviously true. But all this is saying is that organizational structures and organizational production technologies are both chosen by managers. Choice, and the factors which influence management choice, become critical. If management choice is central to decisions about organizational structures then it is possible that managers will make wrong choices or ill-informed choices. Which they do. According to the fit theorists fit is problematic; it must be achieved, but it may not be. The implications are clear: managers choose organizational structures, and they can make good or bad choices. Organizational structures are not determined by some causal imperative.

An important article by John Child argued this key point powerfully. It is now recognized as true that managers can choose the structures of their organizations. Organizational structures are not imposed or determined. Of course, if managers make inappropriate choices which negatively influence organizational performance then over time there may be a tendency for successful and surviving organizations in the same industry or with the same strategy to begin to look alike as competitive and shareholder pressures penalize those organizations whose inappropriate structure or capability negatively affect their business performance, while more appropriately structured organizations achieve greater shareholder value. But this process is simply a reflection of the quality of management choices. Child draws attention to 'The process whereby strategic decisions are made (which) directs attention onto the degree of choice which can be exercised in respect of organizational design'. He notes how this concern with the scope and nature (and consequences) of managers' choices of organizational design contrasts with earlier approaches which 'imply that organizational behaviour can be understood by reference to functional imperatives rather than to political action' (Child 1972: 2). This puts the nature and quality of management decision-making absolutely centre-stage, as indeed it is in all models of organizational change discussed in this book: 'strategic choice is the critical variable in a theory of organizations' (Child 1972: 15).

These, then, are the core ingredients of the fit approach:

- That organizations differ in their shape or nature.
- That the key dimensions which can differ are: structures, systems and cultures which influence how employees behave.
- That these differences determine the nature of the organization's capability.
- That organizational capability should 'fit' strategy – i.e. should encourage, enable and require employees to behave in ways which are consistent with, and which contribute to, the overall purposes of the organization.
- Different strategies will require different capabilities.

Although structures should follow strategy, there is no reason to believe that they will, except for the pressure of long-term evolution, which will be little comfort to managers and staff in organizations that are inappropriately structured and which therefore fail. Therefore it is the duty and responsibility of managers to ensure organization fit and capability – to ensure that structures do follow strategy.

But how can they do this? There is one key question: what sort of organizations are required for what sort of strategies?

▶ Designing Effective Organizations

A warning is necessary before embarking on a consideration of this key question. Despite what consultants and gurus and management experts tell us, despite the passion and conviction they exhibit in their performances and books, there is very little certainty in this area. There are some rule-of-thumb principles, there is some research evidence, there are criteria that can be used to assess change proposals. But there is little certainty in this matter. This is partly because, as noted in chapter 1, thinking on organizational structures and change has a tendency to be cyclical, fashion-driven, over-optimistic, non-incremental. It is also partly because of the enormous complexity of organizations. Boulding has argued that organizations are among the most complex systems possible: complex, diverse, dynamic multi-dimensional, highly interrelated entities. Changing these is not easy or simple. Even working out cause-and-effect links in organizations is difficult, since manipulation of one variable may well have unforeseen and unexpected consequences. Think, for example, of the common consequences of introducing measurement systems: behaviours change, priorities change; but not always as expected or desired.

The difficulty of designing efficient organizations is also a result of an important paradoxical feature of organization: it is likely that not all organizational problems can be solved; any 'solution' to a problem reduces some of the negatives but generates others. Think for example of some common issues addressed by programmes of organizational change: centralization versus decentralization; controlling staff versus encouraging empowerment and commitment; encouraging autonomy and innovation versus installing standardized best-practice procedures, etc. All these are dichotomies, tensions where each position has both positive and negative outcomes. The result is that any form of organization which seeks to change the balance between these various sets of dichotomies is likely to change the way people behave and to generate improvement against the identified weaknesses of the previous position – but also to generate its own distinctive dysfunctions.

Nevertheless, it is possible to say something, albeit at a relatively general level, about the relationship between structures and strategies – about 'fit' or alignment. In order to consider how organizational capabilities should be organized to fit different strategies, it is necessary to have some way of talking about strategy – some classificatory system. Some researchers have focused on the stages of organizational development, or the life-cycle, arguing that different stages – start-up, growth, maturity, etc. – require different strategies and thus different types of organizational capability.

Table 3.1 offers an example of this sort of approach. It bears a resemblance to the Boston Consulting Group's framework – of businesses classified in terms of product growth prospects and product life-cycle which reflect start-up, growth, maturity and decline – discussed in chapter 6.

Different authors tend to use a rather limited conception of the organization, or in this case rather limited HR dimensions that vary with stages of business development. By human resource management they refer to what we describe as personnel systems – recruitment, selection, appraisal, training, etc. This is a limited approach to organizational capability development, since very obviously there are other aspects of organization – structures and cultures for example – which have a major influence on how employees behave. But this limitation of these authors (which derives from the period when these analyses were written) need not distract us from the central argument they advance: that different stages of organizational development – however classified – which reflect different business strategies may be associated with different organizational strategies or capability – i.e. attempts to produce different sorts of employee behaviour.

Another way to classify different types of business strategy is not by life-cycle stage but by the priorities of the strategies themselves. Again the basic idea is simple and has been foreshadowed in earlier work – for example Burns and Stalker's work, discussed earlier in this chapter. Essentially those authors wanted to explain the different levels of performance of firms in the developing electronics industry, which was characterized by rapidly changing technical and/or commercial conditions. They concluded that, of the two types of organizational system – bureaucratic and organic, 'Organic systems are adapted to unstable conditions, when problems and requirements for action arise which cannot be broken down and distributed among specialist roles within a clearly defined hierarchy. Individuals have to perform their special

Table 3.1 Critical human resource activities at different organizational or business unit stages

Human resource functions	Introduction	Life-cycle stages		
		Growth	Maturity	Decline
Recruitment, selection and staffing	Attract best technical/ professional talent	Recruit adequate numbers and mix of qualified workers; management succession planning; manage rapid internal labour market movements	Encourage sufficient turnover to minimize lay-offs and provide new openings; encourage mobility as reorganizations shift jobs around	Plan and implement workforce reductions and reallocation
Compensation and benefits	Meet or exceed labour market rates to attract needed talent	Meet external market but consider internal equity effects; establish formal compensation structures	Control compensation	Tighter cost control
Employee training and development	Define future skill requirements and begin establishing career ladders	Mould effective management team through management development and organizational development	Maintain flexibility and skills of an ageing workforce	Improve productivity and achieve flexibility in work rules; negotiate job security and employment adjustment policies

Source: Kochan and Barocci (1985).

tasks in the light of their knowledge of the firm as a whole' (Burns and Stalker 1961: 121). Their conclusion (in 1961) reflects the basic position of the 'fit' approach: 'We have endeavoured to stress the appropriateness of each system to its own specific set of conditions. Equally, we desire to avoid the suggestion that either system is under all circumstances preferable to the other ... *The beginning of administrative wisdom is the awareness that there is no one optimum type of management system*' (Burns and Stalker 1961: 125, our italics).

More recent classifications of the links between business strategy and organizational capability have built on this basic argument – that there is no optimum type of management system, but that what works best will depend on the objectives and strategy being pursued.

We now consider two classic examples of this sort of thinking. The first (table 3.2) – from Schuler and Jackson – relates different organizational factors (different types of job, payment systems, career structures, training and development) to three different business strategies: innovation, quality and cost reduction. Note how the organizational strategies associated with innovation and cost reduction are similar to, albeit developments of, Burns and Stalker's mechanistic and organic types.

Table 3.3 relates aspects of organization to the widely known strategy classification: defender, prospector and analyser. The features of organization isolated for attention in this classification include the conventional personnel processes (recruitment, appraisal and compensation), but also include organizational structure.

It will help to illustrate these suggested links between strategy and capability. We can do this by considering an empirical example of this linkage drawn from research conducted by one of the authors with a colleague, John Storey. The research concerned the management of innovation. It involved a series of interviews with senior managers in organizations with a serious and strong commitment to a strategy of innovation. One of the key areas of exploration was the extent to which these managers saw the structure, systems and culture of their organization as encouraging or discouraging innovation. Remember, formally the organization was strongly committed to a strategy of innovation. But did actual organizational practices and structures support this priority? The managers insisted that in some important respects it did not.

The organization in question, Teleco, was a telecoms company, designing and manufacturing telecoms equipment. It had all the hallmarks of a traditional British engineering company. It had a long and relatively distinguished history with some important past product innovations to its crédit. In recent years it had found a need to respond to a rapidly and substantially changing environment. It had enjoyed a close and reliable relationship with its main customer – an arrangement which in the past amounted to a cost-plus pricing policy. At that time too, the major customer had been party to the planning of future technological and product developments. Following deregulation, privatization and rapid technological change, most of these erstwhile comfort zones had been removed.

In 1998 the company had a number of main divisions each offering different products and services. It remained a very big player with a large workforce, substantial revenues and healthy profits. But there were major uncertainties about the future. Aggressive international competitors were entering its traditional markets and the rapid growth in mobile telephony, innovations such as telephone services via cable and even via power lines, as well as the potential

Table 3.2 Schuler and Jackson's model of employee role behaviour and HRM policies associated with particular business strategies

Strategy	Employee role behaviour	HRM policies
Innovation	A high degree of creative behaviour	Jobs that require close interaction and co-ordination among groups of individuals
	Longer-term focus	Performance appraisals that are more likely to reflect longer-term and group-based achievements
	A relatively high level of co-operative, interdependent behaviour	Jobs that allow employees to develop skills that can be used in other positions in the firm
	A moderate degree of concern for quality	Compensation systems that emphasize internal equity rather than external or market-based equity
	A moderate concern for quantity	Pay rates that tend to be low, but that allows employees to be stockholders and have more freedom to choose the mix of components that make up their pay package
	An equal degree of concern for process and results	Broad career paths to reinforce the development of a broad range of skills
	A greater degree of risk-taking	
	A high tolerance of ambiguity and unpredictability	
Quality enhancement	Relatively repetitive and predictable behaviours	Relatively fixed and explicit job descriptions
	A more long-term or intermediate focus	High levels of employee participation in decisions relevant to immediate work conditions and the job itself
	A moderate amount of co-operative, interdependent behaviour	A mix of individual and group criteria for performance appraisal that is mostly short-term and results-orientated
	A high concern for quality	A relatively egalitarian treatment of employees and some guarantees of employment security
	A modest concern for quality of output	
	High concern for process	Extensive and continuous training and development of employees
	Low risk-taking activity	
	Commitment to the goals of the organization	
Cost reduction	Relatively repetitive and predictable behaviours	Relatively fixed and explicit job descriptions that allow little room for ambiguity
	A rather short-term focus	Narrowly designed jobs and narrowly defined career paths that encourage specialization, expertise and efficiency
	Primarily autonomous or individual activity	Short-term, results-orientated performance appraisals
	Moderate concern for quality	Close monitoring of market pay levels for use in makingcompensation
	High concern for quantity of output	Minimal levels of employee training and development
	Primary concern for results Low risk-taking activity	
	Relatively high degree of comfort with stability	

Source: Storey and Sisson (1993: 66), adapted from Schuler and Jackson (1987: 209–13). Reproduced by permission of the Open University Press.

for telephony over the internet – let alone new developments in switching technology across all capacity levels from rural to metropolitan and international – all represented major disturbances to the system. It was against this backdrop that our key informants sought to reflect and make sense of the place, priority and nature of, and the opportunities for and obstacles to, innovation. Fundamentally, there was a collective sense that international competitors were handling product and process innovation far more proficiently, and that this adverse comparison represented a serious threat to the future viability of the Teleco organization in the medium to long term.

Teleco's managers held strong views about innovation. Innovation was a top strategic priority, a central concern, a naturally occurring source of interest and speculation. It was seen as critical to the business's success, and was central to the business strategy. Teleco's managers were in no doubt about the importance of innovation for their business. Yet despite the public and internal commitment to the importance of strategy, despite the fact that innovation was clearly a major success factor in the rapidly changing telecoms business, managers in Teleco identified a number of features of Teleco's organization which in their view obstructed the actual achievement of innovation.

One obstacle arose from the structure of the organization. Teleco was a wholly owned subsidiary of a larger engineering conglomerate. Managers insisted this had implications for innovation: 'Our parent organization is at a mature stage of the product life-cycle; they have plateaued. They have a completely different approach to innovation from ours. We are in a young market that will grow. Yet all [the parent company] asks about are quarterly financial returns.'

There were other structural implications: for decision-making about the encouragement or funding of innovation. Although *in principle* Teleco was committed to innovation, *in practice* the business was geared up to encourage some forms rather than others – to encourage incremental improvements to existing products rather than longer-term and more speculative development of radically new products. One major reason for this was the location of responsibility and funding of innovation within the existing product businesses. This was because of the perceived importance of innovation being 'accountable to', or 'owned by', the businesses in order to avoid the perceived risks and extravagances of unaccountable innovation for innovation's sake. Whatever the reality of that risk, Teleco managers vigorously maintained that the positioning of innovation within the product businesses meant that, because of the performance pressure on these businesses, long-term radical innovation was sacrificed to short-term incremental modifications:

> What are we, in essence, organised to achieve? Now you might say that the way we're organised reinforces the reactive element (to innovation) in the sense that new product development tends to be given to the existing product divisions whose main interests are of course maintaining their revenue stream because

Table 3.3 Miles and Snow's model of business strategies and HRM systems

Organizational/managerial characteristics	Type A (Defender)	Type B (Prospector)	Type AB (Analyser)
Product-market strategy	Limited stable product line	Broad, changing product line	Stable and changing product line
	Predictable markets	Changing markets	Predictable and changing markets
	Growth through market penetration	Growth through product development and market development	Growth mostly through market development
	Emphasis 'deep'	Emphasis 'broad'	Emphasis 'deep' and 'focused'
Research and development	Limited mostly to product improvement	Extensive emphasis on 'first-to-market'	Focused, emphasis on 'second-to-market'
Production	High-volume–low-cost	Customized and prototypical	High-volume–low-cost: some prototypical
	Emphasis on efficiency and process engineering	Emphasis on effectiveness and product design	Emphasis on process engineering and product or brand management
Marketing	Limited mostly to sales	Focused heavily on market research	Utilizes extensive marketing campaign
Organization structure	Functional	Divisional	Functional and matrix
Control process	Centralized	Decentralized	Mostly centralized, but decentralized in marketing and brand management
Dominant coalition	CEO	CEO	CEO
	Production	Product research and development	Marketing
	Finance/accounting	Market research	Process engineering
Business planning sequence	Plan-Act-Evaluate	Act-Evaluate-Plan	Evaluate-Plan-Act
Basic strategy	Building human resources	Allocating human resources	Acquiring human resources

	Emphasis: 'make'	Emphasis: 'buy'	Emphasis: 'make' and 'buy'
Recruitment, selection and placement	Little recruiting above entry level Selection based on weeding out undesirable employees	Sophisticated recruiting at all levels Selection may involve pre-employment psychological testing	Mixed recruiting and selection approaches Limited outside recruitment
Staff planning	Formal, extensive	Informal, limited	Formal, extensive
Training and development	Skill-building Extensive training programmes	Skill identification and acquisition Limited training programmes	Skill-building and acquisition Extensive training programmes
Performance appraisal	Process-oriented procedure (for example, based on critical incidents, or production targets) Identification of training needs Individual group performance evaluations (for example, previous year's performance)	Results-oriented procedure (for example, management by objectives or profit targets) Identification of staffing needs Division/corporate performance evaluations Cross-sectional comparison (for example, other companies during the same period)	Mostly process-oriented procedure Identification of training and staffing needs Individual/group/division performance evaluations Mostly time series, some cross-sectional comparisons
Compensation	Oriented towards position in organization hierarchy Internal consistency Total compensation heavily oriented towards cash and driven by superior/subordinate differentials	Oriented towards performance External competitiveness Total compensation heavily oriented towards incentives and driven by recruitment needs	Mostly oriented towards hierarchy, some performance considerations Internal consistency and external competitiveness Cash and incentive compensation

Source: Miles and Snow (1984: 48–9). Reproduced by permission of Elsevier Science.

that's how they are judged. So that raises the question: are we really organised for innovation? Should we not find new ways of doing things such as spin-offs or spin-outs – where we identify new markets and ring-fence them to incentivise the management so they are like entrepreneurs?

Existing businesses focused on innovations that supported their business ends. The structural emphasis on production and the location of innovation within product units tipped the balance against radical innovation and encouraged an antipathy towards investment in longer-term innovation by starving such projects of resources. A respondent argued: 'We are developing our own operating system but we have been directly obstructed in the development of this key component by [the plc] which has been diverting funds and has stopped us employing the necessary engineers so there is a risk we will miss the market.'

Not only were tightly focused product businesses likely to look askance at expensive innovation projects, but the more successful these businesses were, the less likely they might be to see the need for them to support such research. The dilemma was not simply operational activity versus radical research, or certainty versus speculation, but also success versus risk-taking:

> The current process of thinking and decision-making may allow us to ask, should we be in this or that business? And should we move into this or to that? But the way they think [i.e. at the corporate level] about these issues always seems to bring us back to what we already do. Being highly profitable is also highly restricting and constraining. It's funny but if you are highly profitable it's very difficult justifying risks that might threaten those returns.

The problem with this is that businesses have products in different stages of their life-cycles and so, according to some respondents at least, someone had to take a broad view which extended beyond the concerns of any product champion. It was suggested that it was necessary 'to start new ventures, ideally sprinkled with individuals who are prepared to take risks and innovate in pursuit of their belief in a new market opportunity. You may have to do both in parallel which is actually quite hard to do in many organizations because the product barons don't give up their positions very easily.'

In summary, these managers saw an inappropriate balance between radical and incremental innovation, and they interpreted this as reflecting a structural confusion on the part of the organization as a whole. Principles of structuring that were applicable for one end (production) were applied to other strategic objectives (innovation) for which they were less appropriate.

This is a structural constraint on the achievement of a strategy of innovation. But there were others.

Like most organizations with a strategic commitment to innovation, Teleco had a formal innovation management system. The intention of this system was to ensure that only good-quality and promising ideas were funded. However, managers argued vigorously that in effect this innovation management system was an obstacle to the encouragement of innovation.

Teleco managers recognized the need for an organizational process that encouraged innovation. But they were concerned about the nature and implications of the system. Essentially they questioned its purpose, arguing that it was more geared to stopping innovation than to encouraging it. They argued that the implicit values and priorities of the process reflected operational and production concern for short-term benefits and product reliability which was at odds with the sort of attitude to risk and innovation that was necessary. They argued that the logic of the Teleco innovation management process was more concerned to reduce risk than to encourage innovation; to eliminate technical failure rather than elicit success; to ensure engineering functionality rather than marketing impact. Thus, as one said: 'The review process is a filter, not a catalyst. The preordained product business structure is crucial: new products raise questions of how and where they will fit. We need people to think outside of what their brief says.'

Overall, respondents argued that the process enshrined an inappropriate attitude to risk by applying to product development old-fashioned engineering attitudes to risk: 'It applies excessive engineering logics (testing and demanding reassurances) to the development of innovation.'

Some saw the innovation review process as inherently paradoxical, particularly when the need for certainty and reassurance became excessive: 'In dealing with innovation, by definition, you are dealing with things you do not fully understand. Therefore, pressing for detail is foolish. You are killing it. The watchword should be: Try It!' By demanding reassuring information, the process stifled projects. This happened especially when a product was slightly unusual and when the trajectories of the marketplace were less well known and understood. 'You need people with courage; there seems to be something wrong with how we do it. We lose heart, pull out, focus too much on early sales and lose future ones.'

The managers argued that historically established and culturally valued modes of thinking and decision-making which contributed to organizational success at the operational level were dysfunctional when applied to innovation. They appeared to argue that, at least in Teleco, organizing (capability in our terms) and innovating (the core business strategy) were in tension. Organizing meant applying established cognitive schemas and values based on engineering logics, achieving predictability, making events routine. Innovation is to disorganize, to embrace and even to seek variety and unpredictability (Weick and Westley 1996). For example, technical engineering excellence was accepted as a necessary element in innovation but it was also defined as not *sufficient* and even a drawback if engineering logics and values dominated the attitude towards risk.

Teleco managers thus argued that in two main respects the capability of the organization was inappropriate for the encouragement and achievement of a major strategic objective. The structure of Teleco, however appropriate for the organization and management of production, was seen as far less appropriate for the encouragement of innovation; furthermore, requiring innovation to be tied to the product businesses meant that it was subject to production priorities and systems, with discouraging consequences. They argued that organizational systems – specifically the innovation review process – were imbued with priorities and logics which reflected the values and assumption of the engineering culture of the organization, but which effectively worked to such high standards as to be more concerned with eliminating risk than encouraging innovation. In short, they argued that the dominant culture of the organization might have negative effects for the encouragement of innovation.

The Teleco case suggests some of the strengths and appeal of the 'fit' approach: it makes sense to ensure the organization is capable, in the widest sense, of achieving its strategic objectives. It makes sense to ensure that all aspects of an organization's structures, systems, and culture are arranged in a way to encourage the appropriate types of behaviour. But the Teleco example also illustrates some of the difficulties associated with the approach.

First, organizations often pursue more than one strategy, as Teleco did. Sometimes these strategies can conflict or fail to mesh together. When businesses pursue a number of strategies – for example, a low-cost high-volume strategy in a manufacturing operation but an innovative strategy in the R&D arm – this can cause difficulties. A business might find it difficult simultaneously to achieve the two very different sorts of organization each of these strategies requires. The Teleco case illustrates precisely these difficulties. In theory of course there should be no problem: each business or department pursuing a different and distinctive strategy would have the type of organization appropriate for its strategy. An organization would therefore consist, potentially, of a variety of different types of organization. And of course this does happen. But there can be difficulties achieving this in practice. One problem occurs when a particular strategy and its associated type of organization is in some way more powerful and dominant than others. Again Teleco is an example of this. Managers with a concern for innovation argued forcibly that because of the historic significance of manufacturing and engineering, and as a result of the significance of these activities financially, they had assumed a dominant status within the business to the extent that senior managers from these operations were able to dominate discussions of, or even consideration of, alternative organizational forms. This dominance can be both political and cultural. It is most significant when it is both.

Politically, senior managers representing key historical organizational processes (and the organizational forms characteristic of these processes) may well have the political clout to be able to discourage the development of organizational forms which deviate from the principles they see as fundamental to the business's historic success: they might see the encouragement of such new or alternative forms as threatening, irresponsible, or undisciplined.

This reaction may be cultural in origin. Culture refers not only to shared values but also to 'shared meanings, shared understanding and shared sense-making' (Morgan 1986: 24). Senior managers with a long, shared background in a particular type of organization or a particular part of the organization with distinctive strategies and organizational principles may find it hard to think about or countenance radically different types of organization which are based on values and principles in opposition to or different from those to which they are committed. Their reflex response to such forms would be one of concern and opposition. For example, if managers who are strenuously committed to achieving predictability, co-ordination and efficiency in a low-cost high-volume operation (a manufacturing unit or a call centre), where operations are standardized, employees are closely monitored, payment is by results, skill levels are kept as low as possible, attendance is closely watched, and costs are pared to the minimum, are faced with another department where none of these conditions exists and where staff are loosely controlled, are allowed to pursue their own initiatives, where discipline is low but salaries are high, and where standards of behaviour are relaxed, they are likely to have difficulty recognizing the virtues of such a type of organization even though this may be exactly what is required in a department concerned with encouraging innovation.

For example, consider a typical UK insurance company of 10 or so years ago. The traditional strength of the business lay in the tight control of an efficient national network of underwriters and claims processors. Given the nature of this work, strict and clear underwriting control and claims guidelines were essential to ensure the minimum exposure to risk and thus good business margins. Carefully and thoroughly devised actuarial principles allied to close managerial control, guidelines and training reduced the scope for individual discretion which could, through unwise underwriting decisions, result in very high levels of exposure. This type of organization worked. It fitted the technical nature and strategic objectives of the branch network, at least under conditions of gentle and stable competition.

But this organization, seeking to widen its range of business, might have moved into more speculative and innovative lines of work: special niche forms of insurance for example, or types of insurance allied to warranties on consumer products, which required new types of people with new types of skills – initiative, enterprise, commercial judgement, marketing, as well as technical insurance knowledge.

This could pose a challenge to the senior management. Logically and rationally they may recognize that this new type of business with new types of strategic objectives required new forms of organization. But it could well be difficult for them to encourage or allow forms of organization which differed from – indeed even conflicted with – those to which they had been committed for many years. Starbuck has noted that organizational thinking – on structures and strategies – becomes trapped within historic ways of thinking and established routines which, because they are so familiar, become taken for granted.

This is a major reason why senior managers may find it difficult to think about or tolerate forms of organization which differ radically from those with which they are familiar, even though the objectives of the organization make such differentiation necessary.

So far we have stressed the potential practical difficulties of combining – or even of allowing – different types and principles of organization within one overarching organization. However, it should also be noted that it is possible that not all the different types of strategy as classified by those authors who have devised frameworks and classifications of strategy may in practice be mutually exclusive. This is, for example, a point that has been made about Porter's classification. In practice firms may pursue more than one objective at the same time: many Japanese firms, for example, pursue both quality and low cost. In this case presumably the firms in question have managed – or must try to manage – to achieve a type of organization that fits both goals.

There is another potential difficulty with the fit approach, and it's one we have mentioned briefly earlier in the book. This approach to organizational change assumes a coherent and intelligent process of strategy formulation. There is little point in changing organizational structures and systems to make them match the organization's strategy if the strategy itself is poorly thought out, misinformed, unintelligent, imitative. The approach furthermore assumes a certain sequence of activities, with thorough environmental analysis leading to intelligent analysis, resulting in the development of alert and appropriate strategic objectives and strategies for their achievement which in turn and in due course produce organizational change. This sequences implies a top-down, sequential, highly controlled rationalistic and centralized business-planning process.

In practice neither of these important assumptions can always be made: strategies are not always sensible and intelligent and the sequence of operations assumed by the fit approach does not always occur (and arguably should not always occur – but this will be discussed in chapter 5).

The way in which organizations construct strategies is critical to any of the approaches to improved organizational performance discussed in this book. Whatever the nature of the relationship between structure and strategy, the capacity to develop intelligent, well-based, realistic strategies is crucial to any proposal to improve organizational performance. But not only is strategic thinking frequently flawed and limited, the grounds for these limitations often lie in the very nature of the organization itself. The features of an organization that make it operationally efficient at producing goods and services can also restrict its ability to think strategically. James March has described this paradox neatly:

> organisations are plagued by the difficulty of balancing exploration and exploitation. By exploration is meant such things as search, discovery, novelty, and innovation. It involves variation, risk-taking, and experimentation . . . By exploitation

is meant refinement, routinisation, production, and implementation of knowledge. It involves choice, efficiency, selection and reliability . . . Exploration cannot realise its occasional gains without exploitation of discoveries. Exploitation becomes obsolescent without exploration of new directions. Finding a good balance between exploration and exploitation is a recurrent problem. (March 1999: 5)

It's a problem organizations often fail to solve. The significant feature of the paradox is that an organization's strength (operational efficiency – 'exploitation') is a source of weakness (impaired strategic thinking or 'exploration'). Understanding why and how strategic thinking can be limited by features of the organization itself is an issue that merits separate discussion, since a central and critical way in which organizational performance can be achieved is by improving the quality of strategic thinking.

Furthermore, the fit approach's implicit sequencing of activities – environmental analysis (E), strategic development (S), organizational capability (C) – may also be unrealistic. The top-down, centralized, logical sequence of activities which reflects the classic sequence of problem-solving or of the learning cycle – data, analysis, selection, action – is only one of a number of ways in which strategy development and organizational change may actually occur.

Thirdly, while it may be obvious that structures and strategies are less than well matched – as in Teleco – it is often less obvious what form of organization would be better matched. There simply is not a clear or consensual view as to what sorts of structures best fit what sorts of strategies. Of course certain broad-brush agreements have been reached, many of which are set out in the earlier discussion of the possible linkages between strategies and structures.

This problem is compounded by two factors, one of which is that at any particular period the insistence of consultants and management experts and writers often combines to stress the merits of particular forms of organization which are advocated as fashionable solutions in particular epochs. For a time – often quite a short time – managers are almost deafened by a chorus of exhortations, all advocating more or less the same type and direction of organizational change: delayering, BPR, culture change and so on. Very frequently this form of organizational change, although announced as entirely new and revolutionary, in fact bears a striking resemblance to earlier and now largely forgotten approaches to organizational change.

But even the fact that new ideas might be versions of old ideas does not affect their appeal and impact. And during the period that a particular approach to organizational change is in the ascendant it is very hard for managers to avoid seeing this idea as an attractive and compelling solution.

The danger of course is that this results in much organizational change being solution-driven rather than problem-driven. Brunnson and Olsen (1993) have noted wryly that organizational change needs two things: a supply of problems and a supply of solutions. Frequently the supply of solutions is more influential in management choices about organization than the nature of organizational problems, a key one of which is of course the nature of the organization's objectives and strategies.

Available and fashionable, recommended organizational change is often powerful not only because it is so widely accepted and encouraged but also because at certain times certain sorts of organizational solutions may seem 'right'. Some writers have suggested that the appeal of a number of recent recommendations is a consequence of the resonance of the proposed approach and the principles it articulates with wider societal or political values and movements. One example of this is Guest's analysis of the appeal of the 'Excellence' prescriptions, which he attributes to their affinities with basic US values. Guest, writing in the early 1990s at the height of interest in the 'Excellence' approach, noted: 'Those outside the field of organizational behaviour may be forgiven for wondering what all the fuss is about and why an apparently rather poorly researched book by two consultants should create so much interest' (Guest 1992: 5). Despite the weaknesses of the argument of the book, Guest argues that we should take it seriously, not because it is a particularly convincing argument but because of its impact on management practice. The appeal of the book may lie in its linkages with the shared values of its readers. In particular, he argues for the close links between the values inherent in the book and its recommendations and assumptions and US values: the American Dream, the idealized sense of possibility, the focus on individualism and enterprise and the emphasis on the heroic leader. Grint (1994) has taken a similar line in explaining the appeal of the BPR movement, arguing that it lies in the ways in which BPR texts claim to revive or rediscover forgotten US values in the face of threats from the Japanese; BPR offers a way back to basic, true, American values (see also Clark and Salaman 1998: 145). Grint writes: 'The language of reengineering renders opaque developments clear, not by providing a more objective analysis of the situation and the solution but by providing a more persuasive rendering of these. Moreover, part of the persuasive essence lies in the resonance that it "reveals" between the old and new, particularly between American past glories and future conquests' (Grint 1994: 194).

Available and fashionable approaches to organizational change may also seem 'right' because they resonate with wider societal and political programmes and principles of change. A striking and obvious example of this is the enormous stress laid on the market as a principle of economic and financial management by UK and US governments over the last 20 years, as discussed in chapter 1 above.

The problems noted so far suggest some of the difficulties that managers may have in thinking about and selecting an organizational form that is appropriate for the organization's purposes. But, despite these difficulties, is there any evidence that certain structures are associated with specific strategies and that achieving this fit impacts on organizational performance?

It has to be admitted that the evidence is scanty. A useful recent book by Karen Legge lists and summarizes this empirical material. She notes that much of the fit literature is prescriptive rather than descriptive. Empirical assessment of the fit thesis offers some support for a connection between product or organizational life-cycle and organizational features, particularly HR features (Rowland and Summers 1981; Kuhn 1982; Smith-Cook and Ferris 1986). Legge also notes that studies have documented an empirical connection between different strategies and very specific HR elements – such as selection, training and development, and compensation systems. And a study by Fox and McLeay (1992) argues that in the UK electronics and engineering sector corporate strategy is related to a wide range of HR features. Legge also notes that researchers have found some correlation between Porter's strategy types and features of organization – particularly, once again, HR features. But these are relations of correlation or of causation, and once again they are not apparently related to performance indicators.

Part of the difficulty in assessing the empirical nature of a fit between strategy and type of organization is that, although senior managers like to claim that they have an explicit, coherent and strategic approach to their organization whereby the organization, and its structures and systems, is designed to fit its strategy, in practice it is not always easy to find evidence for this. Legge quotes some researchers who studied the nature and realities of UK managers' HR strategies:

> it is difficult to escape the conclusion that although the great majority of our respondents claim that their organisations have an overall policy or approach towards the management of employees . . . it would be wrong to place very much store by this . . . the general weight of evidence would seem to confirm that most UK-owned enterprises remain pragmatic or opportunistic in their approach. (Marginson et al. 1988: 120)

However, things may be changing. Although historically those responsible for issues of organizational capability and structuring (personnel specialists) have usually not been involved in the organizational implications of strategic issues (Legge 1995: 119), recently this has changed significantly, with personnel specialists increasingly being involved in such matters.

One of the reasons for managers' apparent 'opportunism' and lack of clear organization strategy may be that, even if in principle organizations and their HR specialists try to fit their structures to their strategic objectives, and this is clearly a sensible ambition, there is a possibility that short-term pressures and considerations may overwhelm the effort to establish the sort of organization required. This may be one reason why senior managers claim to have an organizational strategy, but empirical evidence to support such strategies is less clear. This is particularly likely when the strategy is one that requires the development of committed, skilled, innovative, knowledgeable, specialist professional staff over the long term. If the strategy requires these sorts of people and attributes, the possibility then arises that achieving fit between strategies of quality or innovation (for example) and the appropriate type of organization – which will require a consistent and long-term approach – may be blown off course by short-term crises and pressures. There is evidence of this. Purcell, for example, in a review of the evidence available in the early 1990s, comes to a 'pessimistic conclusion': that a short-term focus on cost control, or maximizing margins, or on tight financial controls, makes it harder (and less likely) that firms will develop or implement longer-term integrated organizational strategies. He concludes:

> It becomes harder to develop integrated and meaningful institutional strategies or management styles at the corporate level, and – to the degree that short-run rates of return on investment, emphasis on margin improvements, and tight financial controls impose on unit managers – harder at the unit level to develop and maintain long-run human resource policies. (Purcell 1989: 79)

All this may seem a rather gloomy prognosis: fit is hard to achieve, hard to find. Many factors separately and in combination conspire to distract and divert managers. It assumes an idealized notion of strategy and the strategy process. All this is true: there are undoubted problems with the approach. But there are also great strengths. Fit makes intuitive sense. Although hard to achieve it makes obvious sense to try. It's true we may never reach our destination, our Ithaca, but the journey itself will be enriching, and without the promise of the destination we would never set out. And none of the difficulties of the approach entirely undermines its value. Indeed some of these problems actually strengthen it. The value of the fit approach is less that organizations can achieve fit – this remains an attractive aspiration but may, as we have seen, be difficult in practice – and more that seeking to achieve fit supplies a welcome rigour and discipline to management thinking about organization and capability. If numerous factors are likely to encourage managers to adopt fashionable, generic, off-the-shelf consultancy packages then the application of the fit approach may well help to identify the deficiencies and inappropriateness of fashionable solutions. Fit thus becomes a methodology, a set of questions and challenges that can usefully be used not only to assess the relevance and value of recommended courses of action, but also to audit the nature and contribution of existing structures and systems. It is surprising how powerful and productive it can be to ask such questions as:

- 'To what extent and in what ways does the existing structure of the organization contribute to, or obstruct, the achievement of our strategic objectives?' or,
- 'What sorts of attributes and behaviour do we need from our employees if they are to be able and willing to contribute fully to the business's objectives, and how far are these attributes and behaviours encouraged by current structures and systems?' or,
- 'If we were to start again with a clean sheet of paper and design in totality the sort of organization we want, what would it be like?'

It is precisely because of the power of the fit approach as a diagnostic tool that this approach has become enshrined in a number of quality assurance frameworks. Kaplan and Norton's (1992) 'balanced score card', the British Quality Foundation's framework, the principles of the Investors in People framework, all in slightly different ways try to encourage managers to explore the nature of their objectives, the nature of their systems, and the relationships between them. Sometimes this focus is quite explicit. Investors in People, for example, focuses managers' attention on the existence and nature of 'organizational systems which encourage employees' developments and relate this to organizational objectives'. This then is the strength of fit: despite its weaknesses and difficulties it remains a powerful way of thinking about the nature of organization and principles underlying organization and the ways in which organization – or capability – supports the purposes it is intended to deliver.

We should not leave this discussion of fit without noting another approach to the improvement of organizational performance. Unlike the fit approach, this approach argues for the value of a set of measures which are, it is claimed, of value in any circumstances, for any organization pursuing any sort of strategy. This is the closed or absolute approach to organizational performance.

▶ The Closed or Absolute Approach to Improved Organizational Performance

The closed approach to organizational transformation is very common. This approach has three slightly different variants.

1   The first approach argues that there are certain rather unambitious but sensible organizational changes which always improve performance, whatever strategy the business is pursuing. This is the good practice or good housekeeping sense. It recommends that things such as good communications, systematic selection and training, teamwork, coherent reward systems linked to performance and flexible job design improve performance in any circumstances. It claims that in any organization, under all circumstances, in pursuit of all strategic objectives, these measures are beneficial.

2   The second version of the closed approach is far more ambitious. It is not concerned with simple and obviously sensible organizational procedures, with organizational measures, but advocates in effect a theory of organizational functioning. It argues that organizations work better when employees are treated in ways which generate a level of commitment and that employee commitment is related to improved performance. It claims, therefore, that gaining employee commitment is central to the achievement of improved performance. The qualities are consistent:

Guest stresses 'Optimal employee commitment to enterprise goals and practices'; Beaumont emphasizes 'teamwork, flexibility, employee involvement and organizational commitment' (Beaumont 1992: 25). We are familiar with this argument from a previous chapter. Walton (1985) made precisely the same point. He advanced the theory that certain organizational measures are important and valuable – those that promote 'mutuality' (he spells them out); these measures elicit employee commitment. Employee commitment produces 'better economic performance'.

This may seem an attractive idea. It certainly has a moral, social and possibly an individual appeal. And it may be true. But there are still difficulties surrounding this closed approach to organizational improvement, however attractive and intuitively appealing it may be. Apart from the serious practical issues surrounding the likelihood of the success of measures aimed at achieving employee commitment (which we'll discuss later) the main problem is the conflict between the open and closed approaches to organizational change. Gaining employee commitment may always be beneficial. But that's not the point. The point is the degree of priority that should or will be given to the goal of achieving employee commitment under various and varying organizational circumstances. The key issue is the *relative* importance – and relative cost – of gaining employee commitment. If, due to organizational circumstances, a company must downsize, should it reject this option because of its potentially damaging effect on its attempts to gain employee commitment? If an organization is committed to a low-cost, high-volume strategy in an industry which is cost-driven, it may prefer that its employees should be committed through policies that promote mutuality ('mutual goals, mutual influence, mutual respect, mutual rewards, mutual responsibility') but decide that it is relatively more important to automate as far as possible, to deskill, to reduce wages, to move to less attractive employment contracts. Such steps may simply be necessary in the face of conditions in the industry. And they will have obvious implications for the way employees feel about their employer.

3 Another form of this type of closed, invariant approach advocates a single measure or approach which is defined as the single most important and most beneficial change that can be introduced: the universal cure for all organizational ills, the sovereign remedy, the single truth around which the organization must be based. Projects such as BPR, corporate culture, downsizing, decentralization, the introduction of market relations within the organization: each and all of these has in its day been presented by its proponents as the single, unvarying basis for organizational renewal. Regardless of local circumstances, regardless of differences in strategy and purpose, these single-theme approaches to organizational renewal are claimed not only to offer benefits but also to

be essential to organizational transformation. It is the duty of managers to install and manage these schemes. The benefits: salvation, total renewal and transformation.

Consider just some of the claims that have been made for culture change programmes. 'Organizational culture' is considered 'the managerial formula for success' (Jaggi 1985) that determines an organization's 'success or failure'; managers are promised a 'culture of 'productivity' (Akin and Hopelain 1986) if they understand the elements that all cultures of productivity have in common. The 'right' culture may 'reap a return on investment that averages nearly twice as high as those firms with less efficient cultures' (Denison 1984). 'Sustained competitive advantage' (Barney 1986) is expected from the 'right' culture, which is also characterized as 'strong' (Bleicher 1983: 495) 'rich' (Deal and Kennedy 1982: 14), 'healthy, blooming' (Ulrich 1984: 313), 'consistent' (Hinterhuber 1986), and 'participatory' (Denison 1984: 7; Sackmann 1990: 119; Mabey et al. 1998: 462).

There are some ambitious versions of this approach which argue that certain ways of treating employees will always be beneficial. Guest offers such a view. He notes that a number of writers have in effect argued that certain measures have positive effects on performance. They are:

- integration of relevant employee activities into general organizational strategies and policies
- fluid and adaptive organizational structure
- high-quality staff and internal practices to achieve high-quality products
- optimal employee commitment to enterprise goals and practices (Guest 1987).

Now there are two arguments here: that these measures produce improved organizational performance, and that they *always improve performance regardless of the circumstances or the strategic goals*. The former seems intuitively likely, but the latter is less likely to be true. Imagine, for example, an organization committed to a low-cost strategy in a commodity marketplace. Guest's measures may be attractive and may in principle have positive effects on staff attitude. But if they raise production costs they will have negative effects on the organization's performance.

Some authors have tried to argue that the fit approach and the absolute or closed approach can be consistent. Beaumont, for example, writes:

The key messages . . . in the human resource management literature . . . are a strategic focus, the need for human resource policies and practices to be consistent with overall business strategy, and the need for individual components of a human resource package to reinforce each other, while the individual components of the package should particularly emphasise teamwork, flexibility, employee involvement and organisational commitment. (Beaumont 1992: 25)

But this is a bit of a fudge. If the key essential is fit of organizational features with strategy, it is not feasible or logical also to argue that certain stipulated measures will always be necessary and always be beneficial regardless of strategy, unless the fit approach is jettisoned.

Which is what some researchers have done in effect. A number of researchers have identified a series of measures which they have sometimes labelled 'high-commitment human resource systems', and sometimes 'high-performance work practices'. These are characterized by: higher levels of employee involvement in managerial decisions, formal participation programmes, training in group problem-solving and socializing activities (Arthur 1994: 672). Huselid has listed the features of 'high-performance work practices' as 'extensive recruitment, selection and training procedures; formal information sharing, attitude assessment, job design, grievance procedures, and labor-management participation programmes; and performance appraisal, promotion, and incentive compensation systems that recognise and reward employee merit' (Huselid 1998: 105). Huselid – and others – found that the use of these practices was related to organizational performance: 'Across a wide range of industries and firm sizes, I found considerable support for the hypothesis that investments in such practices are associated with lower employee turnover and greater productivity and corporate financial performance' (Huselid 1998: 124). This author also attempted to assess the impact of fit approaches on improving organizational performance. But while acknowledging the difficulties of developing measures of fit, he notes that he found 'only modest evidence of . . . an effect for internal fit and little evidence for external fit' (1998: 124).

However, Huselid's overall conclusions are also interesting because, despite these empirical findings, he acknowledges that the 'theoretical arguments for internal and external fit remain compelling', even if to date the empirical evidence remains thin. This is a conclusion other researchers have also drawn. Although there is some evidence that a set of measures has positive impact in all circumstances, even those who advocate this approach recognize that different organizational environments and strategies will require different types of employee and different types of structures and cultures: 'just about everybody who writes about human resource strategy subscribes to a contingency hypothesis to some extent' (Dyer and Reeves 1995: 665).

4

The Resource-Based View of Strategy

The most important sources of business rents are business-specific: industry membership is a much less important source and corporate parentage is quite unimportant.

(Rumelt 1998: 104)

INTRODUCTION

There is a story, probably apocryphal, that during the UN campaign in Kosovo in the late 1990s, when large numbers of Muslim Kosovans fled the country to become refugees in neighbouring Albania, the British army recognized that it needed to become more adept at quickly and efficiently assembling large quantities of tents and building temporary encampments. They didn't know to whom to turn for help. Then someone had a brainwave: ask a circus. Who would know better than those in a circus how quickly and efficiently to assemble temporary tent structures? They do it all the time.

The point of this story is not that the British army is capable of lateral thinking. The point is more germane to the themes of this chapter: that organizations can use what they are good at as the basis for what they produce and sell. It is unlikely that the circus people had ever realized that their ability to erect tents quickly and efficiently was something marketable. They probably thought that they were in the entertainment business, not the training or consulting business or tent-erection business. They probably thought that what they offered was the *output* of their work: people flying through the air, ladies in tights on horses, strong men in leotards breathing fire and swallowing swords, those awful clowns. They probably never considered that their processes and skills were marketable, or even that they had any.

And the analogy with the themes of this chapter goes further: it is also very likely that the circus people didn't even know they were good at erecting tents (far less that this was something marketable); they probably took their skills at this for granted. Indeed it is highly likely that they didn't even know what they knew: the skills, habits, patterns of co-operation, knowing what order to do things in, how to stow the ropes, the danger signs to watch for, the times when certain participants might need a hand, all this and much more was so embedded in their relationships, and shared culture, history and routines, that they didn't know what they knew. The circus people's skills were part of the way they and their organization worked: they were in the air they breathed. They were not formalized in a manual or training courses. If they were they would not be so precious, because they would then be available to anyone.

These are the elements of the approach to strategy and improved organizational performance that we discuss in this chapter: that business performance can be built and competitively sustained through the organization's possession of a distinctive and attractive, marketable and hard to copy, organizationally based capability.

The previous chapter, in discussing how organizational performance can be improved by improving the fit between strategies and organization, assumed a view of strategy that is distinctive (and potentially vulnerable) in two ways. First it assumed that strategy could be – is – developed in a rational, systematic way. It assumed that senior managers or their staff scan the environment comprehensively, systematically, objectively; that they analyse the data they capture sensibly and with detachment; that they then review all the strategic options and finally identify and select objectives and strategies. This is a wonderfully rational way for strategies to be developed. No doubt this is how things should be done. But is it how it happens in any organization known to you? Probably not: many factors interrupt and distort this model of how strategy is developed, and many of these factors arise from the very nature of organization itself. What a paradox: in order to be efficient and effective, organizations develop ways of working which make them efficient at what they do but which can seriously limit their ability to think about what they do or should do; can have implications for – and can seriously limit – how they think, including how they think strategically. So being good at what they do can have implications for organizations' ability to think clearly about what they should do.

But there is another key feature of the fit approach which is limiting and distinctive and in some cases simply wrong: it assumes a certain sequence or logic of strategy development.

The fit model assumes a process of strategy development which starts with an understanding of the business environment and moves to the development of strategies which will enable the organization to exploit market opportunities and avoid market threats – to position itself advantageously. The organization is then adjusted to ensure it supports the achievement of these strategies.

But there is another view: that, rather than build the organization around its strategies, strategies should be built around organization. Rather than try to modify the organization – possibly painfully and laboriously – to make it capable of supporting new strategies for which it was not originally developed, why not try to find existing organizational strengths around which strategies could be built?

This is the essence of what is called the resource-based approach to strategy. As one commentator notes, this differs from the fit approach in the following way: 'In this view, strategy becomes a patient, inwardly aware process, rather than the fluid, externally oriented pursuit of opportunity' (Whittington 1993: 27).

This approach requires three key elements. First, what is the nature of the organizational 'strengths' around which strategies could be built? Secondly, what is the sources of these strengths – on what are they based? Finally, what are the practical implications of this approach? What can be done from the point of view of the concerns of this book to build and protect such organizational strengths and their sources?

In this chapter we shift the emphasis to the resources that an organization possesses, or may need to possess, as the possible basis of strategy. Actually the resource-based view of strategy is misnamed: the essence of this approach is not the resources that an organization owns but its capacity to use and develop and combine them: 'capabilities represent the capacity to deploy resources' (Kamoche 1991: 46–7). Resources alone are not enough. Resources are reasonably generally available. They can be rare and the subject of competition, but when this is the case the organizational ability to find, monopolize, or retain scarce resources – if it isn't sheer luck – itself owes something to the capabilities of the organization. And it is the capability to exploit and combine resources that is the key here. What makes the difference is how resources are combined, combined in new ways, cherished, nurtured. This is the essence of capability. The question we address in this chapter, which is key to one major way in which organizational performance may be improved, is 'How can we explain and predict why some firms are able to establish positions of sustainable competitive advantage and so earn superior benefits?' (Grant 1996: 110).

The resource-based view of strategy defines a business in terms of what it is distinctively capable of doing well rather in terms of market analysis. It

Table 4.1 Views of resources and competences

Definition	Metaphor	Source
'A competence is a bundle of skills and technologies rather than a single discrete skill or technology.'	The 'genetic code' of the organization	Prahalad and Hamel (1994: 202)
'A firm's competence is defined as the specific tangible and intangible assets of the firm assembled in integrated clusters, which span individuals and groups to allow distinctive activities to be performed.'		Winterscheid (1994: 226)
'"Distinctive capabilities" are "architecture", "innovation" and "reputation".'	The 'passing game' of a football team	Kay (1993)
'Organizational competence – the firm's ability to mobilize its organization, combining people of different skills to work together.'	Ability of a cook to generalize experience to new recipes	Miyazaki (1994: 19, 24)
'Technological competence . . . a firm's capacity to generate change in regard to technologies.'		
'A core competence is a combination of complementary skills and knowledge-bases embedded in a group or team that results in the ability to execute one or more critical processes to a world-class standard.'		
'Proprietary assets not easily purchased, stolen, imitated or substituted for. The most potent of such assets are posited to be intangible or tacit.'		McGrath et al. (1995: 254)

Source: Scarborough (1996). Reproduced by permission of Blackwell Publishing Ltd.

locates the sources of competitiveness in characteristics of the firm, not the positioning of the firm in the wider environment.

Different authors have used different terms and defined them differently to try to describe these competences or capabilities. This is an important issue and one which this chapter addresses: what are these competences and what are the sources and characteristics of these strategically relevant features?

This table illustrates some of the key features of strategic competences. Note some key words: 'bundle', 'intangible', 'architectures', 'innovation', 'mobilize the organization', 'technologies'. These words indicate some of the key and distinguishing features of strategically relevant organizational competences. That is:

- They involve 'bundles' of skills – i.e. they consist not simply of skills (which are relatively easily obtained) but of combinations of skills, or of distinctive ways in which skills are assembled. The expression 'bundles' also points to the relationships between skills and holders of skills – i.e. stressing habits and patterns of co-operation and mutual support.
- They can be based on, or consist of, tangible or intangible elements. For example achieving capabilities requires more than simply assembling resources; it requires 'complex patterns of co-ordination between people and between people and other resources. Perfecting such co-ordination requires learning through repetition' (Grant 1991: 186). Institutionalizing 'learning through repetition' is an intangible element of a competence. Similarly the skills, attributes, habits and knowledge of employees are intangible.
- They are 'architectural' – i.e. they are to do with how the organization is structured and how it works, not bolt-on additions. Strategically relevant capabilities grow slowly, uncertainly and incrementally and the result, when embedded in habits, routines and expectations (which could well be so familiar as to be taken for granted), is what can be called part of the organization's architecture. The capabilities are built in (Mueller 1998: 159).
- They concern how people are mobilized and combined.
- They can concern technology and the ability to generate technological change – as for example in a production technology.
- They involve knowledge: the knowledge in an organization including, crucially, tacit knowledge: the knowledge the organization does not know it has – until it loses it. This knowledge is often embedded in routines which establish how information flows, is generated, shared, challenged. An organizational routine is a regular and predictable pattern of behaviour made up of a sequence of co-ordinated actions, and often developed historically (Grant 1998: 186).

This chapter starts by briefly mapping the terrain of the resource-based view (RBV). This is followed by an analysis of sources of advantage. We then consider how know-how and tacit knowledge contribute to RBV. Critical questions, from a practical point of view, that follow the adoption of the RBV approach are: What are the business's real competitively advantageous strengths? and, therefore, What should it be doing and what should it stop doing? We then consider a number of practical applications arising from the approach discussed in this chapter. Because the development and nature of capabilities are crucial to organizational success, we analyse some of the issues raised by a business's analysis of the its boundaries. Issues of where the boundary of a business should be drawn are best conducted in the light of analyses of its core capabilities: to ensure it does what it does distinctively well. We then move on to analyse the sustainability of capabilities and the capability to innovate. The chapter concludes by considering dynamic capabilities.

▶ Resources and Capabilities

At the heart of the resource-based approach is the idea that organizations possess unique bundles of assets and that 'ownership' of these bundles of assets, together with the use the business is able to make of them, determines the difference in performance between one organization and another in the same sector (Penrose 1959; Prahalad and Hamel 1990; Barney 1991; Peteraf 1993). This approach to strategy emphasizes the role of managers in determining how well or poorly they use the assets which their organizations possess, and the role of organization – cultures, structures, processes, ways of working, established routines, and history – in determining how people behave and how their behaviour produces unusual, important and hard-to-imitate outcomes from readily available resources.

The resource-based perspective focuses attention on the skills and 'know-how' that organizations may take for granted. It sees capabilities as things that must be developed and built over time, and, crucially, cherished and deployed. Even if 'bought' as part of an acquisition, getting the old and new resources to work together to produce an enhanced capability (often described as a 'synergy' at the time of a merger) is itself dependent on the organizational capability to integrate two sets of resources post-acquisition. Indeed a key type of organizational capability may be precisely the ability to plan and manage change effectively and coherently.

From this perspective, strategy is about 'choosing among and committing to long-term paths or trajectories of competence *development*' (Teece et al. 1990: 38; our emphasis). These authors call this a 'dynamic capabilities' approach, to emphasize that the building of distinctive capabilities is a process, and one which must be carried out over long periods of time. So, capabilities are not fixed, but evolve in response to the changing strategic intent of the organization. This is one way in which the resource-based approach can contribute to our understanding of how organizational performance can be improved: by building, nurturing and deploying capabilities, or, put negatively, by ensuring that they are not inadvertently damaged or weakened by ill-considered programmes of off-the-shelf organizational change. Examples could be breaking up businesses into strategic business units (SBUs) and thus destroying historic patterns of co-operation or mutual support between groups and individuals now separated into different SBUs; or programmes of delayering which remove older employees, with all their historic knowledge and experience; or redundancy programmes which subtly change employees' sense of the psychological contract between them and their employer and which therefore reduce their willingness to commit themselves to their employer's goals and priorities.

How does this approach to strategy development relate to the classic industry-led approach of Michael Porter and others? Some commentators have described the resource-based view as complementing that of the industry structure approach. But if the complementary view is accepted, this implies that some industries are intrinsically more attractive than others, and that the resource-based view explains why firms differ *within* an industry. On the other hand, it may be more accurate to say that, in dynamic industries and sectors, capabilities are the key source of superior performance and profit, because the competition is so dynamic. This view could mean either that the market positioning view is generally wrong or incomplete, or that it is applicable only to a particular (more stable?) group of industries, and that in other industries the resource-based view is more relevant.

Prahalad and Hamel (1990) argue that 'The critical task for management is to create an organization capable of infusing products with irresistible functionality or, better yet, creating products that customers need but have not yet imagined.' They go on to note that, while in the short term competitiveness derives from the price/performance attributes of current products, in the long term competitiveness derives from an ability to build core competences that lead to unanticipated products. In other words, in some way competitiveness comes from the nature and workings (or architecture) of the organization itself.

The key lies then – according to this view – in management's ability to consolidate corporate-wide skills and resources into competences that enable individual businesses to adapt quickly to changing environments. Prahalad and Hamel (1990: 82), for example, define core competences as 'the collective learning in the organization, especially how to co-ordinate diverse production skills and integrate multiple streams of technologies'. Grant develops this theme and argues that, where environmental features are rapidly changing, the firm's resources and capabilities are a better basis upon which to develop strategy. His statement of this argument is very important and clear – and ultimately practical. He advocates a view of organization and strategy in these terms: 'a definition of a business in terms of what it is capable of doing may offer a more durable basis for strategy than a definition based upon the needs which the business seeks to satisfy' (Grant 1991).

Organizations of course may have the same resources but different capabilities. Any asset that exists in an organization constitutes a resource: buildings, systems, people, equipment, technology, finance, etc. Daft (1983) has suggested that resources are all assets, capabilities, organizational processes, controlled information or knowledge which enable that organization to develop and implement strategies that improve its efficiency and effectiveness. But this confuses the important and key difference between resources and capabilities. Capabilities are the outcome of using groups of resources in particular ways (Amit and Schoemaker 1993). Grant argues that

> There is a key distinction between resources and capabilities. Resources are inputs into the production process – they are the basic units of analysis . . . But, on their own, few resources are productive. Productive activity requires the co-operation and co-ordination of teams of resources. A capability is the capacity for a team of resources to perform some task or activity. While resources are the source of a firm's capabilities, capabilities are the main source of its competitive advantage. (Grant 1991: 118–19)

Such 'teams' of resources are certainly not just human teams. They are any combination of the mixture of buildings, systems, people, equipment, finance or technology.

An important aspect of the resource-based approach to strategy is that, in order for a capability to be 'distinctive', it must be hard to imitate. In order for a capability to be difficult to imitate, it will usually involve drawing on combinations of resources from any and every part of the organization. It thus extends strategic thinking into human resource management, financial management, organizational development, R&D, and technology development and implementation, and so on. In fact, it is more often the way in which organizations combine their resources in bundles that creates uniqueness, which is what we mean by distinctive capabilities. Many of these combinations are a blend of 'hard' tangible elements (such as buildings, equipment, training manuals) and 'soft' intangible elements (such as how well teams work together, or the internal culture or external image of the organization) which simply cannot be recreated by another organization.

Because resources are the source of an organization's capabilities, while capabilities are the main source of its competitive advantage, organizations in the same industry are usually heterogeneous rather than homogeneous. This does not mean that every organization within a given sector will be different from every other in that sector. But it does mean that certain organizations within any particular sector will be endowed with resources that enable them to produce more economically and/or better satisfy their customers' needs. This is usually because such resources are in relatively scarce supply and all organizations cannot have equal amounts of them.

For example, some teachers are rated as better than others in teaching skill, experience, subject knowledge, commitment to pupils, etc. Schools differ in their ability to attract and retain such people. Supermarkets may all wish to situate themselves at locations which have good catchment areas of population and good travel connections. But such sites are of limited geographic availability and will be acquired by the larger retail chains who can afford to pay high prices for the land, or who can persuade local government agencies to give them planning and development permission because they are able to promise a given level of investment or jobs in the area.

Therefore, amongst organizations in the same sector, their approach to, and their efficiency at, clustering resources will determine their performance (their level of profitability and their ability to secure and sustain advantage in meeting customer needs). The resource-based approach to strategy assumes such heterogeneity of resources and capabilities between organizations. This has consequences not just in exploiting existing assets specific to individual organizations (organization-specific or firm-specific assets), but also for the (dynamic) development of new capabilities through learning and capability accumulation. In fact Grant (1991) argues that 'for most firms, the most important capabilities are likely to be those which arise from an integration of individual functional capabilities'. Such strategic capabilities are what Prahalad and Hamel (1990) describe as 'core competences' and what Kay (1993) calls 'distinctive capabilities'.

In general, 'distinctive' capabilities refer to pools of cumulative experience, knowledge and systems that exist within an organization and that can be used to reduce the cost or time required to create a new resource or extend an existing one. They include the ability to access, internalize and apply new knowledge. Indeed, this may be regarded as the defining characteristic of a capability-building organization. This is because resources may diminish in value or relevance over time, yet organizations may be unwilling or unable to develop new ones. Thus, existing sets of resources may become prisons of strategic thinking ('recipes'). Companies can get locked into thinking of their existing resources and capabilities as unique and fail to notice that what was unique has been copied by competitors, so that everybody can do it and the whole sector standard has moved on.

Analysing Sources of Advantage

We have noted that organizations differ in their ability to secure advantage from resources and capabilities. Amit and Schoemaker (1993) see capabilities as being 'developed over time through complex interactions among the firm's resources'. They argue that *uncertainty*, *complexity* and *conflict*, both inside and outside the organization, *constitute the normal conditions under which managers have to manage*. However, this leaves room for 'discretionary managerial decisions on strategy crafting'. In other words, it is precisely such uncertainties that create the opportunity for heterogeneity between organizations to develop, often as a result of better or worse decision-making by managers about the external environment or the internal resource mix. The challenge facing managers is to identify a set of 'strategic assets' directly arising from the organization's resources and capabilities. These will be developed as the basis for creating and protecting their organization's sustainable sources of advantage. The basic idea then inherent in the whole resource-based view of the organization is to gather and nurture a set of complementary and specialized resources and capabilities.

Advantage arises from the way a firm links together its resources into combinations which are hard for competitors to reproduce. This is what is meant by the concept of *causal ambiguity* (Lippman and Rumelt 1982), where potential imitators do not know exactly what to imitate. In particular, capabilities that develop and accumulate within an organization from the interconnectedness of the resources that contribute to them will be particularly hard to imitate. These are capabilities which have a large tacit dimension and are socially complex. They rely on complex processes of organizational learning, which are themselves contingent upon earlier stages and levels of learning, investment and development. They have followed certain pathways of development to arrive at the complex resource bundle they now form. For example, certain companies may have a research orientation or culture. In 1993 ICI de-merged itself into two separate businesses: ICI, which retained the low-value, volume-driven chemicals and aggregates business, and Zeneca, which focused on the high-value, research-driven pharmaceuticals business. This was the conclusion of the view that these two represented fundamentally different businesses, dependent on fundamentally different resources and capabilities which needed managing in different ways.

Peteraf (1993) argues that heterogeneity in an industry is a fundamental condition for competitive advantage. Indeed, heterogeneity is a fundamental concept of strategy. However, heterogeneity is a necessary, but not a sufficient, condition for sources of advantage to be sustainable.

These ideas can be applied to both single-business strategy and multi-business corporate strategy to show some of the implications for managers of resource-based strategy. At the single-business level this analysis may help managers distinguish between resources which form the basis of a potential advantage and therefore attract investment and other resources which do not. Clarity about the imitability of key resources which the organization possesses should help decide whether and for how long a resource can be protected. This, in turn, should influence the decision on, for example, how rapidly to license out an innovation. An analysis of the quality of resources an organization possesses should help managers use available resources more effectively and have a better idea of the purposes for which they will be used. Resources which are time-path dependent or which require organization-specific or firm-specific co-specialized assets are difficult to create or reproduce, but since they cannot easily be imitated they are worth further investment and nurturing.

Know-how and tacit knowledge

Hamel and Prahalad note that core competences are 'the collective learning in the organization . . . communication, involvement and a deep commitment to working across organizational boundaries . . . skills (which) coalesce around individuals' (Prahalad and Hamel 1990: 82).

Other writers have noted that a major source of resource-based advantage is the way in which organizations manage to develop habits, skills, relationships, values, routines and ways of working, and particularly ways of generating and sharing knowledge within the business. Mueller, for example, argues that, while formal (and obvious and easily imitated) HR policies are probably of little competitive benefit, what is useful from a resource-based viewpoint is the 'social architecture that results from ongoing skill formation activities, incidental or informal learning, forms of spontaneous co-operation, the tacit knowledge that accumulates as the – often unplanned – side-effect of intentional corporate behaviour. Thus corporate prosperity typically rests in the social architecture that emerges slowly and incrementally over time, and often predates the tenure of current senior management' (Mueller 1996: 777). An important implication of this of course is that senior management, particularly if they are in thrall to some currently fashionable package of organizational change, may introduce measures which damage these historic patterns and routines.

Mueller and many other commentators note the importance and role of tacit knowledge as a key element of organizational capabilities. Tacit knowledge is usually defined as that which cannot be written down or specified. It is the knowledge that people and organizations do not know they know. This can be easily lost, taken for granted, or overlooked. It is probably not a coincidence that formal programmes of knowledge management have been developed and installed at exactly the same time that programmes of organizational restructuring (see chapter 1) have either fragmented and broken the organization in ways which damages historic lines of sharing and communication (for example, the move to SBUs), or altered traditional relationships and made them contractual and market-like, or, by delayering, have actually removed key personnel with key knowledge, producing the amnesiac organization.

Tacit knowledge is embedded in the interactive routines, rituals and behaviours of individuals within their organizations. Many now argue that knowledge, particularly tacit knowledge, is strategically the most significant resource of the organization (Quinn 1992; Grant 1991). That is because tacit knowledge in particular demonstrates one of the most valuable characteristics for resource-based sources of competitive advantage – it is almost impossible for rivals to imitate or replicate.

Knowledge is largely an intangible resource, and as such is more difficult to imitate than tangible resources such as buildings or machinery. Nonaka (1991) argues that tacit knowledge has a cognitive dimension in that it consists of mental models that individuals follow in given situations. These mental models are internal processes of sense-making and decision-making and may be personal to an individual or shared by members of a team or a department. We use such mental models all the time in our daily life. Think, for example, of what makes a good doubles team in tennis; it is the mutual anticipation of play and moves by the two partners. That suggests some of the reasons why resources of this type are extremely hard to imitate and hence particularly valuable. One of the strongest reasons for the high value and low imitability of tacit knowledge is that it illustrates once again the concept of 'causal ambiguity': uncertainty regarding the causes of effectiveness in organizations. Often the organization itself does not fully know the precise nature of its source of advantage. This, too, makes the resource impossible to imitate and inherently sustainable.

Some professional service companies (such as the US consulting firm Accenture – formerly Andersen Consulting) go to great lengths to develop internal systems and procedures for storing and reproducing and making explicit such implicit knowledge. They attempt to replicate and thereby standardize and routinize as many organizational procedures as possible. Their manuals are updated continually to disseminate best practice company-wide. Their content covers every aspect of professional work, such as how to approach a potential client, or how to bid for an assignment. Utilization of these procedural manuals is mandatory throughout the company. Although such manuals are an attempt to capture and codify tacit knowledge, what they actually capture is what Nonaka (1991) calls 'explicit knowledge' or objective knowledge. That is, knowledge which can be shared so that at the end of the communication the recipient knows as much as the provider. This is never the case with tacit knowledge, which contains experience, skills (Nelson and Winter 1982) and know-how.

While Chandler (1962) championed the view of the top-down hand of management controlling systems and procedures, Nonaka (1991) argues for the middle-up view of management, emphasizing the critical role of middle managers in knowledge creation and knowledge capture. To quote Nonaka: 'Middle managers synthesized the tacit knowledge of both frontline employees and senior executives, made it explicit, and incorporated it into new technologies and products. In this respect, they are the true "knowledge engineers" of the knowledge-creating company' (1991: 104).

▶ The Practicalities of Strategic Capabilities

This book is about five distinct ways in which the performance of organizations can be improved, each approach to performance enhancement being apparent within the literature known as SHRM. What, then, are the practical applications that arise from the possibility that some organizations may have distinct capabilities on which they can build competitively advantageous strategies? There are a number.

It is important that organizations are able to assess if they have such capabilities or not. To build a strategy around what is thought to be a distinctive capability when it clearly isn't would be disastrous. The criteria by which such capabilities can be identified are important. If an organization does have such capabilities, it should be the focus of attention to cherish and nurture them, or at the very least to ensure they are not inadvertently damaged by ill-considered or short-term initiatives. Organizational capabilities can also be used to make decisions about the location of the organization's boundaries, excluding activities which are not central and retaining those which impact directly on, or derive from, the organizational capability. This section discusses a number of practical aspects of the capabilities approach to strategy.

Make or buy?

One obvious practical issue arising from this approach is that it offers a basis on which to make decisions about which activities to retain and which to outsource or position outside the organizational boundary. The fundamental rationale underlying this question was most elegantly put forward by Oliver Williamson. 'A Study in the Economics of Internal Organization' is the subtitle he gave to his original study *Markets and Hierarchies* (Williamson 1975), in which he used the transaction cost approach as the basis for deciding the shape, size and optimal boundaries of an organization. The argument is a simple one. Transaction cost economics suggests that the most efficient way to carry out a transaction is whichever way will minimize the costs of that transaction to the organization. Such costs may include the setting up and running of a contract, internal costs of management time and resource, costs of operating at less than optimal scale efficiency, and so on. The idea is that the level of the costs of the transaction will determine whether it is most appropriately carried out internally (within the organizational hierarchy) or in markets (buying in the product, component, or service from outside). When making these calculations it is the total cost over the lifetime of the transaction which is the relevant comparison to make with the cost of keeping the transaction in-house.

This may appear rather an academic argument. But it is very practical. We have become completely accustomed to it as the practice of 'contracting out' facilities, functions or services to the most efficient provider. This is now commonplace within both the public and the commercial sectors in most developed economies. It is being popularized world-wide as part of the process of privatization of the state sector. Transaction costs were the theoretical underpinning for looking at the provision of services by both local and national government on the basis of the most efficient use of resources and the lowest costs of the transaction. Should local government employ its own street cleaners? Should schools and hospitals provide their own catering? Should national agencies build and operate power generation and transmission facilities? Or should these services be bought in from outside contractors which specialize in them and can therefore pass on both their expertise and their greater potential scale economies to their customers?

Similar arguments have been explored in private companies also. They encompass not only cleaning, catering and security services, but also entire functions such as provision and maintenance of computer systems, routine data-processing functions such as payroll, and even strategically important information systems. These decisions have formed the basis of massive growth in new business services companies such as EDS (electronic data systems) whose phenomenal business growth since 1980 is largely due to the explosion in demand for facilities management. On this basis the entire computing and IS (information systems) functions of an organization (whether public, like tax-collection agencies, or commercial, like airlines) are carried out for the client by EDS. As part of this reallocation of resources, EDS and other similar firms usually take the staff from the client company who had previously performed that function internally onto their own payroll. Organizations need to be clear about the strategic significance of such decisions for the overall balance of their resources and capabilities, both current and future.

Transaction cost economics is central to a discussion of strategy as competing through capabilities. What it means is that transaction decisions determine the shape, size and resource base of the organization. It contributes to answering these fundamental questions:

- What is it important that we do internally to secure our customers and markets?
- For which parts of what we do is it better to carry out activities outside our boundaries and buy in?

The answers to these kinds of 'Make or buy?' question have transformed the size and boundaries of schools, hospitals, local government departments and prisons, as well as companies. Table 4.2 summarizes the conditions under which either hierarchies (internal markets) or external markets are preferred.

An obvious point on which to begin is that of doing something in-house if there is *risk of information leakage*. For example, should EDS take over all IT and IS functions for the police, or is criminal information too sensitive to outsource even if the data-capture and data-processing function could be handled more efficiently? Should commercial printing firms be allowed to print the official publications of procedures and debates in the European Parliament?

The condition of 'fewer opportunistic actions' means that keeping a resource in-house will affect management behaviour regarding that resource. It may encourage a longer-term view on development of its possible uses. It may

Table 4.2 Hierarchies or markets?

For hierarchies if:	For markets if:
• economies of scale, scope or learning	• fewer opportunistic actions
• in thin markets (with few choices)	• in complex uncertain asset-specific situations
• where information is uneven	• risk of information leakage
• strategic capabilities	• commodity products
• where market mechanism needed	• profit maximization and motivation important
• entrepreneurship necessary	• bureaucratic difficulties and/or high governance costs
• routine situations	

encourage more imaginative uses, perhaps in collaboration with other resources. This may affect, for example, organizational decisions about investing in training or professional and personal development. That is not to say that external suppliers do not train their staff. It is more that the nature of the training is more likely to be designed for their objectives rather than yours.

Consider a different example. Computer reservations systems are the central nervous systems of the modern international travel industry. They are the means by which airlines, hotels, car-hire companies, etc. manage reservations and ticketing services to customers and between themselves. They are also an invaluable source of market data about customers for marketing purposes. However, they are extremely expensive to set up and maintain. Only one airline owns its own system: American Airlines has its Sabre network. All other airlines either share jointly owned systems such as Amadeus or Galileo, or buy transactions from competitor airlines' shared systems. This represents a cost to them and a revenue stream to the rival airline. When the Scandinavian airline SAS was forced for reasons of cost to leave full membership of the Amadeus computer reservation system of which it had been a founder member, it did not lose access to the system. It could access the system by paying on a transaction-by-transaction basis. What it lost was the ability to influence the future design and development of the system to suit SAS's business needs. It also lost access to the database that Amadeus represented.

Every organization should be able to distinguish between activities which it regards as core activities and those which it regards as peripheral. Much of the time people do not think about the difference between core and peripheral activities until they have to. The reason may be a change in government policy towards funding (for example for schools or local government authorities) or competition from a lower-cost competitor (for example, telephone-banking companies such as First Direct offer all banking services to customers over a telephone line and therefore, unlike traditional high street bank branches, don't need to buy and maintain buildings). Whatever the cause, the effect is to make necessary a review of what the organization does, why and how. This in turn requires an understanding of its current use of resources and whether those resources are essential to a core capability.

A further point to note is that designating a resource 'peripheral' is not always the end of the matter. It may not be quite so clear-cut. Not all organizations feel able or willing to contract out their IS function or their bone-setting. That may be because, on analysing the situation, they realize that the data gathered and processed within their IS function is highly valuable market data about their customers, which they would do better to gather and process themselves. Even more critical are management information systems which gather information from across all business functions to provide managers with the information they need to understand their organization.

The complexity of capabilities

In understanding how strategy can be developed, a key task is to assess the organization's capabilities relative to those of its competitors. A successful strategy can then be developed to exploit these relative strengths. Because capabilities involve complex patterns of co-ordination between people and between people and other resources, Grant (1991) identified a number of issues that illuminate the relationship between resources, capabilities and competitive advantage:

> The relationship between resources and capabilities, while not predetermined, does have an impact on what the organisation can do. An important element in the relationship between resources and capabilities is the ability of the organisation to achieve cooperation and coordination between teams. Style, values, traditions and leadership are key dimensions here. (Grant 1991)

The trade-off between efficiency and flexibility is concerned with the limits of the organization's ability to articulate its capabilities, because many of its routines involve a large element of tacit knowledge. So while a limited number of routines can be performed highly efficiently, this may limit the organization's ability to respond in novel situations. Economies of experience derive from an organization's ability to perfect organizational routines over time and length of use. However, while this may give established organizations an edge over newcomers in some industries, in industries where technological change is rapid commitment to old routines may hinder established firms.

The complexity of capabilities refers to the idea that some capabilities derive from the contribution of a single resource, while others involve a complex series of interactions between many different resources. Complexity may lead to the development of sustainable competitive advantage.

We have noted that Grant (1995) insisted on the distinction between resources and capabilities, with resources being the necessary but not sufficient

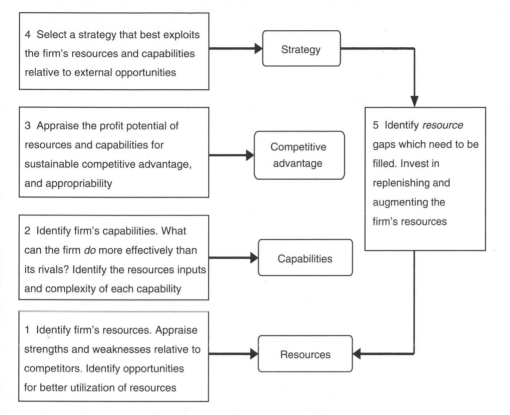

Figure 4.1 A resource-based approach to strategy analysis
Source: Grant (1995). Reproduced by permission of Blackwell Publishing Ltd.

basis for capabilities. This implies that the important strategic issue regarding capabilities is that it is not capabilities *per se* that matter, but capabilities *relative to* other competitor organizations. Grant captures the process in figure 4.1.

However, crucially, consideration needs to be given to the limitations of managers' objective assessment of the organization's resources. These can be misunderstood, over-valued or under-valued. Stevenson found that an individual's cognitive perceptions of strengths and weaknesses are strongly influenced by factors associated with both the individual and the organization's attributes: 'Position in the organization, perceived role, and type of responsibility so strongly influenced the assessment that the objective reality of the situation tended to be overwhelmed' (Stevenson 1976). Stevenson's study indicates that a variety of influences impinge upon the manager as he or she analyses strengths and weaknesses. These influences are shown diagrammatically in figure 4.2.

In addition, Stevenson's research found that most attributes are both strengths and weaknesses because of the ambiguity of the definition process.

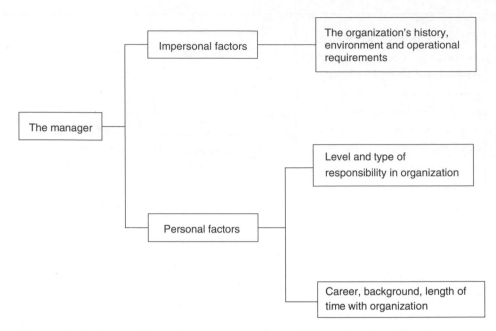

Figure 4.2 Factors influencing a manager when defining strengths and weaknesses
Source: Stevenson (1976).

Management therefore needs to apply judgement to develop a useful tool for action, judgement that needs to be exercised in the context of the decision-making process in the organization.

Stevenson concludes that managers use different criteria in defining strengths and weaknesses. He identifies three types of criterion:

Historical

- past experience of the organization
- intra-company comparisons
- budgets.

Competitive

- direct and indirect competition
- other companies.

Normative

- consultants' opinions
- rules of thumb
- management's understanding of management literature
- opinion.

Historical criteria were used to identify strengths and normative criteria to identify weaknesses. The use of historical criteria for evaluating strengths occurs because managers are constantly searching for improvements in previously identified problem areas, so the base from which these improvements are made is the standard by which the current attributes are judged. Conversely, in the case of weaknesses, the organization's current position is only a step on the way to where the managers wish it to be. The gap between the current position and the goal reflects a normative judgement of what ought to be.

To conclude, it is important to remember that the items being evaluated are not specific events but directions, strategies, policy commitments and past decisions. The process of analysing and assessing skills and resources can provide a link in a feedback loop, so allowing managers to learn from the success or failure of the policies they initiated.

One increasingly common way of helping organizations appraise, develop and improve their capabilities is through 'benchmarking', which encourages comparison with other organizations. Benchmarking against the standards or practices of other organizations can encourage rapid improvements. It is a very useful way to encourage individuals, departments and whole organizations to be more realistic about how good they think they are at what they do. Organizations always have a tendency to be inward-looking and self-congratulatory about how well they do what they do. Benchmarking can introduce a more objective perspective, and remind us that it is not capabilities *per se* that matter, but capabilities *relative* to competitors that determine superior performance.

The sustainability and appropriability of returns from resources and capabilities

Grant (1991) identifies four characteristics of resources and capabilities that determine the sustainability of competitive advantage: durability, transparency, transferability and replicability.

Durability

The durability of resources, that is, the rate at which they depreciate or become obsolete, varies considerably. The current pace of technological change is tending to shorten the lifespan of capital equipment and technological resources. Reputation, brand and corporate image appear to depreciate relatively slowly. Capabilities have the potential to be more durable than the resources upon which they are based because the organization can replace individual resources as they wear out or move on. The longevity of capabilities depends upon managers ensuring their maintenance and renewal.

Transparency

The sustainability of an organization's competitive advantage depends upon how quickly competitors can replicate its strategy. A competitive advantage derived from a superior capability in relation to a single performance variable is easier to identify and comprehend than a competitive advantage stemming from multiple capabilities. In addition a capability that requires a complex pattern of co-ordination between large numbers of diverse resources is more difficult to identify and comprehend.

Transferability

Having established the sources of superior performance, an imitator must acquire the resources and capabilities to develop a competitive challenge. If the resources can be acquired on similar terms then the competitive advantage will be short-lived. However, most resources and capabilities are not freely transferable between organizations, so potential competitors will be unable to obtain them on equal terms. Imperfections in transferability may arise for several reasons:

- *Geographical immobility*. The cost of relocating large items of capital equipment and highly specialized employees puts firms which are acquiring these resources at a disadvantage to those that already possess them.
- *Imperfect information*. Assessing the value of a resource may be difficult due to the heterogeneity of resources and imperfect knowledge of the potential productivity of individual resources. The established organization's knowledge of resource productivity gives it an advantage over any prospective purchaser of the same resources.
- *Firm-specific resources*. The value of a resource (for example a brand reputation) may fall when transferred, owing to a decline in its productivity. Where a brand reputation is associated with the firm that created it, a change in ownership of the brand name will tend to erode its value. Employees may suffer a similar decline in productivity when transferred to another organization.
- *The immobility of capabilities*. Because capabilities require interactive teams of resources they are far more immobile than individual resources. Even if the resources that constitute the team are transferred, the nature of organizational routines, especially the role of tacit knowledge and unconscious co-ordination, make the recreation of capabilities uncertain.

Replicability

Given the difficulty of transferring resources and capabilities, it may be possible to imitate them by internal investment. Some can be easily imitated by replication. Capabilities that are based on highly complex organizational routines are much less easy to replicate.

The implications for developing the organization's strategy are clear. The organization's most important resources and capabilities are those that are durable, difficult to identify and comprehend, not easily replicated, and are clearly owned and controlled by the organization. These need to be protected and maintained. Furthermore, designing a strategy around them limits the scope of the strategy to those areas where the organization possesses clear competitive advantage, the sustainability of which is determined by the durability, transferability and replicability of the resources and capabilities. This will in turn influence the time-frame of the strategic planning process. In industries where competitive advantage tends to be short-lived (for example retailing, fashion, toys) then the organization should focus on creating the flexibility and responsiveness that will enable it to create new advantages at a faster rate than that at which its existing advantages are eroded.

In using capabilities as a cornerstone for the development of a competitive strategy, Stalk et al. (1992) identified four principles. First, they stated that strategy should be based on business processes as opposed to products and markets. Second, they argued that success depends on transforming key processes into strategic capabilities to provide superior value to the customer. Third, these capabilities are created by investing in support infrastructure that links together and transcends traditional strategic business units and functions. Finally, because capabilities are cross-functional their development needs the support of the chief executive officer.

A danger of focusing on capabilities is that the firm becomes too inward-looking. Stalk et al. note that a capability is only strategic when it begins and ends with the customer. Using capabilities as the focus does allow the organization to create processes that are sufficiently robust and flexible to serve a wide range of businesses. While reinforcing the need to examine the organization's resources and capabilities, managers must first identify the strategic capabilities that it is crucial to sustain and develop. Prahalad and Hamel (1990) identify three essential features of core competences:

- They must provide access to a wide variety of markets.
- They should make a significant contribution to the perceived customer benefits of the end product.
- They should be difficult for competitors to imitate.

Prahalad and Hamel note that few companies are likely to achieve world leadership in more than five or six fundamental competences. They also note that it seems strange that managers are willing to compete for cash in the capital budgeting process, but are unwilling to compete for the organization's most prized asset – its people.

The issue that lies at the heart of the resource-based approach, and which is implicit rather than explicit in Grant's work, is implementation, 'making it happen'. By that is meant the ability to use the resources, structures and routines within the organization to create capabilities. This ability is itself a capability, and perhaps the most critical one an organization possesses: the organizational capability to transform resource potential into dynamic capabilities.

The capability to innovate

One of the key capabilities that transforms knowledge into competitive advantage is innovative capability. This explains in part why some companies are so good not only at developing, but also at exploiting new products or services.

Early entrepreneurial models of innovation, which focused on the heroic individual, gave way in the mid-twentieth century to a model based on the large corporation. Chandler (1962) documented the efficiency advantages of the divisionalized form of organization in which the R&D laboratory played a major role. Corporate R&D was viewed as the locus of innovative activity, as the requirement for a significant 'critical mass' of research capability began to dominate in sectors such as electronics, pharmaceuticals, chemicals and aerospace.

One way of thinking strategically about this problem is to distinguish between *core* technology and *peripheral* technology. The core technology of an organization is that which forms the basis of current activities, and therefore it is the area in which it must continually maintain a core capability. Peripheral technology is on the edge of current mainstream activity and capability. However, the problem is that technology regarded as being peripheral today may, over time, become the basis of the future core business. Organizations must find ways of tracking new technological developments while maintaining capabilities in their core technology areas. This presents challenges in generating the resources and developing the expertise to do this.

Innovation results from inputs of all kinds of knowledge or intellectual capital, including the know-how and expertise accumulated by individuals. Much of this knowledge in individuals is not captured by any formal systems – it is tacit knowledge that is difficult to codify. Other forms of knowledge, such as design briefs, specifications, patents, manuals of procedures and guidelines, are written down or otherwise codified, and therefore easier to transfer between individuals, departments and organizations, or to reproduce over time. Tacit knowledge is recognized as valuable, but few organizations have management tools which enable them to evaluate, grow, protect and value informal and tacit knowledge.

Organizations must find ways to orchestrate the knowledge inputs to innovation. They must decide what they need to 'own', and what they can afford to sub-contract, buy in, or acquire through alliances or other means. One major requirement for innovation to occur concerns the transfer and assimilation of knowledge.

Pavitt (1989) emphasizes that the cost of assimilating knowledge and technologies from outside a firm is very high. The knowledge applied by commercial enterprises tends to be firm-specific and cumulative. Corporate technological competences are built over many years through R&D and 'learning-by-doing' processes, and thus often involve tacit skills which are not easily transferable. This view has recently been confirmed in a detailed international study of the opto-electronics industry (Miyazaki 1994).

One of the reasons why firms undertake R&D is in order to be able to track external developments and to assimilate knowledge or technology from outside the firm's boundary. Cohen and Levinthal's (1989) empirical analysis confirms that R&D has a dual role: in addition to the generation of information and innovations, its function is to enable organizations to understand external developments and to learn from their environment.

This process is not only dependent on the ability of the organization to access, assimilate and learn, but is also conditional on the types of knowledge being transferred. Much of the knowledge generated by R&D is tacit knowledge which is difficult to transfer between organizations, as is aptly illustrated by a study of collaboration between Western and Japanese firms. Hamel et al. (1989) found that Western companies tended to bring easily imitated technology to a collaboration, whereas Japanese firms' strengths were often 'difficult-to-unravel' competences which were less easily transferable.

Collaborations and alliances with other organizations in R&D consortia or joint R&D projects offer opportunities to pursue a wider spread of technologies and access a broader range of expertise than would otherwise be possible, but require experienced and cautious management.

Capabilities and change

A sense of dynamics is critical in strategy because strategies are always being developed and refined, reviewed and implemented against a set of moving targets which combine every aspect of industry conditions. Industries change, markets change, competitors change or may become partners in certain activities. These changed industry dynamics and competitive dynamics can affect current and future resources and capabilities.

The point to emphasize is that organizations do not need to own all the resources they use – they simply need to ensure that they have access to them, together with the *internal* capability to manage them effectively. Therefore, whereas resources may be internal or external to an organization, *capabilities are always internal*. The organization merely needs to ensure that the resources it needs are available and that it is possible to use them whenever they are needed. It is therefore more a matter of 'control' than of ownership. Ownership may be necessary in order to ensure adequacy and frequency of access to a critical resource. Or it may be possible to pay another organization which owns the resource to rent it out for a fee instead.

The implications of the resource-based view of strategy for the size and scope of organizations lead to the consideration of such questions as: What should we do for ourselves and what should we resource from outside? Where should the boundaries be drawn? Does it matter?

We will look at the consequences of the boundaries of the organization for managing critical resources effectively, over the long term. That means a consideration of capability-building and the management of learning (i.e. to manage the capability to keep building capabilities).

Dynamic capabilities issues: building organizational capability

Miyazaki (1994: 16–17) provides a simple illustration of the process of building capabilities which will be reproduced here almost in full. She describes the owner of a small café in England who specializes in cooking fried breakfasts including sausage and chips, fried egg and chips, omelette and chips, and other similar menu items. His customers are requesting new dishes such as moussaka. The café owner cannot decide which new dish to offer and eventually decides he has no skill in any of them. A friend suggests that he makes a list of what he is good at, that is his capabilities. The list includes:

- purchasing good-quality materials such as potatoes, eggs, bread and raw sausages;
- producing good-quality products at speed, specifically fried eggs, fried chips, grilled sausages and toast;
- listening to customers' preferences.

On considering this list he finally has an idea of what to do that will build on his existing capabilities and also develop additional capabilities over time. He will add hamburger with chips and cheese omelette with chips to his menu within two weeks. He has decided that grilling hamburgers is similar to grilling sausages. Also, selecting raw sausages is likely to help him in selecting good raw minced meat. He will have to learn how to season and cook the hamburger, but feels confident that his existing skills in cooking omelettes will enable him to cope with cheese omelettes easily. He also decides that in three months' time he will add moussaka to the menu as a totally new dish which he can practise in his spare time. Some of the skills required to make moussaka, such as frying aubergines, are completely new to him. However, he must also draw on existing skills, such as chopping onions.

This simple example of capability-building for an individual illustrates the point that capability-building is 'time-path-dependent' and also cumulative – it takes time and effort and needs to build on what has gone before.

Another way of understanding this, for an organization rather than an individual, is to think of the organization as a tree. The roots of the tree represent basic resources; the trunk of the tree represents time-path-dependent learning; and the branches represent various capabilities. New branches are always growing and sprouting new leaves, just as organizations should always be able to evolve new capabilities from new combinations of resources and trajectories of learning pathways.

Learning and innovation are often dependent on what Kay (1993) calls the 'internal architecture' of an organization, rather than being solely technology- or R&D-dependent. Kay uses the term 'architecture' to describe relationships, both formal and informal, amongst staff (internal networks), with customers and suppliers, and inter-firm collaborative arrangements (external networks). Architecture is the conduit for organizational knowledge and routines. The existence of these relationships is not a revelation; in fact they are often taken for granted. This architecture should benefit organizations seeking to obtain economies of scope through the transfer of capabilities across and between different businesses. Indeed, the point is that their importance can easily be overlooked.

Some well-known examples of this type of capability transfer come from the US multinational Procter & Gamble (P&G). The first example is one of transferring a technical capability. As a result of research carried out in Europe in the 1980s for the European market, the formula for a new liquid detergent was so much improved that the technical know-how was transferred to their research centre in the USA and used to improve a similar product already launched in the American market, but not particularly successfully. As a result of the improved research from Europe, P&G's American technical research scientists were able to incorporate improved performance features into the product designed for the US market. The product was subsequently relaunched and became a category leader in its segment. It was the intra-organizational transfer of learning which made this possible.

A second example from P&G concerns its human resource management. As the European market for consumer goods began to change and converge throughout the 1970s and 1980s P&G began to feel it necessary to respond by developing and marketing more Europe-wide products. However, its organizational structure was set up to be autonomous in each European country and the different management teams would not co-operate or share any information. So P&G began to experiment with Europe-wide teams to manage individual products on a Europe-wide basis. To begin with this was a disaster. The 'Euro-teams' were completely ineffectual and were largely ignored in the company. Adjustments were made to the Euro-teams which clarified their remit, enhanced their seniority level and continuity of membership, and balanced the geographical representativeness of the leaders of each team. It took more than 15 years to make these teams work effectively. However, the company felt that this was an experience curve that it was obliged to travel. It is a learning trajectory that is now being followed and emulated by many rivals.

Some general points on the relationship between organizational learning, organizational routines and capabilities may be noted as follows:

- Capability transfer depends upon organizational learning and organizational routines.
- Knowledge represented by organizational learning will live in the organization as organizational routines.
- Organizational routines contain both formal and informal, codified and tacit knowledge.

Miyazaki (1994) defines routines as 'patterns of interactions which represent successful solutions to particular problems'.

There are a number of mechanisms for integrating and co-ordinating teams of resources, particularly human resource skills and knowledge. Two integrating mechanisms are important here: rules and directives, and organizational routines. The first type is based on codified knowledge. The second type is based on regular and predictable patterns of activity made up of a sequence of co-ordinated actions by individuals. This implies that organizational routines involve a high degree of tacit knowledge. The role of management is to enable the development of routines to achieve integration and co-ordination of capabilities, just as in the P&G examples.

Conclusions

We have set out the key dimensions of RBV as an approach to understanding strategy and building capability around the protection and deployment of organizational capabilities. As with all approaches that purport to help managers understand complex strategic issues the views in the RBV literature are to some extent incomplete. Nevertheless, the RBV approach does provide useful insights into how firms can conceive of competition, and, at the very least, it provides a way of developing a sound analysis and, we hope, understanding of what the organization is capable of delivering and why. As such it represents an important and increasingly common way in which managers seek to improve performance by building strategies around capabilities.

The important issue, though, is to recognize that managers may find it difficult enough to analyse their own organization let alone the competitors they may face. Consider, for example, the various stages set out in figure 4.1. It is an elegant and comprehensive approach to the development of a strategy built upon RBV; but it neglects the issue that exists in most organizations: that there is rarely one all-encompassing view of the firm and its particular capabilities, let alone an ability to develop a reasonably comprehensive view of competitors' capabilities.

5

Formulating Strategy

*If you think about Europe, going back to the 1500s, and why
the Europeans came to dominate the world when there were the
Moghuls and the Ottomans and so on and they didn't, it was
because those societies concentrated on the model that made
them successful. And in Europe there was not one single model.
It's the same with companies. And the point is that with a
single powerful model we will certainly succeed in the short
term and in the long term we will not. That is as true for companies as it is for countries.*

(senior manager, telecoms, research interview)

INTRODUCTION

This chapter is about the difficulties senior executives face when they try to
develop strategies for their organizations. The poet and the manager arrive
at the same conclusion: experience, which is such a potent and important
source of guidance, being built on its historic success, sooner or later betrays
us. Learning simultaneously guides and betrays – both individuals and
organizations.

In chapter 2 we argued that all attempts to improve organizational performance can be seen in one way or another as attempts to correct or realign
the relationship between three key factors: environments, strategy and organizational capability. Five basic approaches were distinguished. To reca-
pitulate our argument briefly:

- First, organizations attempt to change in order to improve the fit
  between organization and strategy. This must start with a strategy

which has been developed sensibly in the light of developments within the business environment.

- Secondly, performance can be improved by installing a limited number of best-practice processes which contribute to enhanced organizational performance regardless of the strategy.
- Thirdly, strategies can be developed which build on existing organizational strengths or capabilities. In this case organizational performance can be improved by the identification, nurturing and deployment of such capabilities.
- Fourthly, organizational performance will be improved if the organization is more capable of developing alert and intelligent strategies. Rather than focusing only on adapting the organization to make it more appropriate for the business strategy, it is useful to ensure that the strategies being pursued are sensible and innovative. If they are not, then forcing the organization to change to make it more appropriate for the strategy is likely to be a waste of time and effort.
- Finally, organizational performance can be improved by improving the adaptability of the organization – its ability alertly and effectively to design and implement change. If organizations need to change frequently, their ability to design smart, intelligent, and not 'off-the-shelf' changes ahead of the competition and to install them more quickly and less painfully, while continuing with business as usual without confusing their staff, becomes critical.

It is the fourth approach that is discussed in this chapter. The fifth approach is discussed in chapter 7.

The ability to develop sensible competitive strategies could be seen not simply as a fourth way in which organizational performance can be improved but as a necessary element in all approaches to improving organizational performance. After all, all attempts to change an organization in order to improve the fit between organization and strategy depend upon, or are limited by, the ability to develop sensible business strategies; and developing strategies which build on existing organizational strengths and which are viable within the marketplace also assumes that the organization has not only operational competences but strategic competences.

The development of alert, sensible, innovative strategies is central to the performance of an organization. Strategies determine (or describe) what organizations do. The quality of strategy is central to the quality of performance. Of course strategy is not in itself enough: strategies that cannot be achieved because of inadequate or inappropriate organizational capability are of little use. But organizations that have misdirected or non-directed capability are also in trouble. In fact, this is unlikely. Capability cannot exist alone: it must always be a capability to achieve something – a something which is determined by strategy.

But if strategic thinking is central to an organization's performance – and therefore potentially a major focus of attempts to improve organizational performance – it is also a complex and somewhat mysterious process. In this chapter we are not going to discuss the nature and strengths and weaknesses of the numerous prescriptive models of strategy that are available to managers and students of business on MBA programmes or airport bookstalls (these are discussed and assessed in chapter 6). These models are useful and illuminating. But they obviously do not determine how businesses develop strategies, for since they are available to everyone, how then could we explain the wide disparities in organizational strategic thinking and the obvious fact that some organizations pursue strategies that lead them into serious difficulties? The availability of useful strategy frameworks and models, the availability of bright, enthusiastic MBAs eager to apply the latest strategic thinking, is not enough. Despite these resources strategic decision-makers in organizations still find it hard to develop sensible, distinctive strategies. In this chapter our concern is rather different: quite simply, it is to try to understand the organizational barriers to strategic thinking.

In fact this is something that you have almost certainly thought about too. Why is it that some organizations seem to be always one step ahead of their competitors? Why is that some organizations seem to set the pace, to see opportunities first, to leave declining areas early? Why is it that some businesses, after years of success, suddenly seem to lose the plot and are unable to find a way out of their decline? Managers themselves are aware of these differences and their importance. As a manager in a firm studied by one of the authors as part of a project concerned with the management of innovation put it: 'I look at innovation as the capacity of the organization to reinvent itself in order to be competitively advantaged – sustainable competitive advantage. That means every process: that means every approach to business problem-solving, from price-setting through to feature design and products to system build and configuration. I am talking about corporate competence.'

This chapter is about the decision-making and analytical processes that produce strategic choices: it goes behind the scenes, to look at the processes and people that produce the choices, the decisions. In this chapter we see what happens inside the organization as people struggle to develop alert and intelligent strategies.

The essential and basic starting point for this chapter is simple but paradoxical. It is that the quality of organizational strategic thinking and decision-making depends not simply or even primarily on the intelligence of strategy-makers, or their knowledge of the strategy literature, or their commitment to their organization. All these can be taken as given. The main source of difficulties in organizational strategic thinking arises not from individuals but from organization itself. There are features of organization that systematically impair the capacity of strategy-makers to think about and develop strategy. Indeed it may be reasonable to regard difficulties in strategic thinking in organizations as normal: as the systemic product of the fact of organization itself. What does this mean? And how can this dramatic assertion be sustained? What are these features of the organization that can impair strategic thinking?

Cognitive Limitations

Organizations are systemically prone to two types of cognitive limitation. One consists of a variety of information-processing limitations, as managers short-circuit the classic rationalistic model of decision-making. The second consists of shared structures of meaning and interpretation within organizations.

The way the organizations are structured, the technologies that are used, the way information flows (or is obstructed), the values people hold, the way power is exercised, and many other factors discussed in this chapter influence how senior managers think (and when they think and even *if* they think). As one authority has put it: 'Organisations have cognitive systems and memories. Individuals come and go, but organisations preserve knowledge, behaviours, mental maps, norms and values over time. The distinctive feature of organisation-level information activity is sharing' (March 1999: 243).

For example, as a firm develops products and associated technologies, inevitably its communication channels and information processes and filters (which influence what data are gathered and transmitted and how they are analysed) develop around those interactions and problems that are central to what it does and how it does it. Managers learn that, when they are making widgets, certain sorts of things can go wrong; when they go wrong there are certain indicators. When these indicators occur a limited range of possibilities arises, and, depending on which possibility occurs, certain sorts of tried-and-tested solution are effective. So they watch for the indicators, analyse them in terms of existing categories, and then apply the well-tested solution. This saves a great deal of time and worry and keeps production flowing. It means problems are alertly anticipated and quickly handled. But of course it also means that certain indicators are *not* being watched; that certain solutions are *not* being tried. And it means that managers are preoccupied with maintaining or improving the existing product and process, rather than with longer-term issues. Thinking becomes channelled and almost unconscious. And unconscious skills or routines can be dangerous as well as useful precisely because, being unconscious, they are not noticed, and their limitations are not noticed. As a manager in a research project into the management of innovation conducted by one of the authors remarked: 'However much they tried improve the stagecoach it was never going to turn into an automobile.'

So as organizations understandably and necessarily focus on trying to do what they do efficiently, they inevitably set up potential limitations to their ability to think widely and radically about what they are doing and what else they could do.

> As the task that it [the organization] faces stabilises and becomes less ambiguous, the organisation develops filters that allow it to identify immediately what is most crucial to its information stream. The emergence of a dominant design and its gradual elaboration moulds the organisation's filters so that they come to embody parts of its knowledge and the key relationships between the components of its technology. (Henderson and Clark 1990: 15)

So what an organization does and how it does it influences how and when managers think. 'In effect, an organisation's problem-solving strategies summarise what it has learned about fruitful ways to solve problems in its immediate environment' (Henderson and Clark 1990: 16).

Furthermore, ways of managing and organizing that may make sense when applied to the organization of production may have unhelpful implications for the organization's ability to think about what it is producing and for what market. For example, certain sorts of production process where cost control is critical make centralized control useful. Operatives are relatively deskilled and as many decisions as possible are centralized in management. But, as a senior manager noted, this principle of organization has its limitations when applied more widely:

> The old command and control structure in businesses that we all had in the '50s and '60s required that the people at the centre were omniscient, omnipresent and omnipotent and none of us are that omni anymore and you can't run a business that way in the next century. You can't be everywhere, you can't know everything, and you can't process the information quickly enough because the time between decisions is now greater than the event.

Also, within organizations there may exist shared ways of thinking, shared sets of assumptions – often known as cognitive routines – which are historically based but which have become irrelevant for future success. The future is seen in terms of the past, indeed can be seen as the past repeated. As one commentator has observed, this can result in a potentially dangerous paradox: size, success, age of organizations can result in the development of habitual ways of thinking which threaten adaptation and innovation: 'the older, larger, and more successful organisations become, the more likely they are to have a large repertoire of structures and systems which discourage innovation while encouraging tinkering' (Van de Ven 1986: 596).

For example, one of the ways in which organization itself can limit strategic thinking is that size can easily limit the willingness to think innovatively:

> the need to report a continuous stream of quarterly profits conflicts with the long time spans that major innovations normally require. Such pressures often make publicly owned companies favour quick marketing fixes, cost-cutting, and acquisition strategies over process, product or quality innovations that would yield much more in the long run. (Quinn 1985: 77)

Equally, history and institutionalized products, processes and established routines – all necessary for operational success – can easily limit strategic options. Mindsets become limited, options closed: established companies become preoccupied with what they already have and so spend little time trying to identify anything new. Rather than devote their energy and time to discovering new strategic positions, established competitors spend their time improving or protecting the strategic positions they already occupy. As a result most established competitors miss out on the wonderful opportunities being created all around them (Markides 2001).

For example, a manager in the innovations project carried out by one of the authors noted the role of his company's historic culture on its ability to innovate:

> Organisations that are innovative have a knack of being able to create an imperative for change that others may not see. Banks have had it too good: so why change? We tend to leave change till the platform is burning before we recognise the need to change or work out the direction to change in. We change because we are uncomfortable about where we are, not because we can see the long-term direction.

Understanding processes and outcomes of strategy development raises questions about how organizations work, because the way organizations work – and the way they are designed and structured – has implications for strategic thinking.

This chapter is about the ways in which various features of organizations – many of which are necessary and useful – can, paradoxically, have a limiting effect on the ability of the senior managers of the organization to develop alert and innovative strategies. Being aware of these dangers will help managers – and their advisers – to recognize and avoid this limitation and thus improve the quality of strategic thinking which is the cornerstone of improved organizational performance. There are four features of organization which can impact on strategic thinking and decision-making. They are distinct and different. However, they are particularly significant when they interrelate and support each other, as we shall reveal. The four internal organizational factors are:

- group processes in an organizational context
- organizational politics
- organizational processes
- shared cognitive structures and traditions.

There is a fifth factor which impacts on strategic thinking and decision-making. This one, however, is external to the organization: the nature and dominance of external bodies of ideas which are powerful and taken for granted, and are frequently institutionalized in various ways and which help to define the priorities, processes and structures which are taken as rational and useful.

We shall discuss each of these in turn. First, however, we need to set the scene for our analysis.

▶ Rationality and Strategic Thinking

Central to any understanding of strategic thinking is the notion of rationality. We expect strategic thinking to be rational. This is the norm against which we judge it, and from which it constantly and sometimes dramatically deviates.

If we attribute rationality to a decision-making process we are saying that it follows various steps which we consider to be thorough, logical, systematic, reflecting what we believe to be the proper and necessary stages and elements of an efficient process. Miller et al. describe the rational approach to decision-making:

> decisions are thought to be arrived at by a step-by-step process which is both logical and linear. Essentially, the decision-makers identify the problem or issue about which a decision has to be made, collect and sort information about alternative potential solutions, compare each solution against predetermined criteria to assess degree of which, arrange solutions in order of preference and make an optimising choice. (Miller et al. 1996: 294)

March (1999) has noted that rational approaches to strategic thinking have four components:

- The decision-maker has knowledge of the action alternatives.
- The decision-maker has knowledge of the consequences of the alternatives.
- There is a clear and consistent preference-ordering or agreed set of values by which alternatives can be compared.
- There is a decision rule by which a single action can be selected.

These conditions don't, in reality, apply. For this to work managers have to be willing to learn: they have to be willing to recognize that a problem has arisen; ready to identify and collect relevant data; willing to attribute causation properly; ready to identify and assess a whole range of possible options; willing to grasp new solutions on their merits; and open to challenge and critique.

Some important clarifying points on rationality and its role within the modern organization have been made by Max Weber. He argued that rationality was a key defining feature of the modern organization. This might seem to be at odds with what we argued above: that in many ways organizations can systematically *distort* decision-making. The resolution of this paradox lies in how rationality is defined. Weber insists that the modern organization is distinctive precisely for its central emphasis on rationality:

> Experience tends universally to show that the purely bureaucratic type of administrative organisation . . . is, from a purely technical point of view, capable of attaining the highest degree of efficiency and is in this sense formally the most rational known means of carrying out imperative control over human beings. It is superior to any other form in precision, in stability, in the stringency of its discipline, and in its reliability. It thus makes possible a particularly high degree of calculability of results for the heads of the organisation and for those acting in relation to it. It is finally superior both in intensive efficiency and in the scope of its operations, and is formally capable of application to all kinds of administrative tasks. (Weber 1964: 24)

'Imperative control' simply means the structures and systems of control and management within the organization. But what does he mean by rationality? This is an interesting question because Weber distinguishes two different forms of rationality, formal and substantive, each of which is still apparent; these distinctions are still important today.

First, Weber distinguishes what he calls *formal* rationality. This rationality is concerned less with reality and more with appearance. It is based on the use of, or reference to, means of calculation, and the application of calculation, particularly accounting-type calculation and measurement, to organizational processes and decision-making. This is a form of rationality that has nothing necessarily to do with the *efficiency* of the process involved: it concerns the *language* in which the issue is expressed: the extent to which the decision or choice or assessment is 'capable of being expressed in numerical, calculable terms' (Weber 1964: 185). So, according to Weber – and this usage is still very much with us – a decision could be 'formally' rational in that it is dressed up in the language of calculation (accountancy-speak, for example, or certain sorts of fashionable management-speak, or statistics), but be by other measures irrational, or questionable.

Secondly, Weber distinguishes what he calls *substantive* rationality. This comes in two variants. The first concerns the extent to which 'calculations are being made on grounds of expediency by the methods which are, among those available, technically the most nearly adequate' (Weber 1964: 185). The second variant of substantive rationality concerns not the appropriateness of means for selected ends but the ends themselves:

In addition, it is necessary to take account of the fact that economic activity is oriented to ultimate ends of some kind, whether they be ethical, political, utilitarian, hedonistic, the attainment of social distinction, of social equality, or of anything else. Substantive rationality cannot be measured in terms of formal calculation alone, but also involves a relation to the absolute values or to the content of the particular given ends to which it is oriented. In principle there is an indefinite number of possible standards of value which are 'rational' in this sense. (Weber 1964: 185)

Weber thus distinguishes three types of rationality in total. These are still useful. As we shall see, organizations can produce shared ways of thinking, shared languages and frameworks, which when used are taken by those who share and employ them as evidence of rational and systematic decision-making and analysis – 'formal rationality'. Obviously managers and observers try to achieve Weber's first sense of substantive rationality – but usually (always?) fail because of the limitations of data search or analysis. This means–ends link is obviously also contextually limited by the prevailing state of knowledge and theory. What counts as an acceptable method of ensuring an outcome depends on the prevailing beliefs and theories about causation. And Weber's third type of rationality – when the ends selected are derived from values, or fashion, or prevailing ways of thinking which at any one time are taken to be sensible and beyond question (although later observers may see them very differently) – is very obviously relevant. It is a great mistake to think that, while we can see the fallacies and errors of our predecessors (or our contemporaries in other belief systems), our own beliefs about the appropriate means to achieve ends are beyond dispute: that we (uniquely) are free from error, that we have escaped from history, that our knowledge alone is complete, our truth absolute. One of the objectives of this chapter is to point out how many of the currently widely accepted assumptions about appropriate means for achieving organizational ends are extremely specific to our period: they reflect not rationality per se, but today's limited version of it.

Certain procedures, or frameworks, or types of information, symbolically come to represent rationality within particular epochs, cultures, or ways of thinking. The means that what decision-makers deem appropriate for the achievement of certain ends reflects not a neutral detached analysis and assessment of available options but an unthinking commitment to certain established, shared and powerful values or cognitive systems. And even the processes of decision-making may themselves have an impact on the quality and rationality of thinking and on the choice of means used to achieve desired ends. Finally we shall consider how the ends that organizations pursue are not natural, neutral or given, but chosen (if subconsciously) and chosen within certain cultural regimes which establish their strength and value.

But it's not always easy to identify or assess the rationality of a decision or action. For example, a recent KPMG survey of mergers and acquisitions noted that the annual value of such transactions was running at more than £1.4

trillion and that one in two blue-chip companies was involved in a major deal every year. And the survey, covering the 700 largest mergers between 1996 and 1999, found that 82 per cent of directors thought that the deal they had done had been a success (KPMG 1999). However, the research also showed that less than half of these executives had carried out any formal review. So their assessments were not well researched or well based. And when KPMG assessed the consequences of the deals (by impact on share price) a far less rosy picture emerged: only 17 per cent had added value to the combined company; 30 per cent produced no noticeable difference and 53 per cent destroyed shareholder value.

Despite this, enthusiasm for and confidence in mergers and acquisitions is very high. How do we explain this apparent irrationality? Is it a classic case of the sort of phenomenon described by Weber: managers using the language of rational analysis but not the realities, or using inappropriate or inadequate means and processes of analysis, or even pursuing fashionable but culturally specific ends? Is it a case of managers seeking an objective (organizational success and growth) but using the inappropriate means?

Or is this example not as simple as it seems – managers simply getting it wrong for one reason or another? Might this *apparent* irrationality (from shareholders' point of view) be perfectly rational from another perspective, another set of objectives and interests (those of senior executives)? Is this a case of the wrong means for the right ends? Maybe, but there is of course another possibility: that this is a case of the right means for the 'wrong' ends: that there is nothing irrational here at all. After all, although the preponderance of these mergers do not have a positive impact on shareholder value, is shareholder value the only end pursued by executives? What about their own ends? Isn't it at least a possibility worth considering that from the executives' point of view these mergers make sense? It is certainly possible to argue this, since many executives now own large quantities of share options, which give the owner the right to buy shares in the future at today's price. In 1999 the average CEO of a large US firm owned $50 million of unrealized stock-option profits. The interests of these stock-option-holding executives and ordinary shareholders may not be exactly the same. The sale of the company inevitably increases the value of the share options in the short term, and thus the profit to executives holding such options and making the decision. It is at least possible that some of the executives' enthusiasm for mergers is entirely rational in terms of their personal financial interests, if not those of the longer-term shareholder.

But the case raises other issues. Even assuming a coincidence of objectives, any decision on a merger or acquisition is a step into the dark. It inevitably involves uncertainty. However much analysis and fact-finding may occur before a decision is taken, the managers concerned cannot be certain of the benefits for shareholders. And even when it is, according to systematic analysis of risks, sensible to merge there may still be an appreciable risk of failure. When there is uncertainty (and there nearly always is), then a decision that in hindsight didn't work out may still have been the right decision at the time. Also, the KPMG survey, by measuring success or failure in terms of impact on shareholder value, may fail to take into account the actual options available to the firms at the time of the decision: maybe the status quo simply could not be maintained: the industry was changing, consolidation was taking place. Possibly the loss of shareholder value that occurred was less than the loss that would have occurred anyway.

▶ When Strategy Goes Wrong

When strategy-makers fail to devise sensible strategies; when they fail to scan and analyse the environmental data; when key data are blocked or distorted so that senior managers lose touch with reality; when the processes of strategic thinking become dominated by deference and compliance; when objectives are confused and inconsistent; when assumptions are unchecked, then the consequences can be serious, and not only for shareholders.

The Somme offensive started on 1 July 1916. It was a landmark of the Great War, the graveyard of Kitchener's volunteer army whose soldiers had joined up in 1914. The battle was planned in late 1915 by the French and British commanders (Joffe and Haig). Right from the beginning there were differences and problems of objectives and tactics. The French advocated a broad attack over many miles of front with 40 French and 25 British divisions (a division is roughly 10,000 men). However, in the event the French were only able to offer 16 divisions, of which only five took part on 1 July. But, although this key element altered, the strategy was unchanged. The historian Liddell Hart notes: 'Nevertheless Haig did not adjust his aims to the shrinkage of resources' (Liddell Hart 1972: 133). There were also differences of view on the objectives of the offensive: Joffe favoured a policy of attrition; Haig wanted to achieve a breakthrough. The result was a compromise which 'made it (the plan of battle) largely unsuitable for either aim' (Liddell Hart 1972: 236). There were also differences about the location of the offensive. The French favoured one place, the British another. Ultimately a compromise was reached, to mount the offensive in the worst possible position, located between both sites, which required the attacking troops to attack uphill. The bombardment – the greatest mounted to that date – was not focused on specific sectors to ensure that there were some areas where the defences would be completely destroyed, but was spread over the entire front, with the result that there were no areas which were totally destroyed.

There were two further errors. Haig had suggested that before the attack was mounted the German defences should be tested to check the results of the artillery. But this suggestion was rejected. There was still one factor that might have reduced casualties: if the British infantry could reach the German lines before defenders were able to open fire. But, although Rawlinson pressed for a pre-dawn attack, the French disagreed because they wanted clear vision for their artillery, so 'he agreed to the later hour, apparently without misgiving' (Liddell Hart 1972: 239). There could still have been a chance if the British infantry had been able to race across no man's land before the barrage lifted (for this kept the German defenders in their trenches). But even this possibility was lost: the troops climbed out of their trenches and walked in broad sunlight towards the machine guns. Liddell Hart describes what happened:

> The whole mass, made up of closely packed waves of men, was to be launched together without discovering whether the bombardment had really paralysed the resistance. Under the Fourth Army's instruction, these waves were to advance at a 'steady pace', symmetrically aligned like rows of ninepins ready to be knocked over . . . Each man carried about 60 lb, over half his own body weight, which made it difficult to get out of a trench, impossible to move quicker than a slow walk or to rise or lie down quickly . . . Battalions attacked in four or eight waves, not more than a hundred yards apart, the men almost shoulder to shoulder, in a symmetrical well-dressed alignment. (1972: 240)

The results are engraved in modern memory and on the war memorials of every town and village in the UK, and far beyond: India, New Zealand, Australia, Canada. On the first day there were 57,000 British casualties, 27,000 men were killed. In two hours the 8th division lost 218 of its 300 officers and 5,274 of its 8,500 other ranks. The 10th West Yorkshires and 7th Green Howards were almost completely destroyed. For the battle as a whole, the average Allied casualties were 2,500 a day. Officially the battle of the Somme lasted five months. Do the multiplication.

How could this happen? The generals concerned were intelligent, experienced men, thoughtful, deeply committed to their war aims (although one Australian officer spoke of the 'incompetence, callousness, and personal vanity of those high in authority' (Liddell Hart 1972: 249): the Anzac corps lost 23,000 men in three weeks). But the Somme wasn't an accident: it wasn't the result of things going wrong: this was a catastrophe that was *designed*. It was a systemic product of core features of the organizations involved – their structures, cultures, systems.

Liddell Hart offers an insightful analysis of the factors at work that created this fiasco. As we shall see, his analysis is remarkably similar to that offered by organizational researchers:

> 'Increasing optimism' was shown by Haig as the day of battle drew nearer, though French resources and consequently their share were steadily shrinking owing to the drain of Verdun. What is perhaps more remarkable is the way his chief subordinates joined in the chorus of optimism, singing so loudly as apparently to drown the doubts they had felt during cool consideration of the problem. They did not meekly defer to his judgement: they made it their own. Loyalty could go no further. (Liddell Hart 1972: 237)

'Privately' Rawlinson (a senior British general) 'was convinced that they (Haig's instructions) were based on false premises and too great optimism'. Yet he 'impressed on all at conferences and other times . . . that nothing could exist at the conclusion of the bombardment in the area covered by it', and the infantry would just have to walk over and take possession. This current of optimism was passed downwards with the result that, even when the bombardment was proving ineffective, battalions 'which reported that the enemy machine guns had not been silenced were told by the divisional staffs that they were scared. Terrible words for an official history to record as being said to men who were about to pay with their lives for this disregard of their words' (quotations from Liddell Hart 1972: 237).

This extraordinary optimism requires analysis. It's a common feature of defective decision-making. Liddell Hart identifies a number of causes: deference to authority, self-delusion, a mistaken and misplaced sense of loyalty (a core cultural value of the officer cadre) and an unwillingness to learn, to entertain the possibility that learning was necessary: an unwillingness to look for, identify or recognize the key relevant facts – in this case, the likelihood that the barrage would not destroy the defenders and their machine guns. Liddell Hart concludes: 'One can hardly believe that anyone with a grain of common-sense or any grasp of past experience would have launched troops to the attack by such a method unless intoxicated with confidence' (1972: 239).

Useful analysis of more recent strategic blunders confirms and develops Liddell Hart's analysis. Each of the organizational factors which can impact on organizational strategic thinking is apparent in this terrible example, as you will see as the chapter unfolds.

▶ Group Processes in an Organizational Context

Much strategic thinking in organizations is done in and by groups. There are obvious reasons for this. Groups can be highly creative; they ensure that various key interests are represented; they help to make the decision acceptable if many key figures have played a part in developing the strategy; they ensure that key data sources are involved; they help to spread responsibility. And they can contribute to the quality of decision-making by ensuring that ideas are challenged, by encouraging innovation, by ensuring that assumptions are identified and checked, that the analysis benefits from the combination and contribution of different styles of thinking – the intuitives and the detail-conscious people, the open-minded and the decisive, and so on.

But there are also grave risks associated with group decision-making.

Research into problem-solving or decision-making biases suggests a number of possible sources of group decision-making biases. These biases not only distort decision-making; they also result in unrealistic over-confidence and an illusion of control which makes such biases hard to surface and difficult to confront.

There is a large body of research-based literature that shows that groups suffer potentially from two tendencies. On the one hand they tend towards conformity. Groups can put their members under pressure to adjust their views to the group norm. On the other hand, group decision-making tends to be less risk-averse than individual decision-making. These are characteristics of any group. But our interest is in organizational groups. When groups make decisions within organizations – especially senior-level groups where very senior executives are likely to be present and to have an interest in the outcome – the processes of group decision-making can be particularly affected.

This is because organizations are hierarchical structures where power, status and privilege are distributed differentially and hierarchically. This makes it possible that members of strategy-making teams defer to, or excessively 'respect', the views and arguments of their seniors. It can discourage confrontation and encourage acquiescence, not necessarily because members consciously censor themselves and others (although this may happen) but because, in the face of a lead from a respected superior, junior team members are over-impressed by this authoritative conclusions and feel duty bound to show support. These tendencies are exacerbated if the organization has a culture which encourages respect towards authority, the display of teamwork skills and attitudes etc.

Some years ago Janis described this phenomenon as 'groupthink'. He defines groupthink as the possibility that: 'members of any small cohesive group tend to maintain *esprit de corps* by unconsciously developing a number of shared illusions and related norms that interfere with critical thinking and reality testing' (Janis 1972: 36). Some of the key symptoms of groupthink are:

- *The illusion of invulnerability.* This is a feature of groups where groupthink occurs: the group believes that the organization is invulnerable to 'the many dangers that might arise from a risky action in which the group is strongly tempted to engage' (Janis 1972: 36).
- *The illusion of unanimity.* 'When a group of people who respect each other's opinions arrive at a unanimous view, each member is likely to feel that the belief must be true. This reliance on consensual validation tends to replace individual critical thinking and reality-testing' (Janis 1972: 38).
- *Suppression of personal doubts.* Group members self-censor in the face of apparent consensus within the group. Furthermore, when contrary data are identified the group develops rationalizations which explain away these data, defining them as somehow exceptional for example.
- *Morality.* Members believe in the inherent morality and rightness of the group and its purposes while holding stereotypical views of the environment and the competition.

- *Mindguards.* 'Among the well-known phenomena of group dynamics is the alacrity with which members of a cohesive in-group suppress deviational points of view by putting social pressure on any member who begins to express a view that deviates from the dominant beliefs of the group, to make sure that he will not disrupt the consensus of the group as a whole' (Janis 1972: 41).
- *Leadership practices.* The way the leader behaves is critical to the emergence – or avoidance – of groupthink. If the leader encourages docility within the group so that members do not challenge or question proposals, or if the leader makes his/her own preferences clear, it makes it difficult for members to suggest alternatives or to raise critical facts or questions.

Groupthink thus refers to a situation where, within a group, ties of group loyalty plus deference to authority figures, combined with leadership behaviour which discourages critique and encourages support and loyalty, generate some seriously dysfunctional behaviour. Proposals are not challenged. Team members strive to find evidence to support the leader's preferences rather than to test them; members of the group are pressured to comply with the emerging consensus. The result is a sort of shared fantasy where the team works to sustain an unrealistic and hopelessly optimistic view of the world and the team's strategy.

Some years after Janis's book *Groupthink* was published, a group of researchers carried out a quantitative study of his thesis. It analysed a number of examples of clearly unsuccessful decision-making in order to investigate the empirical validity of his argument. Schafer and Crichlow usefully distinguish three separate elements of Janis's model (see table 5.1):

- antecedents of groupthink: the features of the group that can cause decision-making difficulties
- information-processing errors which result from these antecedents
- the outcomes of these errors: essentially poor strategic decisions.

These authors' conclusions are interesting. They conclude that some of Janis's 'antecedent conditions' are causally more important that others. The ones that really seem to count are leadership style, traditional group procedures and patterns of group behaviour. 'Groups who wish to structure themselves to avoid faulty decision-making are well advised to have impartial leadership and methodical procedures while they avoid overestimation of the group, closed-mindedness, and pressures towards conformity' (Schafer and Crichlow 1996: 429).

This is consistent with what we know of the Somme disaster. Remember – 'increasing optimism' was shown by Haig as the day of battle drew nearer, though French resources and consequently their share were steadily shrinking

Table 5.1 Specification of the groupthink model

Antecedents of groupthink	Information-processing errors		Outcome
Group insulation	Gross omissions in surveying alternatives		
Lack of tradition of impartial leadership	Gross omissions in surveying objectives		
Lack of tradition of methodical procedures	Failure to examine major costs and risks of preferred choice		
Group homogeneity			
Short time constraint	Poor information search		
Recent failure ⇒	Selective bias in processing	⇒	Low probability of favourable outcome
High personal stress			
Overestimation of the group	Failure to reconsider originally rejected alternatives		
Closed-mindedness Pressures towards uniformity	Failure to work out detailed implementation, monitoring and contingency plans		

Source: Schafer and Crichlow (1996: 418), based on Janis (1972). Reproduced by permission of Sage Publications Ltd and Houghton Mifflin.

owing to the drain of Verdun. What is perhaps more remarkable is the way his chief subordinates joined in the chorus of optimism, singing so loudly as apparently to drown the doubts they had felt during cool consideration of the problem. 'They did not meekly defer to his judgement: they made it their own. Loyalty could go no further.'

Organizational Politics

Organizational politics has got a bad name. This is not surprising. For most managers organizational politics are associated with personal backbiting, careerism, opportunism, dishonesty. But these personal and distressing mani-festations of politics should not blind us to the fact that politics are a natural feature of organizations. They are a systemic product of the basic features of organizational structures and are often exacerbated by organizational systems and cultures.

There are two key features of organizations that encourage political attitudes and behaviour. First, organizations are hierarchic structures with power, authority, status and privilege concentrated towards the top of the structure. This can generate attitudes and behaviour on the part of subordinates which either takes the form of efforts to please (or to avoid distressing) senior managers (see above) or (for those with little personal opportunity to progress up the organization) attitudes of resentment and alienation. The hierarchical form of organizations can thus generate excessive consensus, or oppositional and antagonistic conceptions of and attitudes towards the organization. The first stifles debate and results in the blocked or partial flow of frequently censored information as managers cover their mistakes, or try to present the sort of information their seniors have clearly indicated they wish to see. The second encourages a win/lose approach to decision-making with unnecessary and unhelpful (but often understandable) point-scoring.

Organizations are also differentiated horizontally into departments, product businesses, regions, specialisms, etc. This too encourages politics and differences in loyalties, perspectives, and priorities, especially when these business units are managed separately as discrete business units and their managers rewarded for the performance of 'their' business. So divisions divide (this is their purpose). And they focus loyalty and energy (this too is their purpose). Divided loyalties, vigorously pursued, create politics. Indeed this is almost a definition of what politics means.

These political features of organization are not accidental deviations. They are natural and inherent in organization itself. As Cyert and March note: 'an organization is a coalition of members having different goals' (Cyert and March 1965). Pettigrew sets out this view of organizations – and strategy-making – as political arenas in which organizational units with differentiated or opposed interests, loyalties, and mindsets struggle for advantage, with obvious implications for the nature and outcome of decision-making. Political behaviour follows the unequal distribution of organizational resources and the creation of specialized loyalties and perspectives through organizational differentiation. Pettigrew also notes that political dynamics, initiated by organizational structures, are exacerbated by ideological or cultural differences. He notes that if we wish to understand strategy-making, we must 'recognise the operation of an essentially political process in which constraints and opportunities are functions of the power exercised by decision-makers in the light of ideological values' (Pettigrew 1973: 16).

Most important organizational decisions – such as strategic decisions – are political in that they involve decisions on conflicting goals seen in different ways by senior managers with different amounts of power and with conflicting priorities seeking to mobilize power and influence. And these decisions show that the actual processes of decision-making do not display the full systematic rational process of search evaluation and choice but instead display a variety and multitude of adjustments and deviations.

Although power and politics are always present, specific patterns and levels of political activity will vary with organizational circumstances. Pettigrew cautions: 'Theories should be specified in a social context and related to societal structures and organisations' (1973: 22). In other words, although it may be true that politics will always play some role in decision-making, the nature, scope and expression of politics will vary with different circumstances.

Although organizational politics can often be seen to affect strategic decisions through the efforts of identifiable individual(s), it is a mistake to attribute political forces and dynamics to individuals. Politics are expressed through the behaviour and manipulations of individuals, but they remain essentially an organizational phenomenon:

> decisions are not made by individuals or role occupants but *via* processes which are affected by properties of the unit or units in which the decision is to be made. Information failures that characterise 'bounded rationality' [or one could add, 'groupthink'] are rooted in *structural problems of hierarchy, specialisation, and centralisation, and do not just reflect the malfunctioning of thought processes*. Conflict in a joint decision-making process may arise not only as a result of differences in goals and perceptions but with regard to the transference of authority over a particular area from one sub-unit to another. (Pettigrew 1973; emphasis added)

Organizational Processes

According to the rational approach to organizations and strategy making, organizations work like machines because members know what is required of them, understand their priorities, comply with the rules and behave (and think) as if they were programmed by the organization. Pettigrew and others have shown us one serious flaw in this approach. There is another, which we discuss here. Organizations are not 'structures' – the very word conjures up impressions of stability, durability, permanence, fixity. It's true that they give the impression of being fixed and firm structures, but this is a product of a large number of continuous series of negotiations and interpretations and adjustments which produce a sense of 'patterned variability' which we then mistake for permanence. There is order in organizations of course, but it's an order that is created and emerges from managers' negotiations and adjustments.

The focus on strategy-making *processes* focuses on these negotiations and adjustments. It argues that these are less systematic, rational, detached and objective than is normally assumed. Whatever it is that senior managers should do in order to develop rational strategies – identify data sources, collect data, assess the implications, carry out analyses of the data, identify options, test and assess the options, etc. – in practice strategy-making activities will not accord with these formal, systematic, objective standards. This is because in practice organizational goals are ambiguous and uncertain, and data are inadequate, partial and confused. Knowledge is incomplete and variable. Available solutions colour the definition of problems. Values influence and colour preferences.

Decisions are driven by available solutions as much as by analysis of problems. And organizational goals are important not as determinants of action but as *legitimators* of preferences and action. So strategy – or strategic goals – are used to describe and justify action, not to determine it.

Studies of strategy-making in organizations show that managers behave in ways which differ from the formal requirements, but which make sense to them – not only because they hold different interests and priorities but because they do not simply and mechanically follow the formal rules and procedures and frameworks that surround them. Instead they use and interpret and define these in creative and idiosyncratic ways. Managers make sense actively and creatively of their world in ways which differ from the formal procedures. The conclusion is that what formal strategy-making rules and procedures mean in practice cannot be extrapolated from the procedures themselves. The key question becomes not 'What are the rules?' but 'How is the formal plan of an organization (or some aspect of it) used by the organization's members to deal with everyday work activities?' (Zimmerman 1971: 129). The question of what organizational rules, policies and goals actually are when they are 'used' must be seen as problematic.

Some years ago, in a classic analysis of organizations, Silverman argued for the importance of understanding organizational decision-making processes. He accepts the importance of politics – 'it would be more fruitful to analyse organizations in terms of the different ends of their members and of their capacity to impose their ends on others – an analysis in terms of power and authority' (Silverman 1970: 39). But he adds that those who see organizations as political entities may have overestimated the extent to which 'members of organizations are concerned with advancing their power and status'. And they may have failed 'to take sufficient account of the possible existence of shared values . . . when analysing interaction, one ought to remember that there is a plurality of action systems available to the individual any one of which may be invoked as the frame of reference for a particular action' (Silverman 1970: 41). In other words people act and make choices in terms of their understanding of the situation and their values and priorities.

Herbert Simon, one of the forefathers of our concern with strategy-making in organizations, made a key point about strategic decision-making processes. In a challenge to the rational approach to, and description of, organizations, he argued that it

> suffers currently from superficiality, oversimplification, lack of realism. It has confined itself too closely to the mechanism of authority, and has failed to bring within its orbit the other, equally important modes of influence on organizational behaviour. It has refused to undertake the tiresome task of studying the actual allocations of decision-making functions. It has been satisfied to speak of 'authority, 'centralisation', 'spans of control', 'function', without seeking operational definitions of these terms. (Simon 1952: 53)

In other words, there is a risk when we try to understand strategy-making procedures and systems that we pay too much attention to the formal frameworks and concepts and too little attention to how these actually work, failing to recognize that they are different and allocate sufficient attention to the latter.

Cyert and March (2001) offer a similar and fundamental critique of the rationalistic approach to organizational decision-making. They distinguish three key features of processes of decision-making: organizational goals, expectations, and choice (what we want, what we expect and what we choose). This seems sensible. The first concerns values, objectives, ends and how these are agreed. The second concerns information about what is available and likely and how we search for it or analyse it. The final variable concerns how and on what basis choices are made.

Cyert and March note that 'Organizations avoid uncertainty . . . They solve pressing problems rather than develop long-run strategies . . . They avoid the requirement that they anticipate future reactions of other parts of their environment by arranging a negotiated environment . . . they achieve a reasonably manageable decision situation by avoiding planning where plans depend on predictions of uncertain future events.' An example of process being important is these authors' concept of 'problemistic search', where activity is initiated by an immediate problem rather than by an orderly and systematic process of search and analysis.

In what ways do senior managers' strategy-making processes deviate from the rational model?

First, organizational rules governing decision-making do not and cannot specify appropriate actions in all circumstances. The rules and procedures are far from extensive, or clearly stated, or clearly binding. This leads to continual negotiation. Secondly, the processes are inherently ambiguous and non-specific. Managers are unsure of what the formal processes are and how they apply to what circumstances. Rules and procedures are used not to *determine* appropriate action, but to justify what people want to do. Thirdly, although strategy-makers probably share a few major goals, these are usually so vague that they cannot determine specific actions, and may even allow conflict about widely different interpretations of a goal in various circumstances. These vague shared goals may act as a sort of symbolic cement, but they do not supply clear guides to operational priorities. This shared symbol may even hide a measure of disagreement and discrepant and different purposes. It may offer a general consensus but allow very significant differences in implementation. Finally, the ways in which managers interpret these shared organizational priorities and goals may well be informed by their divisional or disciplinary backgrounds and loyalties.

How can we explain this gap between actual behaviour and the formal systems? Is it simply that managers are human and fallible, that their compliance with imposed procedures will always require their subjective interpretation and will thus be prone to variation and reinterpretation? Certainly these are important reasons; but there are others: deviation from the rational approach to decision-making may be *sensible*. What could be the benefits to managers of short-circuiting rational processes and procedures? How can deviation from rational strategy-making procedures be sensible? Brunsson argues that 'effective decision processes break nearly all the rules for rational decision-making . . . irrationalities can build good bases for organizational action' (Brunsson 1982).

For Brunsson these 'deviations' from the rational model are *intended*, and furthermore are *functional*. His starting point is the assertion that managers are actually not interested in decisions, they are interested in actions. How decisions relate to actions is not simple. Some decisions lead to actions; some don't. Some actions result from decisions; some don't. 'A decision is not an end product. Practitioners (managers) get things done, act and induce others to act'. But managers are concerned *with getting things done*. And getting things done requires certain prerequisites, namely energy, motivation, commitment, accountability and responsibility. These factors are seen as crucial to making managers support and achieve action. Therefore the decision-making process is judged in terms of its consequences for these factors. Brunsson looks at various aspects of the decision-making process (estimating consequences, searching for alternatives, evaluating alternatives, etc.), and suggests that the rational model, if implemented thoroughly, would have negative consequences (causing confusion, dissipating commitment, generating uncertainty, reducing energy) and take too much time. It may also reveal underlying differences that managers may feel are best left unexplored. He also suggests that deviations from the rational model – i.e. making decisions quickly without a great deal of discussion and analysis – are functional for managers' commitment, motivation and enthusiasm.

▶ Shared Cognitive Structures and Traditions

> There are all sorts of constraints [on innovation]: particularly money. But it's culture. The dyed-in-the-wool culture. It's change you see. People are comfortable with the way things were a few years ago – business just walked through the door; the market wasn't very competitive. Now things are global. They find it hard to change, hard to see the need and if they talk about change they don't always mean it, and even if they think they mean it they still find it uncomfortable or disturbing when it's proposed or it happens.

This manager is suggesting that, within an organization, ways of thinking and feeling – habits, mindsets and attitudes – based on shared experience, can develop over time, but in time these become dysfunctional. This is the theme of this section.

We know that we are subject to a variety of illusions and biases when we collect and process information. These biases and problem-solving short-cuts

Table 5.2 Selected heuristics and biases

Bias	Effects
Availability	Judgements of probability of easily recalled events distorted
Selective perception	Expectations may bias observations of variables relevant to strategy
Illusory correlation	Encourages belief that unrelated variables are correlated
Conservatism	Failure sufficiently to revise forecasts based on new information
Law of *small* numbers	Overestimation of the degree to which small samples are representative of populations
Regression bias	Failure to allow for regression to the mean
Wishful thinking	Probability of desired outcomes judged to be inappropriately high
Illusion control	Overestimation of personal control over outcomes
Logical reconstruction	'Logical' reconstruction of events which cannot be accurately recalled
Hindsight bias	Overestimation of predictability of past events

Source: Schwenk (1988: table 11.1). Reproduced by permission of Blackwell Publishing Ltd.

affect strategy-makers too. 'The concepts, beliefs, assumptions and cause and effect understandings of strategists determine how strategic issues will be framed' (Schwenk 1988: 42). Simon (1957), with his notion of 'bounded rationality', has pointed out that decision-makers develop and use simplified mental frameworks when dealing with complex issues, and that they can only hope to approximate rationality when they solve problems.

Schwenk usefully summarizes some of the more important types of bias in strategic analysis and thinking – biases to which we are all prone. These are presented in table 5.2.

These mechanisms are serious enough. But they are far more serious in an organizational context, for two main reasons.

First, managers may, as a result of their shared organizational membership, share cognitive processes, assumptions and frameworks – many of them arising from the organization's history and its structures and systems.

Secondly, these shared frameworks and assumptions may be so embedded and long-standing, so integral to the organization and its way of doing things, that they appear as natural and inevitable to the managers who share them.

Recent research in organizations as sources of shared cognitive schema show how these schema influence perceptions, values, and beliefs. The risk is that, because thinking becomes constrained by habit and by unconscious routines, it becomes hard to think outside the embedded paradigm and also hard to respond positively to others who think innovatively. A respondent in the innovation study saw this problem clearly:

There are two scenarios. If someone says something that is strange – you have carried around a notion of the way things are and this questions it. And there are two reactions to this feeling of shock or strangeness. One is to say: this is a silly response and write it off. And the other way is to say: 'tell me more'. And this is a question of attitude – too often the response is: 'That's not right because it doesn't accord with my truth'. Bankers tend to carry around their version of the truth and to say when they find something other than their truth – 'That's wrong because it doesn't fit with my beliefs'. There are lots of people with that attitude – a first reaction; 'No, it's not like that.'

We know that individuals tend to continue to rely on beliefs about the world long after a rational analysis of available data should lead them to discard these beliefs. And we know too that organizations 'facing threats may continue to rely on their old frameworks . . . and hence misunderstand the nature of a threat. They shoehorn the bad news, or the unexpected new information, back into the patterns with which they are familiar' (Henderson and Clark 1990: 17). This of course is what Eliot is talking about too when he says in *Four Quartets* that the knowledge we gain from experience has only a limited value.

Managers' shared cognitive constructs of the external world (markets, competition, industrial structure) are influenced by their membership of their employing organization. In a study of a failure of business strategy, Valentin has argued that the strategic misjudgement was a consequence of a combination of organizational, cultural and cognitive factors. Organizations, he argues, make available to their members shared and powerful ways of thinking, and shared values can affect willingness to challenge or think radically. Worse than all this, established ways of doing things and ways of making decisions or established assumptions and frameworks for analysis – all of which have worked perfectly well in the past – can become limiting. Success can breed failure – 'past successes and ideological rigidities can foster dysfunctional inertia and mindsets' (Valentin 1994: 377). Valentin's research 'centred on a strategy rooted largely in speculative and (predominantly false) analogies and conjectures that became so vivid and available during the planning process that their verity was eventually taken for granted without the benefit of serious objective inquiry'.

Managers' efforts to collect data, analyse the data, identify options, and make strategy are limited by organizational factors which somehow impinge on the quality of collective thinking. Simon, for example, has pointed out that we organize new data in terms of pre-existing schema and world-views. Our capability for dealing with complexity and non-routine data and stimuli is psychologically limited by our shared ways of thinking and frameworks. Organization and rational, thorough, systematic strategy development may be systemically at odds with each other. An efficient and effective organization relies on managers and staff developing and using structures and systems, operational processes, mechanical or computer systems. To organize is to routinize, which makes complexity manageable. But to routinize and to institutionalize is also, definitionally and deliberately, to increase predictability and to reduce variation. And routinized processes and frameworks and mindsets can limit strategic thinking by limiting thinking to established frameworks, established assumptions, established historical precedent. Cyert and March argue that organizations learn how and where to learn. Old learning impedes or structures new learning, and managers' willingness to recognize that a problem has arisen or that it requires significant organizational reorientation (Cyert and March 2001). Organization can obstruct the sort of learning necessary for rational strategy-making. 'Organizing and learning are essentially antithetical processes which means the phrase "organizational learning" qualifies as an oxymoron. To learn is to disorganize and increase variety. To organize is to forget and reduce variety' (Weick and Westley 1996: 440).

The problem is not that organizations don't learn. The problem is that they do: over time, organizations learn. But what and how they learn can become blocks to further learning: 'in order to understand the strategy formulation process, we not only need to have objective information about a firm's performance and environment, but we also need to have data on managers' perceptions and interpretations of this "objective" information. There is a growing body of work in the strategic management literature that suggests that managers' interpretations matter' (Lant et al. 1992: 604).

Organizational structures, systems and history become an established (but unnoticed) feature of managers' thinking, and colour how managers see and understand and think about the present and the future. The future is seen as history extrapolated forward plus another 10 per cent. The way we were and the way the world was become the way we will be. Ways of seeing the world and the position of the business in that world can become fixed:

> Established companies . . . are preoccupied with what they already have and so spend little time trying to identify anything new. Rather than devote energy and time to discovering new strategic positions, established competitors spend their time trying to improve or protect the strategic positions they already occupy . . . [they] find it extremely difficult to even conceive of a 'different' way of playing the game; and easily lose out to any competitor which attacks them by playing a different game. It seems that the better they play their chosen game, the harder they find it to conceive of a different one, and the more easily they fall victim to an upstart who attacks them by playing by different rules. (Markides, n.d.)

Many years earlier, Cyert and March (1965) argued the same point: 'The standard decision rules are affected primarily by the past experience of the organization . . . when an organization discovers a solution to a problem by searching in a particular way, it will be more likely to search in that way in future problems of the same type.' In research into innovation conducted by Salaman and Storey, a senior manager in a telecoms company makes the same point: current strengths of the organization will become weaknesses unless managers are able to see beyond their established (and successful) ways of thinking and doing:

> I think the beginning of wisdom in this stuff is to realise that what you have got today in terms of your product, your organisation, your skills and competences – the way you go to market – is not going to be right tomorrow. And if you can't find it within your organisation you either have to go and buy it, or ally with someone, or train or do something different. That's the innovation thing: the willingness to recognise that the world keeps on changing and you have to change as fast as it. (Salaman and Storey 2002)

But being able to see beyond your usual ways of seeing, to think beyond the established ways of thinking, is difficult, because these established routines and models are efficient: they *work*. Managers learn to focus and minimize data-processing time in order to achieve efficiencies, but these learned frameworks may become counter-productive under new circumstances. Systems of organizational learning may lead to the application of shared cognitive routines and assumptions which are historically based but irrelevant for future success.

This shared cognitive aspect of organizations is fundamental to what organizations are and how they work. Organizations do not simply *have* shared ways of thinking: they *are* shared ways of thinking. Organizations themselves are increasingly aware of the importance of organizational knowledge and knowledge management. And they are increasingly seen in terms of the ways they create and distribute knowledge. 'Organization is defined as the degree to which a set of people share many beliefs, values, and assumptions that encourage them to make mutually-reinforcing interpretations of their own acts and the acts of others' (Smircich and Stubbart 1985: 727). Smircich and Stubbart look at the organizationally specific nature of knowledge: how managers *define* and *constitute* their organizational environments. These definitions are the result of shared socially (or on this case organizationally) conditioned cognition. The authors describe the constituent elements of this: 'the particular theories and frameworks, patterns of attention, and affective dispositions supplied by the actor-observers' (1985: 726).

These shared theories and frameworks can be particularly important when they are based on shared technical or professional knowledge. If a group of strategy-makers share a professional background they are likely – probably without realizing it – to use their shared ways of analysing data and making decisions – which are entirely appropriate within their professional work – to thinking strategically. So academics, when developing strategy, are at risk of developing strategy academically – that is, with much emphasis on data and analysis and frameworks and discussion and participation, but possibly little urgency and little enthusiasm for bold, speedy, decisive action. If actuaries are required to develop strategy they will be prone to applying ways of thinking and values from their professional work to their work on strategy. The result: strong emphasis on obtaining large quantities of data which would enable them to develop models which can be used to calculate risks. But this will take time; and sometimes strategy needs intuition and vision, not simply probabilities . . .

Lant et al. (1992) use a management learning framework to analyse what hinders or encourages management learning: the sort of open-mindedness, flexibility, propensity for critical review and evaluation, and willingness to question that underpin learning. The rational approach to decision-making assumes that managers are able and willing to learn: for example, that they notice when a strategy is not working, that they recognize the causes of producing these consequences, that they are prepared to change the chosen strategy when necessary (as revealed by the data they gather). All of these assumptions are unsafe. These authors argue that organizations tend to encourage and develop 'structural inertia', whereby future activity is based on past performance and strategies. Therefore dynamic innovation is implicitly discouraged because it requires a break with 'tried-and-tested' methods and ways of thinking within the organization. This is particularly likely in successful organizations. But even in unsuccessful ones the very fact of organization itself may predispose against learning and change. The analysis of Lant et al. may offer insights into the 'fatal optimism' that caused hundreds of thousands of deaths at the Somme in 1916:

> The Official History suggests that the root of this fatal optimism among the higher command may be traced *to an astounding failure to grasp the main lesson of previous experience – a lesson that most regimental soldiers had long since learnt.* 'The failures of the past were put down to reasons other than the stout use of the machine gun by the enemy and his scientifically planned defences.' Such an expert 'reasoning' is certainly one of most remarkable recorded cases in all history of missing the wood for the trees. (Liddell Hart 1972: 238; emphasis added)

In new times, not only do new problems arise, but established ways of solving problems are likely to become problems themselves. Established and cherished organizational success recipes become failure recipes.

So far we have largely focused on the cognitive factors that influence managers' thinking and decision-making. But these are by no means all the story. Think once again of Haig and his generals. There were certainly shared cognitive factors that were operative in the planning of the Somme, but there were also normative factors – shared values of respect, deference and loyalty; commitment to a shared purpose; an unwillingness to challenge or dissent which limited discussion, encouraged loyalty and respect for seniors, and discouraged individuals from feeling able to challenge or change the emerging strategic conclusion. These sorts of factors affect thinking – and learning – but they are not themselves cognitive factors. They are cultural or normative factors.

Morgan notes that 'Shared meaning, shared understanding and shared sense-making are different ways of describing culture. In talking about culture we are really talking about a process of reality construction that allows people to see and understand particular events, actions, objects, utterances or situations in distinctive ways' (Morgan 1986: 24). This sense of organizational culture as a system of shared cognition is directly relevant to our concerns in this chapter.

Similarly, Smircich has noted that organizational cultures can also be seen as a 'social or normative glue that holds the organization together' (Smircich 1983: 344) through shared values and symbols. This normative element of organizational cultures is also pertinent to the capacity of the organization to develop alert innovative strategies. Strategy-making is much more likely to be history-bound, to be unable to see or initiate changes in the rules of the game, to be more concerned with being better than with being different, if strategy-makers share values that discourage challenge and innovation, if they are averse to risk, if they share a respect for the authority to which they defer. Shared values concerning authority, uncertainty and risk, can impact on employees' willingness to engage in radical, innovative or challenging reviews of innovative processes they regarded as inadequate.

Bate (1992) has explored these normative or cultural factors and their possible role in strategy-making. Culture in this sense applies to 'the type and quality of interpersonal relationships, which in turn affect the approach to joint problem-solving processes. To be more precise, certain shared cultural meanings, once established, define what are acceptable, natural, desirable and effective ways of relating and acting. Taken together they constitute people's "dominant relational orientation"' (Bate 1992: 228).

Bate starts with a puzzle: why do some companies which apparently need to change, fail to change? Bate looks for the explanation to this apparent puzzle in the nature of the organizations themselves. Something, as he puts it, 'was enmeshing people in their problems in a persistent and repetitive way' (Bate 1992: 214). They were stuck and they didn't know they were stuck and they were unable to get out of it. Why? 'Why were situations allowed to persist when they were accepted by the parties themselves as problematical and undesirable?' (Bate 1992: 214).

Bate's answer to this question is fascinating. He suggests that the managers were actively colluding in a situation which stopped them resolving their problems. They were willing prisoners. They were trapped by their own attitudes. They were powerless because they believed themselves to be powerless – a nice example of a self-fulfilling prophecy. How did this happen? His answer is to invoke a particular sense and application of organizational culture. Bate's concept of organizational culture is that it is implicit, strongly held (and defended), shared, transmitted and enforced. Bate argues that in the organization in question managers shared a culture which contained elements – shared values and assumptions – which had a strong impact on organizational problem-solving. He identifies six shared values: unemotionality, depersonalization, subordination, conservatism, isolationism and antipathy. Unemotionality discouraged people from expressing their feelings about problems so that issues were not fully opened up and explored. Problem analysis was seen as dangerous. Depersonalization resulted in people being unwilling to address issues of accountability or responsibility so that attempts to resolve problems dissolved into vague general discussions which avoided the real issues and failed to identify individuals' responsibilities for resolving them. Subordination resulted in an unwillingness to challenge authority or to take personal responsibility – attributing this to senior colleagues. Conservatism meant that things were unlikely to change (so why try?), and if they did they would probably be worse. Isolationism meant that managers were expected to focus on their separate areas of authority and not interfere in the affairs of others. This had consequences for the flow of information and for a reduced sense of corporate responsibility. Antipathy was revealed in combative and oppositional relationships between the various divisions and specialisms as managers defended their areas and defined relationships with other areas as win/lose.

Bate argues that the elements of corporate culture can negatively affect how managers interrelate, how they approach problem-solving, how they define a vision for their organization, how they think – indeed even whether they think – strategically. It is hard to overestimate the role of this sense of corporate culture. It is of course particularly important when managers are so deeply imbued with shared values that they are unable to see that they share values – assuming that their particular shared approach is normal, generally shared, and inevitable.

▶ External Bodies of Ideas

There are two basic types of explanation for the nature of strategy-making within organizations. One relates strategy-making processes and outcomes to the impact of internal features of the organization at the organizational or group level. This approach, which itself consists of three different types of explanation (politics, processes and cognitive perspectives), is the subject matter of the previous sections. The other approach, which has only been touched on so far, relates strategy-making criteria, objectives and rationalities to wider societal ways of thinking which legitimate and normalize the assumptions and logics of decision-making. These establish what is accepted as rational and modern and, as they say these days, 'best practice' in any particular epoch.

This is the subject matter of this final section, which moves the focus from the internal working of organizations to the relationship between organizations and their societal, ideological context. It addresses the question: What determines what is taken for rationality within organizations? This section looks at the ways in which some basic assumptions underlying organizational decision-making derive from the wider society.

This section identifies some widely accepted organizational standards of rationality and shows their location within and dependence upon a certain cognitive and political context which renders these ideas and assumptions natural and powerful. This section problematizes what many of us, most of the time, take to be the truth. It sees truth as relative. It suggests that the standards used by members of organizations to assess the adequacy of means to ends themselves derive from the larger society. Actually writers on organizations have always been aware of this crucial connection. Weber, for example, recognized that bureaucracy was only possible and could only develop in societies where there was what he called a 'rational-legal' basis for authoritative power.

What people may regard as true is temporally and culturally and geographically relative. The priorities which managers pursue and the means they regard as appropriate for achieving them are derived as much from powerful, available ideas and proposals current within the society and within business thinking as from an objective analysis of the problems themselves. The fact that a particular solution at a particular time is widely accepted – for example the installation of market relations in organizations in the 1990s, or the decentralization into separate business units – does not necessarily mean that solution is always the right one. The impression that it is may owe as much to popular fashion or to the ideas that are powerful and dominant at that time. In other words, the perceived 'truth' of a body of ideas does not follow from its correspondence with objective reality or other truth tests but from its dominance within a particular regime. In organizational matters ideas are not powerful because they are true: they are true because they are powerful (Hall 1997).

> Truth isn't outside power. Truth is a thing of this world; it is produced only by virtue of multiple forms of constraint. And it induces regular effects of power. Each society has its regime of truth, its general politics of truth; that is, the types of discourse which it accepts and makes function as true, the mechanisms and instances which enable one to distinguish true and false statements, the means by which each is sanctioned the status of those who are charged with saying what counts as true. (Foucault 1980: 131)

In this section we will explore the nature and bases of these powerful hegemonic (dominating) bodies of ideas. The more powerful they are the less relative and contingent they will appear: their truth, it will be claimed, is unquestionable, natural, should be taken for granted. These are the assumptions and ideas that are particularly worth analysing.

Of course the idea that systems or bodies of ideas prevalent within a society at a particular period can differ fundamentally and can affect the criteria and priorities and assumptions of decision-makers is not new. Economic historians and academics who have taken a cross-cultural approach to organizational analysis have been arguing this point for many years. A striking example of this is the particular characteristics of the approach to the management of labour by UK employers and how this differs from other management approaches. Thirty years ago Ron Dore, in a classic study of British and Japanese factories, argued that each country used a strikingly different approach to management. The UK approach was a market-based one, with labour seen as a commodity like any other commodity, and where legislation operated to maintain the unencumbered labour market. The philosophy of laissez-faire was seen as being as necessary to the efficiency of labour markets as to other markets. On the whole, the British employer was not interested in developing an elaborate management system and instead relied on the market: 'they accepted little responsibility for employment security and welfare; job tenure was precarious for most workers and benefits were minimal. It was expected that wages would fluctuate with market forces and with levels of output and, from the late nineteenth century, there was an increased reliance of payment by results' (Gospel 1990: 172). The Japanese system, in contrast (and Dore argues that it is a *deliberate* contrast since Japanese employers, as late industrializers, were able to see the weaknesses of the UK system), adopted a more managerial, paternalistic approach where the vicissitudes of an external labour market were replaced by an internal system which sheltered employees and supplied considerable security, promotion ladders and welfare benefits (Dore 1973).

Each system had its own logic (and, Gospel, Dore and many others argue, its particular consequences for organizational performance and labour relations). But the point to make here is that each distinctive national system or ideology of management and organization had fundamental implications for management decision-making on a range of issues: organizational structure, business strategy, investment policy, labour relations, wage systems, and many more. And each system became, for those within, something natural and obvious, beyond discussion, taken for granted. It is this phenomenon that this section addresses: how pervasive ways of thinking current within a society and an epoch come to dominate the way in which we make decisions.

There are two rather different ways of approaching this issue.

One is to analyse the extent to which ideas and priorities held as reasonable and attractive by managers are time- and culture-specific, or, at the most extreme, are fashion-bound. Many commentators have noticed that the prescriptions and analyses of management consultants who make a living selling solutions to managers are particularly prone to this possibility (see, for example, Clark and Salaman 1996, 1998; Gill and Whittle 1993; Keiser 1997; Abrahamson 1996). This makes the explanation of managers' enthusiasm for ideas which are powerful simply because they are fashionable necessary. Ramsay is one of many commentators who recognizes the need to understand why managers are drawn to fads and fashions: 'The recognition of faddism is an important and welcome step.' However, he also notes that simply recognizing managers' vulnerability to fashionable ideas 'affords little progress towards a response without a coherent explanation of the phenomenon' (Ramsay 1996: 159). The role of academic researchers is clear: 'to expose and help to moderate the unproductive consequences of management fashions' (1996: 167).

'Today's management fashions hold much in common with the early ones: bold promises, bustling consultants, magic, and sporadic references to strict academic science' (Keiser 1997: 50). The failure of earlier packaged solutions seems not to interfere with the attractiveness of the latest ones. Managers, it seems, like consultants, want to move on. Managers 'seem to proceed from deep disillusionment with one panacea that has run its course to high enthusiasm for the next' (Gill and Whittle 1993: 282). 'Since the Second World War, personnel management and human resource management have been exposed to a plethora of new and constantly changing ideas and approaches'; but the real question this raises of course, is: 'Why do these different fads come in and go out of fashion?' (Huczynski 1993b: 443–4).

But management strategic thinking and decision-making are not influenced only by ephemeral fads and fashions. They are also influenced by more powerful, and deeper, strata of ideas. Brunsson and Olsen have emphasized the nature and role of extra-organizational forces in determining how managers within organizations think, and the priorities they think about. In Weber's terms, they have noted how at any one time the ends managers pursue and the means they see as reasonable ways of achieving these ends are strongly influenced by extra-organizational factors. They demonstrate that internal organizational processes and priorities are influenced (possibly in some areas *determined*) by external environmental factors and priorities. These authors argue that, with respect to managers' attempts to change their organizations (the same could apply just as well to strategic thinking): 'attempts at reform are only loosely connected with any direct improvements in structure, process, or results' (Brunsson and Olsen 1993). Instead, they claim, they are inspired by efforts to demonstrate the modernity and efficiency of the organization in terms of prevailing standards and ways of thinking. This requires that organizations demonstrate their adherence to and compliance with whatever are currently seen as the canons of modernity and efficiency, regardless of their actual value. External factors (current ways of thinking about organizations, prevailing orthodoxies in management and business thinking, etc.) determine what are seen as rational and efficient processes and structures.

The same point has been made by those who note the nature and role of management discourses. The notion of discourse was developed by the French sociologist Michel Foucault (quoted earlier). He wanted to analyse how human beings understand themselves in different cultures and different historical periods. A discourse is therefore historically grounded. What this means is that what is seen as true is true only within a particular historical discourse – what Foucault calls 'regimes of truth'. A discourse is not simply a linguistic concept (although that is how the term is used in an everyday sense), it is about talking *and* thinking *and* doing. A discourse supplies a way of thinking and talking about a topic, a way of knowing it. Hall puts this well:

> Discourse, Foucault argues, constructs the topic. It defines and produces the objects of our knowledge. It governs the way that a topic can be meaningfully talked about and reasoned about. It also influences how ideas are put into prac-

tice and used to regulate the conduct of others. Just as discourse 'rules in' certain ways of talking about a topic, defining an acceptable and intelligible way to talk, write or conduct oneself, so also, by definition, it 'rules out', limits and restricts other ways of talking, of conducting ourselves in relation to the topic or constructing knowledge about it. (Hall 1997: 44)

So discourses produce the objects of knowledge. This may seem an odd idea. Of course, Foucault was not denying the existence of the material world. But he claims that the meaning we attribute to the world comes from discourse, not from the objects themselves. And this is true of organizations. How senior managers understand their organizations, how they try to achieve their goals (even the goals themselves), are derived from prevalent and powerful ways of thinking about and understanding organizations and businesses, and the business environments which are dominant within the wider society.

Foucault used the concept of discourse to focus on the relationship between knowledge and power. He defined power not in terms of coercion and repression, but in terms of the power implications of knowledge and the knowledge implications of power. He writes: 'There is no power relation without the correlative constitution of a field of knowledge, nor any knowledge that does not presuppose and constitute, at the same time, power relations' (Foucault 1980: 27). An implication of this is that when knowledge is allied to power it can become true.

You can see the implications of these remarks for our analysis of strategy making in organizations. What Foucault is suggesting is that the logics, assumptions and theories that managers use when seeking to achieve their strategic purposes, however right and natural and true they may seem to them and to others, are in fact aspects of a 'regime of truth', which is temporally and culturally specific, and that their apparent strength and solidity is a result of their authority, not their truth.

Du Gay and Salaman (1992) have explored these possibilities in their analysis of the role of the market – or the discourse of the 'market' – in organizational restructuring. This analysis starts at the level of a variety of common organizational change projects – TQM, competences, restructuring, etc. For anyone working in an organization – and certainly for academics – many of these are very familiar indeed. They derive their rationale and legitimacy from a particular and distinctive way of thinking about and understanding organizations and how they work and therefore how and when they have to change. This is the discourse of enterprise – a discourse which is defined explicitly in terms of its opposition to the notion of bureaucracy. These authors argue that much organizational change is derived from a shared (but often unquestioned) commitment to the idea that organizations – and employees – work better when exposed to market forces, which requires them to behave in an enterprising manner. In short, much organizational thinking is – or has been – dominated by a conviction that the market is the only basis on which organizations should be structured and employees employed and managed. This is the discourse of the market and its associated quality, enterprise. The discourse of enterprise derives its power and apparent truth (its lack of rivals) from its connections with wider socio-political discourses of the market and its role in government and organizations.

The notion of the market and of enterprise is a powerful, pervasive and prevalent discourse of organization. It informs change by supplying a logic – or regime of truth – which defines what is seen as problematic and what are seen as solutions. Enterprise is closely and directly related to the iconic, almost sacred, importance attributed to the idea of the market in current thinking about government, organization and many aspects of contemporary life. According to contemporary discourses of organization, 'enterprise' is the quality organizations – and individuals – must develop if they are to thrive successfully in markets. The market is seen as the only force capable of regulating economies and organizations (and departments within organizations). When markets don't exist they are invented.

Du Gay and Salaman focus on what is still the dominant conception of and rationale for organizational restructuring, which seeks to redefine and reconstruct the organization in terms of the culture of the customer: it is focused on and designed in terms of achieving responsiveness to the customer. The authors draw connections not only between the political and economic priorities of successive recent UK governments and the restructuring of the firm in terms of enterprise, but also between enterprise as a principle of organizational restructuring and current definitions of the character of the new employee.

You may remember Weber's comments on what he called 'formal rationality', that is, rationality which achieves its status of rationality by virtue of its compliance with what are currently accepted as the canons of rational, sensible analysis and problem-solving. The sort of discourse discussed by du Gay and Salaman offers a way of thinking about and solving organizational issues; it shows how some prevailing ways of thinking supply the basis of a formal rationality, by supplying a way of thinking about how organizations need to be structured and how they should behave strategically. It thus 'rules in' some ways of understanding how to restructure the organization, or treat staff, or develop strategies, and 'rules out' others.

Conclusion

Organizations do things. They create products or services. And they try to think about what they are doing and what else they could be doing: what products or services to produce with what features for what market at what price. Both these activities are crucial. There is little point in an organization being highly accomplished at producing beautifully designed and manufactured products if nobody wants them; and there is little point in spending time developing intelligent ideas for new products in new markets if the organization is incapable of producing them.

This chapter has considered how the ways in which organizations do things affect how they think about things. It has analysed how various features of organizational structure and the values and knowledge that build up in organizations over time can influence the ability of senior members of organizations to develop sensible, well-based realistic competitive strategies. This is a crucially important issue and one that organizations are increasingly seeking to address: that organization itself creates barriers to thinking about the organization and its products. But many organizations have not grasped this simple point. They see organizations as machines for doing things, and assume that those running these machines, as intelligent, sensible people, are perfectly able in an objective and systematic manner to develop ideas about the future direction of the business. But our analysis raises some doubts about this. It suggests that all organizations are vulnerable to the possibility that being good at doing things may make them less good at thinking about what they are doing and even less able to recognize that the former can influence the latter. That is one of the main intentions of this chapter: to sensitize the reader to the possible ways in which ways of organizing affect ways of thinking. This is not always something that senior managers want to hear or are prepared to consider. They assume that their thinking is clear and uninfluenced by distorted or incomplete information gathered from limited sources; they would probably not be pleased to consider that they may share knowledge and values deriving from their shared experience which limit how they think and work together. And they would probably reject the notion that their thinking was in any way influenced by pervasive and powerful assumptions deriving from the society around them. But these possibilities exist and are powerful and pervasive influences on organizational performance. They therefore merit the attention of senior managers and of those who try to improve the performance of organizations. If organizations are to perform better they need to be better at identifying what it is they want to do (and better at achieving it). This means that the processes of strategic thinking and formulation must themselves be exposed to rigorous analysis and critique in the sure knowledge that they can be influenced – albeit unconsciously – by taken-for-granted assumptions, beliefs and values. Recognizing this possibility is a major step towards addressing it.

chapter

6

Developing Strategy

INTRODUCTION

This book is about SHRM and how it is possible to see this literature (at its best) as offering five different ways in which organizational performance can be improved. Central to the improvement of performance is the achievement of strategy, and we have noted that one approach to performance improvement focuses on improving strategy development. But we also need to discuss strategy itself. Although we recognize the many difficulties associated with strategic thinking in organizations, and although we recognize that strategies can be organizationally based as well as industry- or market-focused, it is also necessary to devote some time to a consideration of the nature of strategy and the strategic options that are open to organizations. This is our focus here: this chapter will acknowledge the complexities and difficulties that surround the notion of strategy and the nature of strategies, and it will also seek to map and order the literature that faces the curious manager.

Strategy is about organizational change. An action or decision is strategic when it allows a firm to become more competitive, i.e. to become better than its competitors. Not all decisions are strategic: some, for example, are simply dedicated to maintaining the status quo. Others might increase a firm's competitiveness but in a way that is not sustainable in the future. Yet not all theorists of strategic management agree on what determines firm strategy. Some describe strategy as a rational and deliberate process, while others describe it as an evolutionary process which emerges from the interaction between different, often unpredictable, processes and events. Some place more emphasis on external factors, such as the structure of the industry to which the firm belongs, while others place more emphasis on factors internal to the organization, such as the way in which operations are organized.

Furthermore, some describe a relatively static relationship between strategy and the environment where firms respond to external conditions, while others describe a dynamic picture of competition, where firms are not only influenced by the environment but also actively seek to change it. Strategy is no longer seen as primarily determined by market conditions external to the firm but also by organization-specific factors, for example the way in which information flows inside an organization and how new knowledge is created.

The 'competitive forces' approach to strategy, developed by Michael Porter in the 1980s, is an example of the view of strategy that places primary importance on external conditions faced by the firm. In this view, strategy is about the firm creating for itself a 'market position' whereby it can defend itself from competitive forces and/or influence them in a way that places it at an advantage vis-à-vis its competitors and suppliers. Porter focuses on the effect of five industry-level forces on strategy and performance: entry barriers, threat of substitution, bargaining power of buyers, bargaining power of suppliers, and rivalry among industry incumbents. This framework is connected to the 'structure–conduct–performance' approach to industrial organization where the structure of an industry (for example, how easy it is for new firms to enter) determines a firm's conduct and strategy (for example, innovation strategies), and hence a firm's performance (i.e. profits).

A different way of thinking about strategy is to give the primary role to intra-organizational factors. This view is best exemplified by the 'resource-based' theory of the firm, which has its roots in the work of Penrose (1959). She suggested viewing the firm as a 'pool of resources'. Resources include not just tangible resources (such as machinery and research laboratories) but also the intangible ones embodied in human resources, such as skills, knowledge and the ability to interact effectively. Intangible resources are unique to each firm, and when a firm finds itself with different uses for its excess resources it will often choose those combinations that are tied most closely with its previous activities. The fact that the firm's prior experience and history matter means that firm growth is often path-dependent: where the firm goes tomorrow depends on how it got to where it is today. The main point is that value is created not only by the quantity of physical capital, land and labour that the firm owns but also, and especially, how it combines its resources. This ability to combine resources in an innovative and efficient way was discussed in chapter 4.

Rumelt (1991) is a widely cited and influential empirical study that purports to show that inter-firm differences in rates of return are primarily due to firm-specific factors. He reported that 46.4 per cent of business units' profitability could be accounted for by business-specific factors (i.e. choice of strategy), while only 8.3 per cent could be accounted for by general factors related to the industry to which the business unit belonged. Baden-Fuller and

Stopford (1999) support this by providing case-study evidence of firms succeeding in industries which are considered no longer profitable (or 'attractive'). One of the most innovative areas of research has considered how firm strategy changes over the industry life-cycle and how strategy and structure co-evolve (Klepper 1997). These studies have focused especially on the changing role of firm-led technological change: the structure of an industry will constrain the amount and type of firm innovation at any one moment in time, yet industry structure will itself evolve depending on the characteristics of the innovation activity.

This chapter considers first a variety of perspectives on strategy. We then analyse generic strategies and portfolio approaches to strategy. Because of the importance of innovation we also discuss the difficulty and complexity of using innovation as a cornerstone of competitive strategy.

▶ Different Perspectives on Strategy

In this section we will briefly explore different conceptions of strategy. Whittington (2000) usefully summarizes four different perspectives on strategy: classical, evolutionary, processual and systemic. The classical perspective assumes that the manager understands and has control over how to allocate the resources of the firm. The manager can thus manipulate the internal organization of the firm to better suit these objectives. So strategic behaviour is guided by rationality, opportunism and self-interest. The evolutionary perspective emphasizes behavioural differences between firms and the market selection mechanisms that allow some firms to fail and others to survive and grow. Performance is determined by a mix of the forces of the market, random events, and processes of positive feedback. The evolutionary perspective, therefore, undermines the image of the heroic entrepreneur or manager which is central to the classical perspective. The processual perspective argues that economic outcomes emerge from the interactions between individuals and between individuals and their environment. The result of this interaction is unpredictable because actions are often unintended. Humans are not perfectly rational but bounded in their rationality. This, along with the fact that interaction between individuals is guided not only by self-interest but also by collective bargaining and compromise, causes fuzzy and unpredictable outcomes. The systemic perspective argues that each of the above is characterized by a narrow, Western, often Anglo-Saxon, view of the world. The rationality of a particular strategy depends on its specific historical, social and cultural context. Strategic behaviour is embedded in a network of social relations that includes cultural norms, class and education background, religion and so on. What is labelled as irrational behaviour in one context may be perfectly rational in another. Because much of the argument centres on which of these views prevails, and because we think that it is not a case of either/or, but rather both/and, we will consider two aspects of the variety of views in a little more detail.

One of the most influential thinkers, Michael Porter, claims that decisions can only be described as strategic if (a) they involve doing something differently from competitors and (b) that difference results in sustainable advantage (Porter 1996). Sustainability means being difficult to imitate; activities that simply increase productivity by making existing methods more efficient are not strategic, since they can be copied by competitors. Although a firm must engage in both types of activity, it is strategic activities that will allow it to develop a sustainable superior performance. One of the factors that renders strategies difficult to imitate, and hence unique, is that they are the result of a complex interaction between different activities which are not reducible to the sum of the individual activities. It is this synergy between activities that produces value, not the activities themselves. The other important point that Porter makes is that strategy involves trade-offs. That is, if a firm chooses to pursue one type or form of strategy it may preclude the development of an alternative.

In contrast to Porter, Mintzberg and Waters (1985) explore the process by which strategies develop within organizations. Their empirical work enabled them to develop a typology of strategies along a continuum from planned strategies to emergent strategies. In the planned strategy, intentions are clear and directly translated into actions. In emergent strategies, decisions arise from bargaining, chance and positive feedback. Between these two lie what Mintzberg and Waters call entrepreneurial, ideological and umbrella strategies. What is best for an organization is contingent upon the nature of the organization. They conclude that strategies are usually a mix: 'strategy walks on two legs, one deliberate, one emergent'.

Competition, Performance and Strategic Fit

Superior performance is often expressed in terms of profitability or market share, which are essentially comparative measures. Organizations can and do, however, use a variety of other performance criteria, financial and non-financial. They may measure success in terms of the value of their assets or returns on equity, sales, investment or capital employed. They may also 'benchmark' themselves against similar organizations on non-financial ratios such as output per employee, awareness/favourability ratings and so on.

In thinking about organizational performance and how competitive strategies achieve success, we need to recognize that organizations may have a range of objectives. Shareholders probably assume that management strives daily to build shareholder value, whereas management may have other goals to meet. A taxpayer may assume that hospital consultants strive only to make patients better, when they may also have personal research objectives. Such multiple objectives naturally impact on the choice of strategy.

Objectives and performance indicators may be financial and non-financial. Some of these can comprise a 'basket' of weighted individual measures. For example, university 'league tables' can comprise a basket of the availability of student accommodation, drop-out rates, completion rates, graduate employment rates and so on, aggregated to form a single index. Not-for-profit organizations may deploy resources to achieve high ratings on these indicators as a means of seeking sustainable competitive advantage in the competition for resources.

As discussed earlier, management may seek a strategic 'fit' between the opportunities available in the competitive environment and the organization's internal resources and capabilities. This does not imply the pursuit of some kind of equilibrium or coexistence among competitors. Rather, 'fit' is about exploiting some perceived environmental opportunity, based on a clear understanding of the organization's distinctiveness and competitive advantage. For this it must understand *how* its resources and capabilities give it a competitive advantage in relation to the capabilities of its competitors. An organization's profit potential depends on whether its managers can use or develop its internal resources and capabilities to fit the emerging external opportunities.

▶ Competitive Advantage and Corporate Success

Kay (1993) asserts that corporate success derives from a competitive advantage – which may vary from one market or industry to another. Competitive advantage is based on distinctive capabilities and strategic assets. These assets and capabilities are most often derived from and matched with the relationships that the organization has with its customers, suppliers, employees, the government and so on.

In economic terms, a useful measure of success is superior added value (Kay 1993). Superior returns can, by definition, only be achieved when the organization is performing better compared with others in the same industry. If an organization's capabilities and strategic assets are not distinctive, there is unlikely to be sustained advantage. On the other hand, distinctiveness is a necessary, but certainly not a sufficient, condition for competitive advantage, as we will see later.

Kay suggests that there are three types of distinctive capability:

- architecture
- reputation
- innovation.

Architecture is the term used to describe relationships, both formal and informal, between internal staff, with customers and suppliers, and inter-firm collaborative arrangements (networks). Architecture provides an effective conduit for organizational knowledge and routines, which are often the key source of sustainable competitive advantage.

Reputation is built on relationships with an organization's suppliers and customers. A particular reputation, perhaps for reliability or speed of service, is a source of advantage where a buyer values this reputation over a competitor's at the moment when a contract is placed. Reputations are, however, a wasting source of advantage if they are not maintained.

Innovation is Kay's third type of distinctive capability. Innovation can be a source of competitive advantage when it provides the means for an organization to compete more efficiently, offering a product which is more valuable to a customer; or when it allows the organization to compete in new ways (for example, using new distribution channels). Innovation is only sustainable as an advantage, however, when it cannot be easily imitated or superseded by alternative innovations.

Competitive advantage can also derive from the organization's ownership of *strategic assets*. These can be classified as:

- *Natural monopolies* such as scale economies, or closed systems compatibility standards such as the PC-operating system from Microsoft, or proximity to high-value or low-cost inputs (rare minerals, a labour pool with particular skills, research laboratories or low labour-cost regions).
- *Sunk costs*, such as prior investment in capital equipment (such as plant for oil- and gas-refining), knowledge, or established skills (for example, in managing large and complex projects).
- *Exclusivity*, such as exclusive importation or distribution agreements, licences to use a particular technology, or legislative protection.

Note that competitive advantage involves organizations in finding some way of disturbing the bases of 'perfect' competition in an industry or sector. All organizations must compete in some way or other for scarce resources (indeed, the working capital provided by customers in commercial organizations is no more than a scarce financial resource with which to pay suppliers, wages and salaries, dividends, etc.). Monopoly providers such as UK universities are now forced to compete for students and research grants as universities in the USA have always done, and many charitable organizations are being driven to adopt strategies based on competition as the struggle for scarce funds intensifies.

Porter's Generic Strategies

The opportunity to earn supernormal profits within an industry depends on exploiting some competitive advantage *within that industry*. By casual observation, sources of competitive advantage seem infinitely variable. Competitors continually jostle for customer attention by adding more features or extra services at no charge, by cutting prices or supplying extra product at the same price. We regularly see airline advertisements claiming to service more destinations with more comfortable seating than competitors; business-information providers claim more up-to-date statistics and business trends than other providers; courier services claim faster parcel delivery to more destinations than their competitors.

The work of Michael Porter (1985), and his generic strategies of cost leadership, differentiation and focus, is a useful way of identifying some generic approaches to exploiting competitive advantage. The features and scope of his generic strategies can be summarized as follows:

Cost leadership

Here the organization sets out to be *the* low-cost producer in its industry, using any or all of the various sources of cost advantage. If an organization can achieve and sustain cost leadership, then it will be an above-average performer in its industry, provided it can command prices at the industry average or increase overall sales volumes from lower prices. The organization may price its offerings at a level that is comparable with, or lower than, its competitors, but yet achieve higher gross margins. Note that superior profits and advantage derive from lower *cost*, not price. Low costs do, however, give an organization increased flexibility on the pricing strategies it can pursue. Further, being the lowest-cost producer does not mean that the value package offered to customers is unimportant. The low-cost producer must offer a level of functionality and quality that is acceptable to its market sector.

Differentiation

Here an organization seeks to be unique in its industry along some dimensions that are valued by buyers. It selects one or more attributes that buyers in an industry perceive as important, and uniquely positions itself to meet those needs. The means for differentiation are peculiar to each industry and each organization. It is rewarded for its uniqueness with a premium price. A firm that can achieve and sustain differentiation will be an above-average performer in its industry provided its price premium exceeds the extra costs incurred in being unique. The product or service must continue to be valued by the customer if the price premium is to hold up. Of course, the differentiator cannot ignore cost, since a poor cost position will erode any gains that result from a price premium.

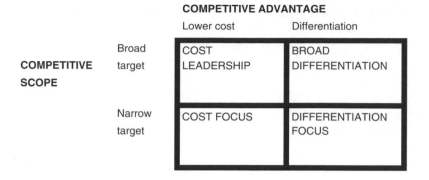

Figure 6.1 Porter's generic strategies
Source: Porter (1985). Reproduced by permission of The Free Press, an imprint of Simon & Schuster Adult Publishing Group.

Focus

A firm may pursue advantage from cost leadership or differentiation, either in the broad market, or by pursuing a strategy of *focus*. Segments, or a group of segments, in an industry are selected for either a cost or a differentiation strategy, to the exclusion of other segments. By optimizing strategy for the target segments, the focuser seeks to achieve a competitive advantage in its target segments. It aims to use its cost or differentiation strategy to out-focus its broadly targeted competitors. This requires a clear appreciation of (a) where its focus is and (b) how narrow or broad a market segment or sector to compete in. A segment may be broadly defined by geographic coverage, product application, distribution channel, or particular customer characteristic (such as age, gender, ethnicity or income group).

Taking differentiation, cost advantage and focus together gives the four generic strategies shown in figure 6.1: cost leadership, cost focus, broad differentiation and differentiation focus.

- A cost leadership strategy involves being the lowest-cost producer across the broad sector or industry.
- A cost-focused strategy aims for cost advantage within a specific segment.
- A broad differentiation strategy involves offering a differentiated product or service across a broad sector or industry.
- A differentiation focus strategy aims for differentiation within a specific segment.

We now look in more depth at the two basic types of generic strategy: cost-based and differentiation-based.

Cost-based strategies

Eight drivers of cost advantage can be identified (Grant 1995):

- economies of scale
- economies of learning
- process technology
- product design
- process design
- capacity utilization
- input costs
- residual differences in operating efficiency.

A broadly targeted *cost leadership strategy* is appropriate where significant economies of scale or scope are possible and where it is difficult to differentiate the product. Take oil-refining and petrol distribution, for example. Here the industry structure has led to established practices for managing large capital investments, and distribution channels are often shared. The competitive arena cuts across many markets and so the competitive scope is broad. This is also true for many cosmetics, such as soaps, deodorants, shampoos and after-shave lotions. These are promoted for everyday use by all sections of the population, at very competitive prices. Most of these products are likely to be mature in terms of their product life-cycles.

On the other hand a *cost-focused strategy* is appropriate where a product or service is clearly defined and offered in a budget-conscious market segment. This strategy depends on the existence of segments whose needs are for products or services with fewer functional features than those aimed at the broad market. The YMCA and YWCA provide examples of 'cost-focus' strategies that aim to provide minimum-cost accommodation to young people. Although they attract travellers with different motivations – the temporarily homeless, tourists, low-paid tradespeople – their common denominator is an overriding concern for the basics of decent accommodation at minimum cost. Then again, car manufacturers such as Lada and Hyundai have established themselves in Western markets by targeting a segment of the population whose needs for personal transport are relatively modest, with extremely low prices. The manufacturers of these cars rely on older-generation technologies and low input costs, such as low labour rates and unsophisticated manufacturing processes.

Cost control is clearly central to competitive strategy, whether the organization is pursuing a strategy of cost advantage or differentiation. A sensible programme for cost reduction is not the same as pursuing a strategy for cost advantage, however. Competitors may also be seeking a cost advantage, and there may be a shared interest in making an assessment of their own cost position in relation to others.

While most managers would agree that the control of cost is critical to their organization's health, there is often wide disagreement within the organization about what those costs are. Furthermore, the cost behaviour of a product or service tends to be poorly understood in terms of knowing how the real costs affect profitability. In some instances, a firm's allocation of costs to its various activities may remain unchanged for a decade or more despite obvious changes in the activities themselves. In addition, firms often have very little understanding of their competitors' cost position, which is essential for understanding their own *relative* cost position. What is needed is a systematic analysis of cost to determine an organization's cost position *relative* to that of its competitors and to identify ways in which an organization may gain sustainable cost advantage. Existing accounting systems have a limited role here.

Differentiation-based strategies

When following a strategy of *broad differentiation* it is important to strike the right balance between providing unique benefits and minimizing the additional cost of the product or service. Getting the balance wrong could result in the erosion of all superior profits. Honda seeks competitive advantage by following a differentiated strategy in terms of enhanced reliability and advanced engine and transmission technologies. Its competitive scope is broad, because it competes globally and across all market segments. Another example of a 'differentiation' strategy is the Swatch watch that is available through retail channels such as jewellers, department stores and airport shops. To its broad market it is differentiated by its modern and unusual designs. As the designs have changed, a thriving collectors' market has developed.

An organization may choose a strategy of *differentiation focus* when a target segment has unique needs and is willing to pay a premium for the right product or service features. This strategy depends on the existence of segments whose needs are for products or services with greater functional or service features than those aimed at the broad market. Here, customers expect or are offered a comprehensive product package, including service features if needed. The competitor operating in this segment is likely to seek out sophisticated design and technologies, whether related to a product or a service. The manufacturers of high-performance cars such as Porsche, Maserati or Lamborghini, for example, are highly differentiated in their aesthetic design, their advanced handling and other sought-after features. They serve a small clientele of enthusiasts drawn from all over the world.

Since differential advantage depends on whether potential customers value their relationship with the supplying organization, the scope for being differentiated is not restricted to extra features on the product or service. There may be scope for differentiating the organization's relationship with its customers in many ways:

- delivering the product or service
- managing the customer's inventory
- financing to help purchase
- training new users
- removing barriers to the ordering process, trial periods, etc.
- establishing close partnerships with customers that facilitate just-in-time scheduling, open-book accounting, joint efficiency-seeking projects, organizational process-development projects, etc.
- providing after-sales service.

These tangible aspects are accompanied by intangible qualities that potential customers weigh up in their evaluation of the relationship. For example, we noted previously that consumers exercise choice on the basis of the image they associate with a particular product, as is common in fashion goods. Or, to take a different example from financial services, there are investors who trade only in shares of companies that are deemed not to harm the environment.

A supplier, whether firm, charity or public service, and its customers are each party to an explicit or tacit contract of expected performance. Suppliers promise, and customers expect, that a product or a service will meet certain levels of quality, reliability, durability, safety and so on. The contract may be underpinned by regulatory constraints such as safety standards that today affect most products and services. Many complex products and services need to comply with both regulatory and voluntary criteria, otherwise there is a risk of reduced safety and standards. Examples include standardized power socket dimensions, computer data protocols, the level of lead in car fuel, and so on. However, while these performance criteria constrain differentiation in particular directions, such constraints are also very often sources of innovation. For example, without common standards, competitors' resources are often diverted to maintaining proprietary standards, and customers generally do not value proprietary standards. On the other hand, where there are common technical standards, competitors can focus their creativity on other areas that potential customers *are* likely to value.

In the same way, market segments are not just static structural characteristics of a market to be taken for granted. The reality is that market segments exist because of patterns in human behaviour, which organize and guide suppliers' thinking about how to differentiate themselves. People buy fashion accessories and cosmetics because they seek a particular identity. Segmentation is thus created and routinely maintained jointly by suppliers and buyers. While such segmentation can be stable over time, competitive forces lend segments a degree of fragility. This is a potential source of innovation, and fragility provides scope for further differentiation if the organization is able to enlist potential customers in creating a new segment.

Generic strategies in perspective

In Porter's view, the choice of generic strategy depends on forces within the industry structure. The competitive environment tends to weed out inappropriate competitive strategies and their organizations on the basis of survival of the fittest. The Porter framework does, however, help in the assessment of the relative strengths and weaknesses of competitors and therefore suggests what strategy a new entrant might follow to position itself, or how an established firm could reposition itself.

Stable industry environments, for example, may encourage cost advantage from economies of scale and experience, as they move towards standardization practices. Unstable environments may encourage differentiation more than cost advantage. For example, rapid and continual technological change in the information technology and telecommunications sectors is characterized by an ever-growing range of products and services. In this environment, new firms enter and leave the industry at a high rate, due to intense competitive rivalry and rapid technological change that often makes products obsolete before they can recover their investment.

Probing and elaborating the generic strategies

Porter's generic strategies are clearly useful for understanding competitive advantage, and they have been very influential. Nevertheless, it is important to critically evaluate their strengths and weaknesses.

Bowman and Asch (1996) find significant problems in practice with the static nature of Porter's analysis in a complex and dynamic world. For example, cost leadership is often confused with competing in low-price segments, and so the question of *where* to compete can be misleading if combined with the question of *how* to compete. It is irrelevant to compare Hyundai with Jaguar because they compete for different customers. Hyundai competes with firms who are perceived by the customer to offer competing products, such as Lada.

Bowman and Asch also suggest that inputs can get confused with outputs. Customers do not particularly care about the input side of a strategy, which is invisible to them. A cost leadership strategy, or even a low-cost producer strategy, is unlikely to be identified as such by the consumer. Cost leaders can gain superior profits from an average market price for an average product, based on their lower costs. Following this practice, cost leaders would probably enjoy an average market share and not gain the volumes necessary to secure 'experience curve' benefits, another route to reducing costs.

In the same way, it appears that not all 'differentiators' command or demand premium prices. Some 'differentiators' actually increase market share instead.

Differentiation in the airline industry – for example, by British Airways or American Airlines – has usually been aimed at increasing the number of passengers carried at similar prices to competitors. This is because the high fixed cost and capacity availability structure of running aircraft flights encourages airlines to maximize overall revenues, rather than a notional profit margin per passenger.

There are other dangers in using the generic strategies framework in too literal or rigid a manner. First, it is a static classification device. It takes no account of the way advantage is created and destroyed over time. Secondly, there is a danger in trying to force organizations exclusively into one box or another. There needs to be a finer grain of analysis in practice to identify what an organization's underlying sources of advantage actually are. Organizations may even gain overall advantage by pursuing *both cost and differentiation advantages*, while being the leader in neither.

Miller (1986) suggests that, in order to achieve differentiation, cost advantage and focus, we must consider how the organization's fixed and current assets are being used. For example, in order to achieve a cost advantage, the organization's assets tend to be selected and organized to maximize efficiency – Miller calls this *asset intensity*. But for a differentiator to achieve superior returns, there is an observed tendency to squeeze the maximum variety out of the minimum of assets, which he calls *asset parsimony*.

Miller also suggests that 'differentiation' can be based on advantage from either (a) product innovation or (b) marketing and branding. Mintzberg et al. (1995) go further in highlighting the role of price as a means of differentiating the value package offered to customers. They identify a total of six types of differentiation strategy:

- price
- image
- support
- design
- quality
- undifferentiated (or non-differentiated).

These differentiation strategies are, of course, often mixed and combined with one another. For example, the cosmetics industry, in selling perfumes, offers an interesting example of the first two strategies, *price* and *image*. The industry often reminds its critics that it is in the business of offering people an image, or identity. Particular fragrances and colours deliver particular identities at a price that is itself part of the image. Unlike standard consumer products, the industry is not prepared to compete on price. One beer brand (Stella Artois) has also promoted itself in the UK on the grounds that it is 'reassuringly expensive'.

A competitor may differentiate itself through the *support* or complementary products it provides to customers, and this could take many forms: technical training, maintenance, finance, home delivery. The *quality* of the product or service also offers scope for differentiation. In Europe, washing machines from Miele, Bosch and AEG stand out from their competitors, not on the basis of features or support, but instead on the perceived *quality* and *design* of their construction. Through quality and image, they are able to command premium prices. Designer-wear, such as jeans, shirts, belts, scarves, watches, bags and other accessories with well-known brand labels, appeal to those who wish to be identified as connoisseurs of unique design.

Finally, there are many firms that get by *without differentiating* themselves in any way. Copying what the competitors are doing is an undifferentiated strategy. For some firms this is a conscious choice, but for others it is the result of managerial inability to be creative or innovative.

In addition, Mintzberg et al. propose four characteristic markets, which provide a finer grain of analysis than broad or narrow focus:

* unsegmented
* segmented
* niche
* customized.

Some firms look for an *unsegmented* mass market, others *segment* the broad market, and some target a particular *niche*. The provision of public transport exemplifies the spectrum of possibilities. At the unsegmented end of the market are the buses and trains. The market is also segmented, with competitors offering taxis and different classes of air travel (club, business, first, economy). Niche markets include taxis specializing in chauffeur hire to airports or for weddings, and very discriminating and wealthy customers receive *customized* travel arrangements that can combine private jets, chauffeured limousines and escorted sightseeing or shopping.

Mintzberg's four market definitions combine with the six strategies of differentiation of the product or service to suggest a matrix of possibilities, some more likely than others. For example, a customized market strategy probably demands a customer-support-differentiating strategy, while differentiating on low price and quality would normally not support a customizing strategy.

Innovation as a Source of Competitive Advantage

Innovation is of interest to the strategist for two main reasons. First, it can be a threat to the returns derived from existing products and services. Second, it can be a source of advantage for innovating organizations and can cause radical shifts in industry structures. This is what Schumpeter (1942) calls 'creative destruction'. Examples of this phenomenon are abundant in such innovations as the printing press, the steam engine, the railways and the semi-conductor. One idea that runs through our earlier discussion on generic sources of competitive advantage from either a low-cost or a differentiation perspective is that both can involve innovation.

From a cost perspective the capability to design products with a low build cost, and to develop or improve process technologies, were identified as key drivers of this form of advantage.

Differentiation advantage can also be based on innovative design and utilization of new science, for example the Swatch series of watches.

Thus innovation has the potential to be a strategic option for all forms of organization. For example, in the service sector, organizations can possibly derive advantage through the application of technology to either their offering or their processes. Such an example is Direct Line, the insurance company that applied information and communication technologies to eliminate a source of cost – brokers' commissions – and to add value for the consumer through differentiation in the form of being able to give prompt approval for repairs to begin.

Freeman (1982) suggests that an invention is an idea, a sketch or a model for a new or improved device, product or process, which may or may not lead to a technological innovation. An innovation is really only accomplished with the first economic transaction involving the new product or service.

It is clear that some innovations do not have the radical transforming impact referred to above. The majority of them are incremental in nature. They are the result of, or actually are, the marginal improvements of the product or service offering. Each is the outcome of a development trajectory that is both coherent and cumulative. Such an incremental trajectory has been shown over time to be capable of even greater technical progress and productivity increases than major transforming innovations. Banbury and Mitchell (1995) conclude that incremental product innovation is crucial to business survival and to performance for firms already established in a product market.

In some cases it has been found that the arrival of a radical new idea actually stimulates a period of innovation in the older technologies. This is known as the 'steamship' phenomenon, because the arrival of the steam-driven vessel inspired a flurry of innovation in sailing ships as they strove to compete.

The strategic management of innovation must take account of the fact that innovations may be interdependent and have a systemic quality. The adoption of any innovation may depend on *complementary innovations* occurring in the marketplace, as with the example of virtual reality computer games and simulations requiring powerful PCs. Freeman (1982) suggests the term *new technological systems* to describe constellations of innovations that are technologically and economically interlinked. Technological interdependence is evident, for example, between petrochemicals, synthetic materials and plastics, and in the innovations in the process machinery required to produce them. Organizational and institutional innovation are also vital components of new technological systems. For example, the availability of consumer credit is an essential component of the creation of markets for new consumer products such as cars or televisions, as is the presence of appropriate skills in the workforce to enable the adoption of product and process innovations.

We now have three categories – *incremental innovation*, *radical innovation*, and *new technological systems*, which include complementary innovations. Freeman suggests an additional fourth category, which he calls a change of *techno-economic paradigm*, a cluster of innovations and new technological systems, as well as associated organizational and institutional changes. The key characteristic of innovations in the techno-economic paradigm is that they pervade the whole economy. They must therefore meet the following criteria:

- clearly perceived low and rapidly falling costs
- apparently unlimited supply over a long period
- potential for use and application throughout the economic system, both directly and indirectly, in products and processes.

These criteria were met by the techno-economic paradigm surrounding oil and petrochemicals, which underpinned the post-war economic boom, and, according to Freeman, are met today by the ICT techno-economic paradigm.
This results in a *typology of innovations*:

- incremental
- radical
- new technological system (including complementary innovations)
- techno-economic paradigm.

To these four we must, of course, add process innovation for, as we mentioned above, organizations also invest heavily not only in developing new products but also the ways in which they transform inputs into outputs.

When making the distinction between product and process innovation we need to be aware that the two types of innovation may have a dynamic interdependence over time. Strategic advantage may be gained by exploiting this interdependence. For example, the major banks developed electronic funds transfer (EFT) as a process innovation to speed up the transfer of money between branches, and then between banks. The productivity benefits and cost savings that resulted from the reduction of paper transfers were significant. The first phase, focused on automation of back-office tasks (basic data-processing), enabled the UK banking sector to improve productivity to a 4.5 per cent annual growth rate by the early 1970s, when the volume of banking transactions was growing by 8 per cent per year. As the demand for banking services slowed from the mid-1970s, the banks continued to invest in ICTs at an increased rate over the period 1975–81. In a period of enhanced competition, innovative banks turned their ICT investment to improving the quality of services. The EFT systems were process innovations that also provided the infrastructure upon which new products could be based. In particular, they enabled the banks to introduce ATMs (automatic teller machines) that provided customers with 24-hour cash withdrawals, balance checks, and other services via the 'through-the-wall' computer terminals at their branches. This is also an example of a classic economy of scope.

▶ Portfolio Approaches to Strategy Development

The view that corporate strategy can be managed as a portfolio of diversified strategic business units has long been a feature of corporate strategy. The idea of portfolio management was popularized by the Boston Consulting Group (BCG) and its founder Bruce Henderson.

The BCG growth share matrix

The simplest and most publicized business portfolio matrix was developed by BCG and is known colloquially as the Boston Box. Each of the firm's businesses is plotted according to the growth rates of the industry or market and its own relative position in that industry. BCG was concerned to produce a framework whereby a range of SBUs could be managed according to their relative position on two axes: relative market share and market growth rate. A dividing-line between 'high' and 'low' market growth is arbitrarily set, the idea being to position the line so that businesses above it can be said to be in a growth phase, while those below are in a mature/saturation/declining phase. Similarly the dividing-line for relative market share should be positioned so that those businesses to the left are market leaders (though not necessarily *the* leader), while those to the right are in a training situation.

The matrix builds on two other concepts: the experience curve (also developed by BCG) and the product life-cycle. Relative market share (the ratio of an SBU's market share to that of the largest competitor in the market or segment) is deemed important in that it gives an indication of an SBU's market power, or its ability to earn higher than average rates of return. It is argued that having a large relative market share will coincide with cost benefits from large average production runs (economies of scale) and from a large cumulative volume of production (experience curve benefits).

The BCG growth/share matrix (fig. 6.2) implies that SBUs with a high degree of market power in a growing market (a 'star' in BCG terminology) should, with property investment, naturally mature with the market to become a 'cash

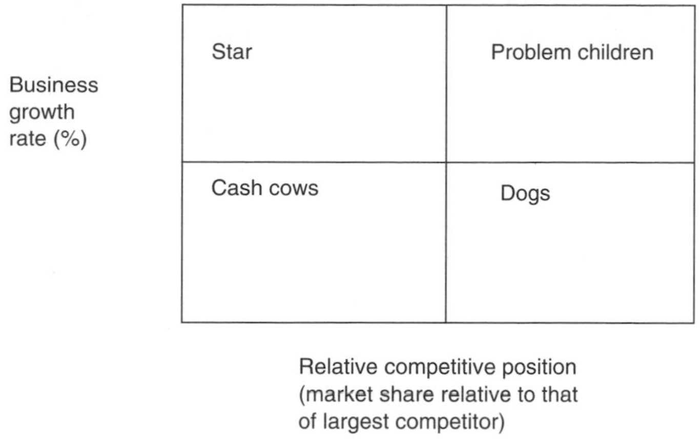

Star	Problem children
Cash cows	Dogs

Business growth rate (%)

Relative competitive position
(market share relative to that
of largest competitor)

Figure 6.2 Growth share matrix
Source: The BCG Portfolio Matrix from the Product Portfolio Matrix © 1970, the Boston Consulting Group. Reproduced by permission.

cow', generating significant amounts of cash and requiring little investment. The portfolio view of these SBUs is that a corporation can secure its future by holding a selection of SBUs, both stars and cash cows, the latter to fund the development of the former through their growth phase. The core notion in the BCG matrix that has led to its popularity as a means of managing (often unrelated) diversified corporations is that a corporation needs to maintain a balanced portfolio of stars and cash cows, the one to fund the development of the other. The simplicity of the idea has probably added to its attraction, but it also matched by the relative simplicity of the task prescribed for the corporate manager – that of managing the cashflow in a symbiotic relationship between cash cows and stars.

For businesses with a low relative market share in a high growth market ('problem children' or 'question marks'), however, the corporation is faced with a difficult choice: should it invest heavily to gain market share, moving the business to become a star and in due course a cash cow; or accept that the business is already at a competitive disadvantage, which makes it highly unlikely that it will ever return above average profits, thus suggesting the corporation should seek to divest itself of the business? Finally, for the 'dogs' – those SBUs with a low relative market share in a low-growth (mature) market – there is deemed to be no prospect of utilizing the market power that market share confers to achieve other than average returns. Once again, the simple prescription might be to divest these SBUs as they do not contribute to the overall wealth of the corporation.

The use of the BCG matrix focuses attention on the cashflow and investment characteristics of an organization's businesses, and how its financial resources can best be deployed to optimize the long-term strategic position and performance of the whole corporate portfolio. The firm's current position can be plotted on such a matrix and a projection made of its future position, assuming there are no major changes in its strategy. Used in such a way these two matrices can help to outline the scope and competitive-advantage elements in the company's corporate strategy, as well as helping to identify some of the key strategic issues facing it. A BCG matrix may also help to isolate some of the basic characteristics of each SBU's strategy.

Research by Haspeslagh (1982) revealed that 45 per cent of all Fortune 500 firms and 36 per cent of all Fortune 1000 firms used portfolio analysis to some extent, and that 75 per cent of large, diversified firms utilized the technique. The following perceived benefits were identified:

- A noticeable improvement in the quality of strategies at both corporate and business levels.
- More selective and focused allocation of corporate resources in an environment with capital rationing.
- A stronger framework for tailoring 'how we manage' to the needs of each business in the portfolio.
- An improved capacity to perform the tasks of strategic management and exert firmer control over both corporate and business-level strategies.
- Less reluctance to face the problem of marginal businesses.

The use of portfolio techniques tended to increase understanding of the role and potential contribution of each business, assist in the construction of a rational framework for resource commitments, and help in prescribing general types of strategy for each business unit. Overall, therefore, the technique helped to clarify what the firm should do with each of its businesses.

▶ The Anti-Portfolio Perspective

The late 1980s and early 1990s saw a distinct move away from the ready acceptance of portfolio management as the means of managing corporate strategy. This was at least partly the result of the perception (supported by the empirical findings of, for example, Grant et al. 1988) that many of the large, diversified corporations who followed the precepts of portfolio management saw a deterioration in their performance, as their management capabilities were stretched beyond their areas of competence. This may have been a function of the relatedness of their diverse SBUs (Rumelt 1976), but may equally have been a result of the sheer size of some of the corporations involved and the difficulties expected in processing and digesting the volume of information required to control the corporations. Given the depths of the early 1990s recession, it would seem reasonable that the fairly well-established tendency of corporations to sell off peripheral or non-core businesses when under pressure to survive (Slatter 1984; Grinyer et al. 1988), may have coincided with a perception of poor performance from diversified corporations to reinforce a view that portfolio management is an inappropriate method of corporate strategy management.

Regardless, there has been a growing tendency for corporations to talk of the need to 'focus', to concentrate on their 'core competences' and 'core capabilities', possibly again reflecting the need for corporate managers to simplify their strategic task. The main theoretical criticisms of portfolio approaches, however, have come from the fields of finance and economics.

Testing Strategy?

Rumelt (1995) suggests the four tests of 'consistency, consonance, advantage and feasibility'. He acknowledges that it may be impossible to demonstrate conclusively that a particular business strategy can, or will, work, let alone be an optimal strategy. He points out, however, that all proposed strategies can be tested for four types of critical flaw.

Rumelt suggests a *consistency* test: the proposed strategy must not present mutually inconsistent goals and policies. This test may be particularly necessary for emergent strategies since these will not have been explicitly formulated and may have formed over time in an ad hoc fashion. Even deliberate strategies may contain compromise arrangements between power groups.

Inconsistency in strategy is not simply a flaw in logic. A key function of strategy is to provide a coherent framework for organizational action. Rumelt cites the practical example of high-technology firms that face a strategic choice between offering customized, high-cost products and standardized, low-cost products. If senior management does not enunciate a clear and consistent view of where the firm stands on these issues, there will be continuing conflict between sales, design, engineering and manufacturing people. The same situation might arise in a public-sector organization where specialized interests conflict with general goals, and where priorities in allocation of resources are difficult: for example, which medical treatments should be publicly funded, or whether pre-school, primary or secondary education should be allocated additional available funds.

Rumelt goes on to argue that an organization relates to its environment in two main aspects:

- It must match and be adapted to the environment – the products or services must create more value than they cost.
- It must compete with other organizations that are also trying to adapt and prosper.

Rumelt therefore proposes a test of *consonance* that focuses on the creation of social value: to evaluate the economic relationships that characterize the business and determine whether or not sufficient value is being created to sustain the demand for the strategy in the long term.

The major difficulty in evaluating consonance is that most of the critical threats or substitutes that come from the external environment will also threaten the whole industry. Management may be so focused on existing competition that the threat is only recognized after the damage is done. Rumelt also points out that many forecasting techniques do not reveal potentially critical changes that arise from *interaction* among combinations of trends. For example, supermarkets came into being only when home refrigeration allowed shoppers to buy in bulk. Similarly, retail parks depend on an increase in car ownership. The key to the test of consonance is to grasp why the organization exists and the basic economic foundation that supports and defines the business, and then to study the consequences of key changes.

Rumelt's third test is about *competitive advantage*, or whether the organization can capture enough of the value it creates. Remember, competitive strategy is the art of creating and exploiting those advantages that are most telling, enduring and most difficult to replicate. The strategy must provide for the creation and/or maintenance of a competitive advantage in one or more of three roots: superior skills, superior resources, superior position.

The fourth test – of the *feasibility* of a proposed strategy – will consider how well it would work in practice and how difficult it might be to achieve. In considering feasibility, businesses need to take into account whether the necessary resources are available, and the firm's ability to achieve the required level of operational performance, say in quality and service levels. For example a strategy aimed at reducing costs in manufacturing may run into problems associated with inadequate managerial resources, insufficient numbers of trained staff, or inadequate process and product technologies. The reaction of competitors should also be considered. In considering the feasibility of a strategy, however, there is a danger of ignoring the challenge of strategic stretch and leverage (Prahalad and Hamel 1994). Feasibility should therefore reflect the challenge as well as the test of ambition.

▶ Risk and Uncertainty in Strategic Choice

Strategy is about charting a course for the future: Will governments alter legislation? How will competitors react? Will war break out in one of the countries where business is carried out? The choice made by an organization is usually made in the face of risk and uncertainty. *Risk* is concerned with assessing the probability of foreseen outcomes. In contrast, *uncertainty* is to do with outcomes that may be unforeseen, or those which are foreseen but against which a degree of estimated risk cannot be set.

Assessing uncertainties and weighing up risks is a difficult, often personal, process and very dependent on the business environment. In making choices about strategy, acceptance of different degrees of risk is often a matter of an individual manager's (or group of managers') personal preferences. Some individuals are very risk-averse, others take risks almost as a matter of routine. In fact, Wilde (1982) suggests that:

- tolerance to risk affects the way in which people assess information
- people behave so as to maintain a certain level of subjective risk at all times.

Strategic risks that would be acceptable in one industry, such as PC manufacture, would be quite unacceptable in another, such as health care or aerospace. Quinn (1978) feels that perceived risk is largely a function of an individual's knowledge about a sector or industry. This raises the question whether managers entering a new industry are best equipped to assess the risks and uncertainties associated with it. For example, would managers used to predicting stable revenues in public monopoly utilities be best placed to identify the risks and uncertainties of, say, software design and manufacture?

Judgement may involve 'satisficing' and compromise. For example, in most organizations there will be a drive to attain the lowest possible cost in order to yield the highest possible added value. Alternatively, the strategic intent might be to maximize market share without regard (within limits) for the cost. With such trade-offs in the face of conflicting objectives, some, such as those involving finance or market share, will be measurable, and others will be expressions of stakeholder preference. Measurement of success in strategic situations is frequently concerned with reaching the most acceptable solution in the face of conflicting objectives, inadequate resources, or unfavourable attitudes.

Conclusion

This chapter has focused on the choices that may exist as firms seek to develop competitive strategies. In particular, the importance of strategy as a means of exploiting sources of advantage has been affirmed as a key consideration in strategic choice.

Ohmae (1982) has written persuasively about the boundary between the rational *prescriptive* approach to making strategy and the *descriptive* approach. Synthesizing successful business strategies never results just from rigorous analysis, but from a particular state of mind. Insight and a drive for achievement fuel a thought process that is creative and intuitive rather than rational. Ohmae acknowledges the role of analysis – indeed, strategists could hardly do without it – but they use it to stimulate the creative process, test the resulting ideas and ensure successful execution of high-potential 'wild' ideas. No matter how difficult or unprecedented the problem, a breakthrough to the best possible solution can come only from a combination of rational analysis (based on the real nature of things and imaginative reintegration of all the different items into a new pattern) and the exercise of individual thought and judgement. Ohmae believes that great strategies, like great works of art or great scientific discoveries, although they all call for technical mastery in the analysis, must originate in insights and judgements that are beyond the reach of conscious analysis.

chapter 7

The Adaptive Organization

In the practice of warfare, however, the star-shaped fortresses which were being built and improved everywhere during the eighteenth century did not answer their purpose, for intent as everyone was on that pattern, it had been forgotten that the largest fortifications will naturally attract the largest enemy forces, and that the more you entrench yourself the more you must remain on the defensive, so that in the end you might find yourself in a place fortified in every possible way, watching helplessly while the enemy troops, moving on to their own choice of terrain elsewhere, simply ignored their adversaries' fortresses, which had become positive arsenals of weaponry, bristling with cannon and overcrowded with men. The frequent result, said Austerlitz, of resorting to measures of fortification marked in general by a tendency towards paranoid elaboration was that you drew attention to your weakest point, practically inviting the enemy to attack it, not to mention the fact that as architectural plans for fortification became increasingly complex, the time it took to build them increased as well, and with it the probability that as soon as they were finished, if not before, they would have been overtaken by further developments, both in artillery and in strategic planning, which took account of the growing realisation that everything was decided in movement, not in a state of rest. And if the defensive power of a fortress was really put to the test, then as a rule, and after the squandering of enormous quantities of war material, the outcome remained more or less undecided.

(Sebald 2001: 16)

INTRODUCTION

The eponymous hero of Sebald's wonderful novel describes, in another but closely analogous context, some of the contradictions and limits of the conventional approach to organization restructuring which seeks to build organizations around existing or new strategies. Changing organizations to fit their strategies takes time; it freezes the strategy (and the emergent organization); it places emphasis on defending the strategy (thus drawing attention to it) rather than on moving beyond the strategy. The elaborate defence of the existing strategy takes time to achieve. And in the meantime other, more alert, less encumbered organizations have developed new strategies which make yours vulnerable. The parallels are many and intriguing. The most important parallel is indicated by Austerlitz's wonderful and telling phrase: 'everything was decided in movement, not in a state of rest'. This assessment is directly relevant to the concerns of this chapter. This chapter is about the attempts by current organizations to avoid the dangers outlined by Austerlitz – that they define the future in terms of the past, that they prepare for the next struggle by re-fighting the last one, that they embark on lengthy processes of change which are out of date before they are complete – and to replace freezing and embedding the status quo with a more alert, adaptive type of organization better suited for a rapidly changing but unknowable and unpredictable world.

▶ Organizational Adaptation

> *Organisational learning is seen to lie at the heart of strategic competence. It [is] a central strategic topic in the context of world-wide processes of business transformation.*
> (Hodgkinson and Sparrow 2002)

The 'fit' theorists argue that the greater the degree of fit between an organization's structure, processes, culture and systems, and the skills and attributes of its employees, and its strategy and environment, the better its performance. The approach, although stressing multiple levels of accommodation, essentially assumes a process that results in a new stability, and that achieves consistency and fit. The result of change is to re-establish order and stability. But another approach stresses an approach to organizational change which is not based on the achievement of order and stability but rather one in which the organization is in constant interchange with its environment and renews itself continuously.

In the adaptive organization strategy is developed by the organization as a whole, and achieved by the organization as a whole as a continuous process. This characteristic underlies three other features: the ability to learn, to innovate and to change.

The adaptive organization is capable of learning. This concern with learning (particularly associated with the notion of the learning organization, which is discussed below) is central to the adaptive organization approach. Adaptation after all – at least successful adaptation – is based on learning – on learning about the environment, and learning about the organization and its products and structures and processes, and being capable of analysing the relationship between organization and environment. The concept of organizational learning receives further examination below. It is crucial. Whipp notes 'the importance of learning in relation to fast changing competitive conditions . . . If in the wake of globalisation, marketing, financial and manufacturing techniques become ever more capable of imitation, then their competitive advantage is correspondingly diminished . . . in this sort of world "the ability to learn faster than competitors may be the only sustainable advantage"' (de Geus 1988: 74, quoted in Whipp 1991: 166).

Finally the adaptive organization has to be able to change. To be able to learn and to innovate but to be unable to design and implement the changes learning and adaptation require, is insufficient. The adaptive organization must be able to make fast and effective adjustments when necessary. It sees the need for, and benefits of, change, and is good at achieving the necessary changes. The ability to manage change is not just a technical competence; it is a fundamental feature of the organization, a systemic consequence of its integration, its ability to overcome the conventional separation of thinkers and doers which is seen as antithetical to the achievement of organization-wide change. The adaptive organization's competence at change (and its competence at recognizing the need for change) stem from its openness at all levels to information-gathering and information-processing, strategy development, and strategy refinement in the light of experience:

> The process of competition often begins from the understanding a firm develops of its environment . . . it is not enough for firms to regard judgements of their external competitive world as only a technical procedure. On the contrary, the requirement is for organisations to become open learning systems. In other words the assessment of the competitive environment cannot be the responsibility of a specialist function. Nor does it happen through neat, separate acts. Strategy creation tends to emerge from the way a company, at all levels, processes information about its environment. (Whipp 1991: 174)

If we are to be able to understand, assess, and if possible apply, the ideas implicit in the adaptive organization then it is necessary to separate out the discrete ideas which constitute this approach and to assess them. This is the task of the following two sections.

One of the paradoxes of the contemporary discussion of ways to improve organizational performance is that, although those advocating these changes stress their newness and the ways in which they represent radical breaks with the past, very often these changes, although frequently relabelled, are in fact old and familiar. There are reasons for this: one of them is that many of the problems of organizations which current change programmes claim to resolve are probably unresolvable and in fact are tensions and contradictions which are basic to the very nature of organization. Another reason is the obvious benefit to consultants and change advocates of persuading clients that a proposed change represents a new approach to old problems.

This applies to all the main approaches to the improvement of organizational performance. The emphasis on achieving 'fit' between strategy and organizational structure is central to the 'contingencies' approach to organizational structure, which argues that different organizational structures are appropriate for different purposes and production technologies. The recognition of the importance of organizational core competences, that differences in the performance of organizations in the same industry are a consequence of the ways in which firms manage their resources, was first advanced by Edith Penrose in 1900. The importance of an organization's capacity to formulate strategy and the role of strategy became clear shortly after the Second World War. And the notion of the adaptive organization as an attractive and appealing (if hard to attain) approach to improved organizational performance is certainly as old as Burns and Stalker's classic work, *The Management of Innovation* (first published in 1961 with further editions in 1991 and 1994), together with other books – for example a stream of publications from Chris Argyris – which not only focused on the merits of innovation and learning but sought to identify the organizational features which encourage them.

The attraction of the adaptive organization approach does not lie in its newness, for it – or at least its basic constituent ideas – is not new. The adaptive organization as an approach to improved organizational effectiveness has been a dream of managers and organizational theorists for many, many years. And at the heart of this dream is a paradox: that, although in modern versions it does not admit as much for this would lessen its credibility, the appeal of this approach to improving organizational effectiveness is an attempt – or a claim to be able – to counteract and overcome organization itself. This approach derives its power as an idea – but possibly also its weakness as a guide to practice – from its claim that it can overcome some of the more persistent, systemic and basic aspects of organization itself. This, in itself, does not entirely undermine the approach; recent thinkers may possibly have identified ways of overcoming the negative consequences of organization. We shall see. But we must remember that these negative effects of organization are also the very features that give organizations their extraordinary power and efficiency. Trying to remove them may not only be difficult: it might, were it to be possible, remove the very features that make organizations effective.

The adaptive organization is, ultimately, not simply a description of a new and (for its advocates) possible and desirable type of organization: it is actually a theory, an assertion. The theory is simple but nevertheless claims, as all theories do, that certain conditions create certain effects. In the case of the adaptive organization, the theory is that certain organizational features – both structural and cultural – permit and encourage organizational learning; that organizational learning encourages innovation; and that innovation and learning, when translated into appropriate organization actions by processes of successful change, create competitive advantage. The adaptive organization thesis mainly focuses on the outputs of this form of organization: 'creating new forms of competitive advantage', 'redefining the industry, anticipating market trends, moving quickly in and out of products and business', 'being willing to abandon what has been successful', and so on.

In what follows we are going to move back from these desirable outputs and beneficial consequences and seek to identify the organizational conditions which create or support them. But the adaptive organization thesis does not simply advocate a list of desirable organizational features: it advances a thesis, and the analysis that follows of its constituent elements will mirror the stages of the thesis. Thus we start with theories of learning in an organization which support innovation and which require successfully designed and implemented change, all of which depend upon a new form of organization which somehow transcends or neutralizes the anti-learning features of conventional organizations. Each of the core ideas that are inherent in the adaptive organization approach is presented and discussed, including, crucially, the nature of the organization that supports learning. The power of this approach resides in the ideas and arguments it subsumes. Its status as an approach also depends on the strengths of these ideas and their application in practice.

▶ The Learning Organization and Organizational Learning

These two ideas are significantly different: possibly qualitatively, certainly in degree. The learning organization (LO) is a set of ideas propounded and advocated by a number of consultants and academics. It claims the importance (and possibility) of achieving an organization that is devoted to learning. This is a very definite and ambitious project. It is discussed below.

However, the notion of the adaptive organization is not necessarily dependent on the achievement of a learning organization; it is dependent on achieving organizational learning, which is a less ambitious and more feasible project. Organizational learning is addressed in the second part of this section.

The learning organization

It is tempting to dismiss the learning organization. It's so easy: it can seem simplistic, poorly researched, poorly conceptualized, hopelessly unrealistic. But we must try not to reject it out of hand. As a number of writers who have commented on similar consultancy-based ideas and theories have pointed out, the fact that the idea is popular with managers and associated with consultancy activity does not necessarily mean that it is not serious and important (Wood 1989; Guest 1990).

In fact the learning organization is an important idea, more important than many academic commentators realize. It merits attention. This is because it is central to current thinking about organizational change and performance and because it actually contains an important and provocative suggestion. But its importance is not the importance it claims.

The contemporary manager is flooded with advice, and the contemporary organization is exposed to unprecedented quantities and programmes of change, some of which reflect this advice. The learning organization movement has a place in this advice and practice. It inspires it and legitimates it and informs it. The learning organization is important as an idea.

What is the learning organization? One useful summary which clearly establishes not only its desirable outputs but also the organizational preconditions for it, is offered by Pedlar, Burgoyne and Boydell 1991 (figure 7.1).

The essence of this approach to improving organizational capability is a view of a new form of relationship between organizations and environments. As Senge comments: 'At the heart of a learning organisation is a shift of mind – from seeing ourselves as separate from the world, from seeing problems as caused by someone or something "out there", to seeing how our actions create the problems we experience. A learning organization is a place where people are continually discovering how they create their reality' (Senge 1990a: 12–13). Senge's notion of the learning organization shares many features with Nonaka and Takeuchi's 'knowledge-creating company' (1995) and Quinn's 'intelligent enterprise' (1992).

It's not difficult to see the appeal of this argument. Both the fit and the resource-based approaches assume an alert senior management cadre capable of anticipating and understanding environmental developments and then being able to redesign the organization quickly and efficiently to ensure its compatibility with strategy. But the learning organization approach argues the merits of achieving a total organization that is endlessly capable of reinventing itself in response to unpredictable environments. The learning organization doesn't have to be made to change and adapt: it does it 'naturally' as an organism adapts naturally to changes in environment.

So the appeals of the metaphor of the learning organization are obvious. It draws on not only a strong underlying link to evolutionary dynamics, but also a long-standing historical interest in flexible, adaptive organizational structures, and in learning in organizations. The LO approach also draws on the value placed on enterprise in contemporary discourses of organization (Du Gay 1991, 1996; Du Gay and Salaman 1992; Rose 1995; Miller and Rose 1993). Enterprise is a key concept in contemporary approaches to organizational change. It acts as a central relay device between organization and employee and external environmental forces. It thus asserts the importance of exactly the same sort of necessary linkage between these elements as is prescribed by the LO thesis. It also defines both organization and employee as actively and autonomously committed to the achievement of flexible, responsive relationships with clients and employers.

Finally, like enterprise, the notion of the learning organization conflates individual and organizational levels of analysis and assumes that one reflects and supports the other. Like enterprise, the LO approach defines organizations in terms of individual attributes. Thus the approach shares many of the elements of the discourse of enterprise but sanitizes the concerns and priorities of enterprise, by replacing an overtly commercial, market focus with the gentler psychological and developmental language of learning. But while we may understand the appeal of the LO thesis we must also understand its practical limitations.

In order to explore the practical feasibility of the learning organization it is necessary to identify the organizational features associated with, or assumed and required by, its achievement. Overviews have been offered by Pedlar et al. (1991), Jones and Hendry (1994), and Pettigrew and Whipp (1991). Many of these commentators note the daunting demands of the learning organization. Pedlar et al. note that its achievement requires that 'the basic assumptions and values underpinning reward systems are explored and shared', and 'all members of the company take part in policy and strategy formation' (Pedlar et al. 1991: 26–7). Another useful statement of the key elements of the learning organization has been offered by Snell (2001), and we will use it for this evaluation of the approach.

However attractive the idea of the learning organization might be, it seems prima facie that it might be systematically at odds with many of the core features of the modern organization. This is a conclusion many commentators have reached. For some the issue is the conflict between learning and the fact of organization itself. Others have approached this via a distinction between types of learning. Various writers using various dichotomies have distinguished learning that involves adjustment around the existing situation from learning that addresses and changes underlying assumptions (Hedberg 1981; Kirton 1976; Senge 1990a). The first involves correcting errors; the second involves addressing the sources of the problems or errors. Argyris, who has contributed enormously to this area, notes that the more radical form of learning – which is essential to the achievement of the learning organization – raises issues of politics, deference and resistance within features of organization. In

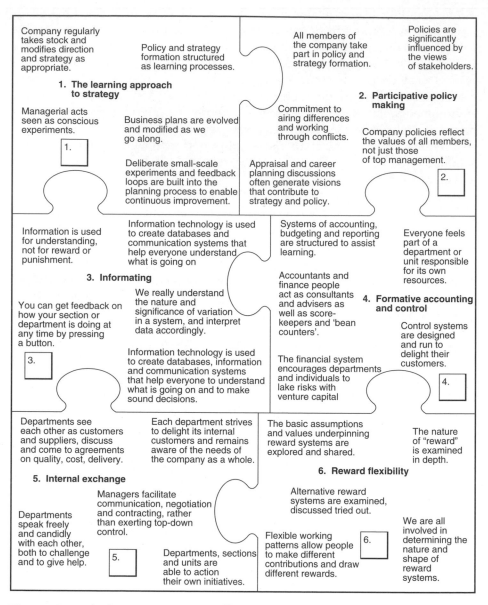

Figure 7.1 The learning company profile
Source: Pedlar, Burgoyne and Boydell (1991). Reproduced by permission of McGraw Hill.

short, he argues, organizations have institutionalized barriers to the sort of radical learning identified by Pedlar et al. as essential to the achievement of the learning organization. They have learned not to learn.

This assertion requires further discussion. It is central to our analysis of the feasibility of the appealing notion of the learning organization. It's useful

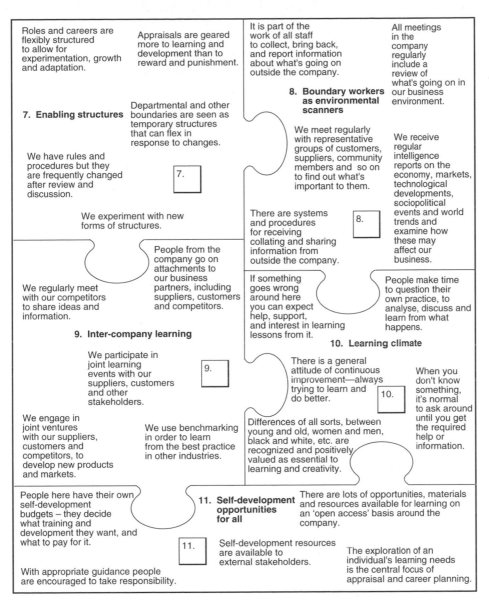

Roles and careers are flexibly structured to allow for experimentation, growth and adaptation.

Appraisals are geared more to learning and development than to reward and punishment.

7. **Enabling structures**

Departmental and other boundaries are seen as temporary structures that can flex in response to changes.

We have rules and procedures but they are frequently changed after review and discussion.

7.

We experiment with new forms of structures.

It is part of the work of all staff to collect, bring back, and report information about what's going on outside the company.

8. **Boundary workers as environmental scanners**

We meet regularly with representative groups of customers, suppliers, community members and so on to find out what's important to them.

There are systems and procedures for receiving collating and sharing information from outside the company.

All meetings in the company regularly include a review of what's going on in our business environment.

We receive regular intelligence reports on the economy, markets, technological developments, sociopolitical events and world trends and examine how these may affect our business.

8.

People from the company go on attachments to our business partners, including suppliers, customers and competitors.

We regularly meet with our competitors to share ideas and information.

If something goes wrong around here you can expect help, support, and interest in learning lessons from it.

People make time to question their own practice, to analyse, discuss and learn from what happens.

9. **Inter-company learning**

We participate in joint learning events with our suppliers, customers and other stakeholders.

9.

10. **Learning climate**

There is a general attitude of continuous improvement—always trying to learn and do better.

10.

When you don't know something, it's normal to ask around until you get the required help or information.

We engage in joint ventures with our suppliers, customers and competitors, to develop new products and markets.

We use benchmarking in order to learn from the best practice in other industries.

Differences of all sorts, between young and old, women and men, black and white, etc. are recognized and positively valued as essential to learning and creativity.

People here have their own self-development budgets – they decide what training and development they want, and what to pay for it.

11. **Self-development opportunities for all**

11.

Self-development resources are available to external stakeholders.

There are lots of opportunities, materials and resources available for learning on an 'open access' basis around the company.

The exploration of an individual's learning needs is the central focus of appraisal and career planning.

With appropriate guidance people are encouraged to take responsibility.

Figure 7.1 *Continued*

to organize this evaluation under two headings: internal and external constraints.

As chapter 5 noted, it is important when admiring the virtues of the learning organization to remember that many core features of organization are either inimical to or at odds with it. Persistence and stability are extremely powerful realities of organizational life. Furthermore, the structuring of organizations

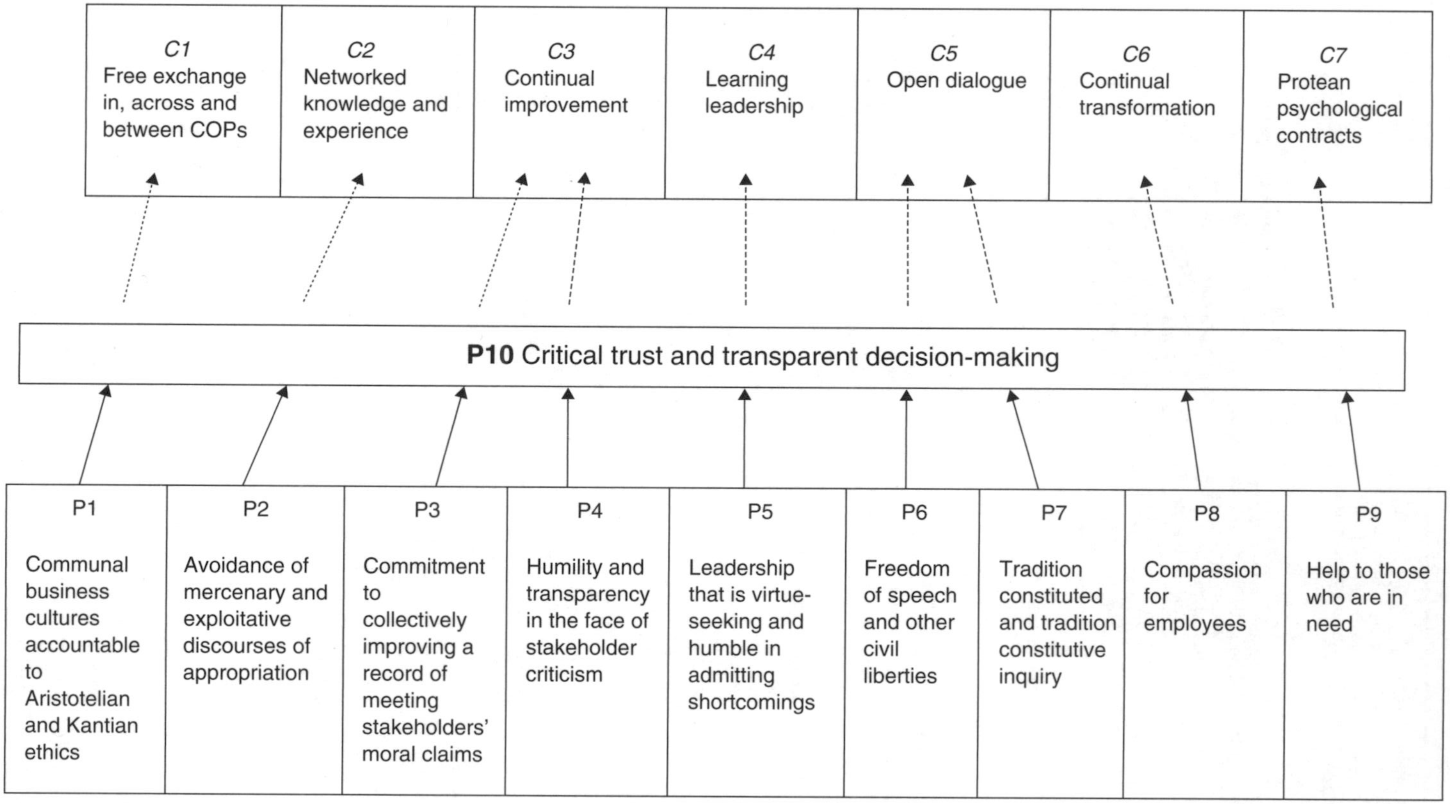

	C1	C2	C3	C4	C5	C6	C7
	Free exchange in, across and between COPs	Networked knowledge and experience	Continual improvement	Learning leadership	Open dialogue	Continual transformation	Protean psychological contracts

P10 Critical trust and transparent decision-making

P1	P2	P3	P4	P5	P6	P7	P8	P9
Communal business cultures accountable to Aristotelian and Kantian ethics	Avoidance of mercenary and exploitative discourses of appropriation	Commitment to collectively improving a record of meeting stakeholders' moral claims	Humility and transparency in the face of stakeholder criticism	Leadership that is virtue-seeking and humble in admitting shortcomings	Freedom of speech and other civil liberties	Tradition constituted and tradition constitutive inquiry	Compassion for employees	Help to those who are in need

Figure 7.2 Moral foundations and their connections with characteristics of learning organizations
Source: Snell (2001). Reproduced by permission of Sage Publications Ltd.

defines boundaries and levels. Horizontal boundaries establish areas of specialism and focus; vertical levels differentiate power and rewards. These structural principles will generate systematically sectional priorities which in turn generate differentiated priorities and interests – politics. Politics influence the flow and distortion of data, the development of priorities, the possibility of deference and careerism. 'Each group fights to preserve and enlarge the area over which it has discretion, attempts to limit its dependence upon the other groups . . . The group's freedom of action and the power structure appear to be clearly at the core of these strategies' (Crozier 1964: 156).

Structures not only establish sectional priorities and loyalties, they also interfere with and distort the flow and nature of information: organizational boundaries become informational barriers. Even Argyris, whose analyses mostly focus on the role of interpersonal skills and behaviour in achieving learning, notes that organizational factors influence the possibility of achieving learning: 'One is the degree to which interpersonal, group, inter-group, and bureaucratic factors produce valid information for the decision-makers to use to monitor the effectiveness of their decisions. The other is the receptivity to corrective feedback of the decision-making unit' (Argyris 1976: 365).

This political aspect of organizations would clearly impact on three major features of the learning organization as defined by Snell: 'free exchange in, across and between communities of practice'; 'networked knowledge and experience'; 'open dialogue'.

Hierarchical structuring introduces a new barrier to learning: strong motivation to distort, divert or censor data. It also introduces the values of conformity and deference as described by Janis's *Groupthink* (1982; see chapter 5) which, although it focuses on group dynamics, identifies a number of organizational antecedents of groupthink, including factors such as 'pressures towards uniformity', which clearly derive from the impact of hierarchy.

There are numerous available examples of the role of hierarchy in encouraging behaviour and attitudes that obstruct learning, specifically with respect to environmental analysis. See, for example, Valentin (1994), Roberts (1992), Presthus (1979) and Janis (1982) (many of these are discussed in chapter 5).

As we have seen, barriers to learning can also arise from the basic nature of organizations and from the ways in which organizational structures and processes themselves enshrine learning and thus limit future learning. Managers learn how to solve recurring problems; they learn what information is relevant and useful and how to focus effort and attention; they become skilful and efficient at problem-solving around existing products and technologies. But all this is at a potential cost of limitations on the issues around which learning can occur and the type of learning that can occur. Established product or process-based problem-solving routines and associated communication filters and processes determine what sort of information is received on what subjects and how it is treated. This is not necessarily a question of the values of the dominant culture determining what may be learned about and how; it is a consequence of the way the organization works. Also important as potential obstructions to the achievement of the learning organization are the cultures which exist within organizations, discussed in chapter 5.

The normative components of organizational cultures are also relevant to the achievement of learning, to the extent that they supply norms and values which define how managers relate to each other, and specifically their willingness collectively to challenge each other, to review, analyse and reflect. Shared values of deference towards authority, unwillingness to confront embarrassing issues of error or failure, unease at radical or creative ideas are likely to reduce the possibility of achieving the learning organization. Snell notes that the LO requires that managers 'challenge assumptions without invoking defensiveness . . . gently confront themselves and their staff with the need for reality testing' (Snell 2001: 4). Hierarchy typically encourages values and expectations of conformity; leadership usually discourages contradiction; groups usually reward loyalty. Managers learn deference towards authority, and interpersonal relations are ordered in ways that reflect organizational values of loyalty and mutual support

Cultural norms may inhibit the achievement of the learning organization. So may shared structures of knowledge that managers apply to data analysis. Managers within organizations actively engage in structured and shared attempts to understand and explain what is happening. Organizations per se involve shared ways of constructing reality (Gioia 1986; Gioia and Poole 1984). Sackmann has argued that organizational cultures involve collective sensemaking, and has usefully identified four aspects of this:

- *dictionary knowledge* consists of shared definitions and labels
- *directory knowledge* defines how things work
- *recipe knowledge* is more theoretical and prescriptive: it suggests what needs to be done for things to be improved
- *axiomatic knowledge* draws on deep-seated assumptions and underlying premises (Sackmann 1992: 142).

Any of these may have implications for the achievement of the learning organization by offering theories or recipes that determine which data are collected and how they are analysed: how and if learning occurs.

Other authors have described the shared theories or recipes made available by organizational cultures and their role in obstructing organizational learning. Prahalad and Bettis (1986) talk about the 'dominant management logic' within organizations, which suggests that what managers know and how they think results from their accumulated (and shared) experience. Weick (1979) has used the expression 'cause maps' as a way of describing how members of organizations share frameworks which they use to translate chaotic reality into a version where cause and effect are located and understood. The concept refers to the subtle ways in which members share ways of making, sharing and communicating sense. Berger and Luckmann (1966) note the importance of the ways in which the organizational order makes sense to participants by defining how things should be put in place. Mastering these 'recipes' is one of the first and most important achievements for the organizational newcomer.

The important point about these and many other writers is that they all share an interest in identifying and understanding the organizational 'recipes', the shared cognitive structures or 'schema' which offer established says of thinking, the taken-for-granted, unacknowledged core assumptions which set limits on what can be thought about and how, and which establish the limits of the possible, the discussible and the imaginable. In order for managers to make their world meaningful they have to simplify it, develop rules of thumb or recipes.

The implication of these schema is that managers learn to focus their analyses and to minimize data-processing time through the use of shared recipes which achieve speedy responses and some efficiencies but that these routines become counter-productive under new or changed circumstances (Stubbart and Ramaprasad 1990). The outcome has been described by Starbuck and others: shared structures of organizational learning may lead to the application of shared cognitive routines which are historically based but irrelevant for future success.

The problem with such cognitive schema is that they may obstruct the achievement of the learning organization by restricting the ability of the organization to conduct environmental analysis, or by influencing how data are analysed. As chapter 5 argued, a number of empirical studies confirm this possibility. Snell notes that, within the learning organization, managers 'surface and test mental models . . . helping to expose hidden assumptions in mental models' (Snell 2001: 4). But Lant et al. (1992), and other researchers, have explored the factors that hinder or encourage management learning: open-mindedness, flexibility, propensity for critical review and evaluation.

These authors identify the possibility that 'structural inertia' limits managers' willingness to recognize when a performance issue arises, or reduces their willingness radically to reorient their organization, and they note that the ways in which managers interpret past performance may lead them to miss or misunderstand key environmental developments, and thus fail to initiate radical change through misattributing the causes of organizational failure.

Barr et al. (1992) analyses the mindsets of senior managers of similar railway organizations in the US over a 25-year period. One organization changed radically and survived; the other ended in bankruptcy. The study gathered data on the use of new concepts, the abandonment of old concepts, the development of new ways of thinking, and new mental maps. Although the mental constructs of managers in both organizations were originally similar, they changed over time. 'All the indicators in mental maps supported the hypothesis that more rapid change in mental maps was associated with organizational renewal and survival. The surviving organization changed its mental model on all measures far more rapidly than the one that eventually declined' (Sparrow 1994: 14). Interestingly the declining organization did not fail to notice the situation, but it failed to respond and accommodate to it quickly enough.

Such phenomena are likely to obstruct the achievement of a key feature of the learning organization. As Snell notes, within the learning organization, senior managers 'surface and test mental models, challenging assumptions without invoking defensiveness' (2001: 14). They balance enquiry with advocacy, distinguish between espoused theory and theory in use, are sensitive to defensive routines and gently confront themselves and their staff with the need for reality testing, helping to expose hidden assumptions in mental models with reality (Senge 1990b: 14–15; Snell 2001: 4).

Researchers have also identified the ways in which organizations make available ways of defining, or even enacting (Smircich and Stubbart 1985), the business environment, and that these definitions vary with national, sector or business context (Calori et al. 1992; Daniels et al. 1994). Sparrow, who summarizes much of this literature, notes that the literature on organizational cognitive processes attends to the ways in which organizations consists of underlying cognitive boundaries that managers use to make sense of the world (Sparrow 1994). A large and rapidly growing body of work suggests that, at a senior level within organizations, processes of environmental analysis (which are seen as critical to the achievement of the learning organization) are influenced by classification processes which structure the ways in which managers see, define and organize the data from their environments (Calori et al. 1992). Others have argued that managers' classifications of their environments should be seen in terms of 'enactments': the creation of their environments through shared sense-making. Managers may create their environments – constitute them – and then respond to these enactments in ways which make them real (Smircich and Stubbart 1985). Such a possibility conflicts with the need within the learning organization for managers to engage in 'generative learning, questioning basic assumptions about self and others, the nature of the organisation and its environment' (Snell 2001: 5).

Researchers have also noted how emotional factors (Fineman 1996; Allbrow 1994; Daniels 1999) and data overload (Weick 1995) may also contribute to distortions in organizational decision-making and learning. It is possible too that recent fashions in management restructuring have exacerbated congenital tendencies towards impaired learning. 'Downsizing' may also damage the 'psychological contract' within an organization, or generate feelings of mistrust, anger or resentment which will also impact on employees' willingness to participate energetically in the activities and processes that underpin learning. The emotions generated within organizations by recent forms of organizational change are unlikely to encourage the sort of attitudes and feelings necessary to underpin the learning organization model. The LO would, as Snell notes, 'treat employees with compassion' (2001: 1).

This second source of limitation on the achievement of the learning organization requires a shift of focus from the internal working of organizations to the relationship between organizations and their societal and ideological content. The achievement of the learning organization is limited not only by internal structures, cultures and shared cognitive schema, but also by external ideological factors which constrain and structure the ways in which managers define and think about organizational problems and possible solutions. The learning organization concept assumes that managers respond to environmental and other cues by open-minded analysis of all options using unrestricted forms of analysis: learning organizations are 'distinguished by the freeness and openness with which ideas and know-how flow' (Snell 2001: 3). As chapter 5 noted, many organizational and contextual factors can limit this possibility by supplying powerful established modes or logics of analysis.

The learning organization is a powerful and attractive idea. It owes its appeal less to its practicality than to its resonance with widely prevalent values and discourses of organization and management. It allows an elegant and appealing convergence of three key ideas. First, it includes the value of organizational flexibility and responsiveness, defined in opposition to the claimed dysfunctions of bureaucracy. Secondly, it subsumes the discourse of enterprise, with its critical role within a dominating discourse of the market as a moral, cleansing force – a discourse which itself acts as a relay between the economy, the organization and the individual. And, thirdly, the learning organization invokes and emphasizes liberal values of learning, individual development and growth, and argues not only the merits of these elements but their inherent interconnectedness.

The evidence therefore suggests that the learning organization is seriously at odds with multiple realities of organization as we know them, at the structural, process and cultural (normative and cognitive) levels. This doesn't mean that it is therefore unimportant – simply a dream. First, dreams *are* important: the learning organization undoubtedly plays a role in inspiring or rationalizing a whole range of organizational change projects. But, more significantly, the learning organization may be useful in bringing to the surface and causing us to confront and assess the nature and the adequacy of current forms of organization. It may be the case that the learning organization and current forms of organization are seriously at odds. This could cause us to reject the notion of the learning organization. But it may also encourage us to try to reimagine the very nature and form of the work organization.

Organizational learning

Although the learning organization may be at best an ambitious project which in effect requires the rejection or overcoming of many of the central features of organization, this does not mean that the adaptive organization approach as a whole should be rejected out of hand. On the contrary this merely makes the search for new forms of adaptive organization all the more important. And some supporters of the adaptive organization approach would advocate another view of learning in organization, preferring to stress the importance, not of the learning organization, but of organizational learning. The difference is used to distinguish an emphasis on the importance of improving the support for learning within organizations from an emphasis on achieving all the components of the learning organization as described by, say, Pedlar et al. (see above).

Those who advocate the value of organizational adaptability argue the merits of achieving an organization that is alert, adaptable, intelligent and responsive. It asserts that traditional monolithic, centralized and hierarchical organizations, in which design is separated from execution – which were geared for repetitive transactions and routine activities – are being replaced by 'flexible and agile organisational forms which can accommodate novelty, innovation and change . . . Rapid change demands quick reactions and continuous re-calibration' (Bahrami 1998: 184–9).

Central to an understanding of the organizational bases of learning (and innovation and change) is the recognition that learning is facilitated by a variety or series of subtle recurring patterns of behaviour – habits, conventions and routines – which underpin learning and make it possible. As Putnam notes, these patterns of behaviour (which may well not be formally structured but which have developed and grown through habit and use) refer to elements of social organization, such as networks, norms and trust, that facilitate co-ordination and co-operation for mutual benefit (Putnam 1993). The Aalborg group of economists in Denmark, and particularly Bengt-Ake Lundvall, argue that modern capitalism now requires that knowledge is the most strategic resource and learning the most important process. Like many commentators, Lundvall argues that, because of the increases in competitiveness and the speed of innovation, learning and knowledge have become critical to organizational success, and therefore the achievement of innovation and learning within the organization becomes critical. The sources of learning within organizations are collective. As Morgan notes, this will require that the organization has 'thick' flows of information between R&D, marketing and production; has decentralized learning procedures; is receptive to multiple channels of information from all relevant sources, and has enabled its employees to feel a real sense of commitment and belonging (Morgan 1997).

Learning is directly related to improvement. And improvement means doing existing things better and quicker and also mastering new responses. Organizational learning refers to more than simply the existence of individuals within the organization who learn, undergo training, study, develop, gain qualifications, etc. It refers to more than the fact that individual learning is encouraged within and by the organization – although this is a component of organizational learning. Organizational learning requires that individual learning is used and applied. It occurs collectively, not only in the sense that learning occurs collectively as colleagues discuss and analyse data, but also in the sense that problem-solving (the application of learning) is collective and joint. Organizational learning also leads to collective responses as new knowledge is invested in new organizational patterns or routines so that successful solutions to problems are made available to others.

Organizational learning, central to the adaptive organization, depends on four conditions:

- the range of things that are learned about: the objects of learning (broad range of objects)
- the degree to which learning occurs in integrated or interconnected processes (integrated and interconnected)
- the temporal nature of learning: is it episodic, occasional or continuous?
- the nature of the learning that occurs (double loop as well as single loop).

Learning in organizations means that organizations are able to develop speedy responses to environmental conditions that are quickly spotted and intelligently understood. It means that organizational responses to support new strategies are well designed and implemented. Competitive advantage follows the organization's ability to learn from its environment and how to adapt appropriately and quickly to it: 'Winners in the global marketplace have been firms that can demonstrate timely responsiveness and rapid and flexible product innovation, coupled with the management capability to effectively co-ordinate and redeploy internal and external competences' (Teece and Pisano 1998: 194).

The range of things that are learned about

The greater the number and range of things that people learn about the greater the degree of organizational learning (all other things being equal). The great danger with organizational learning is that it is limited to safe and established areas – training, for example, which, although important, is probably the least important form of organizational learning and indeed in some cases could be seen as an alternative to organizational learning, as individuals are sent to develop new skills rather than face the organizational sources of the issues which require these skills.

For example, as noted earlier, senior managers' understanding of their business's environments is crucial to the capacity to develop alert and appropriate strategies, but this capacity to learn from and about the environment is often limited by assumptions based in the organization's structure, processes and history. In such cases, the environment could be a subject around which open-minded, radical and thorough organizational learning did *not* take place.

As noted in the discussion of the learning organization above, an organization's structure, communication systems, and knowledge and information base may come to reflect and support its existing products and technologies. And so learning can become limited, become 'path-dependent', based on history and what has worked in the past. History matters: 'a firm's previous investments and its repertoire of routines (its history) constrain its future behaviour . . . an organization's core capabilities can just as easily create "core rigidities" . . . opportunities for learning will be "close in" to previous activities and thus will be transaction and production specific' (Teece and Pisano 1998: 203). If organizational learning is to occur, the organization's structure, cultures and processes must be able to overcome these tendencies. Unlearning must be possible.

Furthermore, the preferences and priorities of senior management are important in this respect. If learning is dominated, managed, monopolized and initiated by senior management then it is possible that learning will be defined by the concerns, preferences and assumptions of senior management. If organizational learning is to occur, senior managers must not just espouse the value of learning and challenge, they must model it, demonstrating *by their behaviour* the value and safety of learning for them as for others.

One of the first things that new members of organizations learn is which subjects can be discussed and publicly challenged and analysed, and which may not – which topics are, as Argyris puts it, undiscussible. One of the routine consequences of conventional organizational structures and systems and cultures is that some issues become difficult and dangerous to discuss, or at least to discuss (and learn about) openly and challengingly. Undiscussibility limits learning by limiting the subjects around which learning can take place and the sort of learning that can take place. Undiscussibility is defined by the powerful and communicated through organizational cultures. And, because undiscussibility is clearly indefensible but also advantageous to the powerful since it limits challenge, undiscussibility is itself undiscussible. If organizational learning is to occur, undiscussibility must be at a minimum.

Similarly, one of the reasons why new entrants to an industry are more likely to develop radical innovations is because incumbents develop organizational processes and structures (and associated mindsets) that are not compatible with the new technology, channel or product. Radical innovation challenges the competence base of existing firms. And some of the knowledge base of existing firms may handicap the firm with respect to innovation (Henderson and Clark 1990: 13).

The degree to which learning occurs in integrated or interconnected processes

The ways in which learning occurs are also crucial – that is to say, the degree to which learning episodes are connected or disconnected, periodic or continuous. The greater the degree to which learning is connected and continuous, the greater the extent of organizational learning. The greater the degree to which learning is distributed throughout the organization and not specialized in specific (usually senior) areas, the more likely it is that organizational learning will take place. Nonaka and Takeuchi argue that one of the distinguishing characteristics of the Japanese company is precisely that no one person or department or group is defined as responsible for creating new knowledge. Learning is too important to be left to specialists. This is a point made by many analysts of modern organizations. Nonaka and Takeuchi note that good ideas can come from anywhere; but management still has a major role in encouraging but also managing and organizing the inevitable confusion that occurs as new knowledge is created within an organization – they supply frameworks for organizing information and ideas and act as a bridge between 'the visionary ideals of the top and the often chaotic reality of those on the front line' (Nonaka and Takeuchi 1998: 317).

Pettigrew and Whipp, in a study of the organizational characteristics of market leaders in a number of different industries, conclude that one important differentiator was that:

> environment assessment occurs across the organization . . . Each function of an organization engages with some aspect of its environment through its routine activities . . . A critical difference between firms is the extent to which this is realized, built upon and exploited. In other words to assume that a single, specialist planning or marketing function can by itself supply an adequate interpretation of a firm's environment is highly dangerous. (Pettigrew and Whipp 1991: 116)

Nonaka has made the same point: organizational adaptiveness and learning requires that 'inventing new knowledge is not a specialized activity – the province of the R&D department or marketing or strategic planning. It is a way of behaving, indeed a way of being, in which everyone is a knowledge worker' (Nonaka 1991: 97).

Learning is more likely to occur if it is continuous and distributed: 'Technological systems evolve through relatively small steps marked by an occasional stubborn obstacle and by constant random breakthroughs' (Hughes 1984: 83). Many commentators note the importance of interconnected learning, whereby the maximum number of bits of information and ideas are connected, generating potentially large possibilities for testing and challenging ideas and for developing new connections and patterns, and of course for overcoming the traditional design/implementation split with all its dysfunctions. Hierarchical structures have been seen by many commentators as antithetical to organizational learning, as hierarchy is associated with senior managers formulating strategy and junior staff implementing it. This damages organizational learning; it 'undermines competitiveness by fostering an elitist view of management that tends to disenfranchise most of the organization' (Hamel et al. 1989: 75). Furthermore, this conventional distinction generates undiscussibility:

> Middle managers buffeted by circumstances that seem to be beyond their control desperately want to believe that top managers have all the answers. And top management, in turn, hesitates to admit it does not for fear of demoralizing lower level employees. The result is often a code of silence in which the full extent of a company's competitiveness problems is not widely shared. (Hamel et al. 1989: 75)

Research into innovation is relevant here. Innovation shares many characteristics with learning, and requires learning. Research into the determinants of organizational innovation supports the thesis that organizational interconnections which distribute information and allow for adjustment support innovation: 'research reveals that few if any major innovations result from highly structured planning systems . . . major innovations are best managed as incremental goal-oriented interactive learning processes' (Quinn 1985: 82). When thinking is a specialized organizational function, learning will suffer: 'Japanese companies win not because they have smarter managers but because they have developed ways to harness "the wisdom of the anthill"' (Hamel et al. 1989: 75).

The temporal nature of learning

'Corporations will have to learn to reformulate strategy and realign their organizations continuously, if they are to survive in an increasingly turbulent environment' (Beer and Spector 1993: 598). There is increasing agreement that, if learning is central to adaptation and innovation (which are themselves key to competitive advantage), then organizational learning itself must be a routine part of organizational functioning and not a specialist or intermittent activity. This is not simply because learning cannot be programmed: the need for learning is likely to be constant or at least unpredictable, and therefore if learning only occurs at specified formal occasions, then opportunities for learning will be missed. It is also because learning itself needs to be a constant process of iterative adjustments and changes as proposals and plans are amended in the light of new information coming from new sources about new developments. Two commentators, for example, stress the need for 'constant' surveillance and for learning to be 'frequently practised':

> In rapidly changing environments, there is obviously value in the ability to sense the need to reconfigure the firm's asset structure, and to accomplish the necessary internal and external transformation . . . This requires constant surveillance of

markets and technologies. The capacity to reconfigure and transform is itself a learned organizational skill. The more frequently practised, the more easily accomplished. (Teece and Pisano 1998: 201)

In their study of the bases of superior organizational performance Pettigrew and Whipp (1991) support this emphasis on the importance of constant, ongoing learning. The instability of organizational advantage, allied to the dynamism of organizational environments, means that processes of internal organizational learning and innovation must be capable of matching environmental change. These authors stress the 'impermanence of given strategic positions and the fragility of bases of competition' which make the process of strategic change creative. But this impermanence 'leads the more successful firms to develop learning processes at all levels of the organisation. Such learning is seldom through orderly progressions . . . the use of the resulting knowledge occurs through a process of untidy iterations and learning spirals' (Pettigrew and Whipp 1991: 277).

Oddly, the notion of redundancy has also been used to draw attention to the organizational features necessary to encourage constant learning. Nonaka and Takeuchi (1998) note that Japanese organizations create knowledge through redundancy – unnecessary duplication. Redundancy in information-sharing and job allocation can encourage frequent communication and dialogue: 'this helps create a "common cognitive ground" among employees and thus facilitates the transfer of tacit knowledge'. This happens because, as people have tasks in common, they can understand what others need to know – or understand what they have learned, or are trying to say. Some companies use exactly this principle in encouraging innovation. New product is divided among competing teams; these can develop different approaches; these differences are then used as a basis for discussion and comparison (Nonaka and Takeuchi 1998: 316).

The nature of the learning

Critical to any understanding and discussion of learning in organizations is a key distinction between different types of learning. This distinction solves the apparent paradox that, on the one hand, adaptability and learning are seen as fundamental, competitive differentiators, while, on the other hand, learning is very obviously a basic feature of every organization. Organizations would not be capable of achieving the remarkable results they produce every day if they were not able, quickly and efficiently, to learn. If organizations learn all the time how can learning be a differentiator? The answer is that the learning that differentiates organizations differs significantly from everyday learning. There are different types of learning within organizations. Some learning simply solves the immediate problem but does not challenge the status quo; adjustments may solve the immediate problem but reduce pressure to identify and address

Types of learning

underlying sources of the problem. Other sorts of learning are more fundamental. Learning how to do things better is different from learning about the
assumptions underlying what the business produces and why. The vast majority of organizational learning is aimed at fixing things that have gone wrong.
Organizations need to be able to master both types of learning:

> Firms must learn in order to survive. They need to respond to new information
> from customers and suppliers, and from other external sources of technology.
> They need to learn from R&D and from the 'doing' and 'using' of their products
> and processes. Very importantly, they need to learn from their mistakes. But they
> also need to learn about themselves, about the reasons why they make specific
> choices, and how they might consider doing things differently in the future. This
> is a higher level of learning, and is the sort that can lead to significant transfor-
> mations of firms' strategies and activities. (Dodgson and Besant 1996: 18)

One commentator has argued that this distinction between different types
of learning and analysis is fundamental to business innovation and, interestingly, is related to business success, not in the expected sense that radical learning could lead to success through innovation (although he does argue this), but
in the sense that successful companies will find it harder to embark on radical
learning. Radical learning is seen as crucial:

> A prerequisite for strategic innovation is a fundamental questioning of the way
> we do business today. It means actively thinking about the business and perhaps
> mentally experimenting with a few 'whys' and 'what ifs'. This is difficult for any
> company to do but it is almost impossible for a successful one. Successful
> companies 'know' that the way they play the game is the right way. After all they
> have all those profits to prove it. Not only do they find it difficult to question their
> way of doing business, but their natural reaction is to dismiss alternative ways
> even when they see competitors trying something new. (Markides 2001: 247)

Other writers have noted that fundamental organizational learning may be
relatively rare as it can seem indelicate or embarrassing because it requires participants to think about and air their underlying premises and assumptions.
This requires skill and courage because, usually, 'individuals make their
premises and inferences tacit, then draw conclusions that cannot be tested
except by the tenets of this tacit logic' (Argyris 1994: 81).

But such questioning is crucial, and represents the sort of learning on which
organizational adaptability is based. Senge (1990a) calls this sort of learning
'generative', contrasting it with 'adaptive' learning. The former is concerned
with new ways of looking at the world, the latter with learning to cope and
respond. This distinction has been made before. Argyris, who was an early contributor to this debate, stressed the distinction between 'single-loop' and
'double-loop' learning. The former refers to learning and action that follows the
recognition of error. A classic example of single-loop learning is a thermostat:
'It detects when the air around is too hot or too cold and corrects the situation

by turning the heat on or off . . . single loop learning solves the presenting problems. It does not solve the more basic problem of why these problems existed
in the first place' (Argyris 1990: 92).

Double-loop learning does not seek mere readjustment; it involves addressing and challenging basic values and assumptions. As another contributor,
using slightly different language, put it: 'Low learning produces successive
replacements or refinements of responses but meta-learning can open up totally
new ways to assemble responses to connect stimuli to responses' (Hedberg
1981: 81). In other words, doing things better is easier than doing things
differently or doing different things. Doing things better uses existing competences and systems and information and mindsets. Doing new things not
only requires new supports but might challenge existing ones.

Achieving double-loop learning is difficult. As previous chapters have
noted, some authors see double-loop learning as at odds with the bases of organization: the search for predictability, the need to routinize, the urge to embed
complex procedures in a combination of reduced systems and processes which
then become hard to change and which filter information and constrain thinking. There may also be a psychological or cultural limitation when managers
are unwilling to accept or encourage challenge: Argyris and Schon, for example,
assert that 'organizations tend to create learning systems that inhibit double
loop learning that calls into question their norms, objectives and basic policies'
(Argyris and Schon 1978: 10). If double-loop learning is important and a key
feature of adaptiveness, then it is important to review what has been said about
the organizational conditions which encourage or discourage this type of learning and, more generally, adaptiveness.

The flexible, 'organic' organization

Argyris identifies differences in organizational cultures and strategies of control
as crucial. Organizational cultures refers to the value placed on open learning,
on challenge and on review and critique by the dominant organizational
culture. Cultural norms relevant to organizational learning would include, for
example, norms concerning attitudes towards authority, or towards risk-taking
If organizational cultures encourage deference and respect towards authority
and discourage risk (for example, by publicly vilifying and punishing failure
or challenge) then radical forms of learning will be discouraged. Culture, of
course, is an over-used concept which is all too often employed to explain
aspects of organization which cannot otherwise be explained. But in this
instance culture is a useful heuristic tool. We know from many attempts to
explore organizational cultures systematically and cross-culturally (Bate 1992;
Hofstede 1980; Kluckholn 1964) that central dimensions of cultures are likely
to have implications for the encouragement or discouragement of behaviours
central to learning. And we know from observation and experience that orga-

nizations differ in these respects. The key issue is the extent to which cultural norms encourage two processes: one is the extent to which good-quality information is produced from every area of the organization; the second is the extent to which this information is analysed thoroughly and radically even when it is unpleasant and challenges the assumptions, structures, strategies and decisions of the organization.

Argyris's work has focused on the individual behaviours which articulate and manifest these cultural pressures, noting how senior managers' behaviour in potential learning situations is critical to the outcome. He has usefully developed a powerful process in which managers' behaviour – specifically their language – is analysed to reveal the inadvertent ways in which double-loop learning is discouraged. But such behaviour is not simply a result of managers' lack of skill. It is also a consequence of the organizational context, not only of powerful cultural norms but also of structures, specifically structures and strategies of control. Argyris himself recognizes this, noting, for example, that single-loop learning that doesn't challenge basic assumptions is associated with top-down, machine-like control structures where decisions are made at the top by controlling management. This structure defines the limits of the possible: what can be thought, what data are legitimate, who can think, who can decide. Learning is clearly closely related to control. Hierarchy typically reinforces the status quo, encourages conformity and compliance and rigorously manages the nature and movement of information. Of this form of traditional bureaucratic model, for example, Burns and Stalker note that it was 'quite explicitly devised to keep production, and production conditions, stable . . . the system defined what information or instructions arrived at any one position in the hierarchy, what information might leave it, and their destination. Such definition was a matter of fixed, clear and precise routine . . . At all levels, decision-making occurred within the framework of familiar expectations and beliefs' (Burns and Stalker 1994 edn.: 82–3).

What sort of organization is necessary if it is to be capable of learning, or being adaptable and flexible? This is the key issue. We may well agree on the value of adaptability and learning, but as Jones and Hendry have noted, 'At present we know a lot about providing individual learning . . . albeit still rather in the "training" than in the "developmental" mode, but our knowledge of how to gather together the fruits of this individual learning . . . to enhance the generic problem solving capacity of the organization is rudimentary. The great challenge . . . is to learn how this can be done' (Jones and Hendry 1994: 155).

However, the above analysis has already suggested in broad terms at least some of the features of an organization that would encourage organizational learning. First, it is one where the four characteristics listed above as key features of organizational learning are encouraged by structures, cultures and systems. Secondly, it is clear that organizations that encourage organizational learning would differ from the traditional, machine-like, hierarchical form of organization. This may be good at routine processes; it may be good under stable circumstances; but it will not encourage learning and adaptation.

The organizational features which are emphasized are those that constitute the key features of organization itself – for example, those identified by writers in the Aston school: specialization, standardization, formalization, centralization. These are the core features of organization. And they contribute enormously to the achievement of organizational goals:

- *Specialization* means that employees focus their attention and work on defined areas.
- *Standardization* means that procedures are made uniform, with great benefits in consistency, predictability, and (where HR procedures are concerned) in fairness.
- *Formalization* means that procedures and rules and expectation and policies are written down and therefore less likely to be ambiguous or uncertain or variable.
- *Centralization* means that activities can be controlled and co-ordinated so that one area or department is informed and knowledgeable.

But these very features, intrinsic to organization – or to some organizations or some parts of organizations – also limit adaptation, learning and innovation. Specialization means a limited focus, a restricted vision, a concern for some things but not other things, for parts but not the whole. Standardization means a concern for predictability and the routine, and less attention to the unusual or the unpredicted. Formalization constrains behaviour to the rules, stressing compliance as the expense of experiment. Centralization assumes that seniority is positively related to wisdom, and limits the flow (and quality) of data within the organization from those who do to those who design.

In traditional organizations, the organization ensures that the tasks it faces are routinized and made predictable and surrounded by organizational processes which reduce variety. The organization develops information channels and filters that control the key issues: the flow of materials, the nature of materials, the processes, the nature and availability of staff for the processes, and so on. These organizational structures and processes are reflected in the organization's knowledge and its information-gathering systems. Knowledge that is known to be important is valued, and relevant information is monitored. Other information is not gathered. What has been learned affects what else is learned and what can be learned. 'In effect, an organisation's problem-solving strategies summarise what is has learned about fruitful ways to solve problems in its immediate environment' (Henderson and Clark 1990: 16).

Central, then, to the adaptive organization thesis is the idea that, if organizations are to be adaptive (learn – innovate – change), they must be different from conventional organizations, since the essence of the conventional organization is a series of elements that hinder these core processes. As Whipp remarks, effective adaptation cannot be based on the assumption that a small group of senior managers has a monopoly of ideas or wisdom; that these managers have more and better knowledge of the organization and its environment than other staff, or that the process of strategy development is best managed as a top-down, one-way process.

The manner in which a firm actively and purposefully engages in the implementation of a competitive strategy – the way it handles competition – must start with (or at least at some stage incorporate) an analysis and understanding of its environment. We have seen how such an understanding may reflect aspects of the organization as much as it does the environment. The environment is not simply or solely 'out there'. Successful environmental analysis is not simply a technical or specialist function. It requires continuous monitoring from all areas of the organization.

But just consider how this organization differs from the normal form: environmental analysis is done by everyone; it is not done in neat separate acts but messily and iteratively back and forward, up and down the organization; furthermore, strategy development emerges from all levels of the organization: everyone is involved. This is definitely different. What would such an organization look like? How would it work?

Burns and Stalker list the features of the traditional organization, which they term – appropriately – mechanistic, and which is in dramatic contrast to the sort of organization required for organizational learning. According to Burns and Stalker, the mechanistic type of organization is characterized by:

- The abstract nature of each individual task, which is pursued with techniques and purposes more or less distinct from those of the concern as a whole, i.e. the functionaries tend to pursue the technical improvement of means, rather than the accomplishment of the ends of the concern.
- The reconciliation, for each level in the hierarchy, of these distinct performances by the immediate superiors, who are also, in turn, responsible for seeing that each task is relevant in their own special part of the main task.
- The precise definition of rights and obligations attached to, and the technical aspects of, each functional role.
- The translation of these rights, obligations and methods into the responsibilities of a functional position.
- Hierarchical structure of control, authority and communication.
- A reinforcement of the hierarchical structure by the location of knowledge of actualities exclusively at the top of the hierarchy, where the final reconciliation of distinct tasks and assessment of relevance is made.
- A tendency for interaction between members of the concern to be vertical, i.e. between superior and subordinate.
- A tendency for operations and working behaviour to be governed by the instructions and decisions issued by superiors.

- Insistence on loyalty to the concern and obedience to superiors as a condition of membership.
- A greater importance and prestige attaching to internal (local) than to general (cosmopolitan) knowledge, experience, and skill.

It is important to stress that this mechanistic form should not be seen as some form of grotesque aberration, which emerged before managers and academics were alert – as we now are – to the limitations of such organizational forms. As well as dangerously overestimating our own freedom from error in issues of organizational design, such a view would fail to recognize that mechanistic forms of organization worked – and in many instances still work. As the authors note, under certain circumstances mechanistic forms are rational and efficient, for example in a stable environment and probably also when cost control is a crucial strategic objective.

The mechanistic form is an extreme type of approach; at the opposite pole is the organic form (an intriguing and prescient choice of name: Burns and Stalker's work was first published in 1961). The organic type explicitly lists many of the key qualities associated with learning and adaptability discussed earlier. See the references to knowledge and experience as 'the common task of the concern', or the 'adjustment and continual redefinition of individual tasks', or 'a network structure of control, authority and communication'. The features of the organic type of organization are:

- The contributive nature of special knowledge and experience to the common task of the concern.
- The 'realistic' nature of the individual task, which is seen as being defined by the total situation of the concern.
- The adjustment and continual redefinition of individual tasks through interaction with others.
- The shedding of 'responsibility' as a limited field of rights, obligations and methods (problems may not be posted upwards, downwards or sideways as being someone else's responsibility).
- The spread of commitment to the concern beyond any technical definition.
- A network structure of control, authority and communication. The sanctions which apply to the individual's conduct in his or her working role derive more from a presumed community of interest with the rest of the working organization in the survival and growth of the firm, and less from a contractual relationship between the individual and a non-personal corporation, as represented by an immediate superior.
- Omniscience is no longer imputed to the head of the concern; knowledge about the technical or commercial nature of the here-and-now task may be located anywhere in the network, this location becoming the ad hoc centre of control authority and communication.

- A lateral rather than a vertical direction of communication through the organization; communication between people of different rank resembles consultation rather than command.
- The content of communication consists of information and advice rather than instructions and decisions.
- Commitment to the concern's tasks and to the 'technological ethos' of material progress and expansion is more highly valued than loyalty and obedience.
- Importance and prestige attach to affiliations and expertise valid in the industrial and technical and commercial milieux external to the firm.

Burns and Stalker's model of two types of organization, each better fitted for different circumstances and one clearly, through its appropriateness to changing conditions, more likely to encourage adaptation and learning, usefully describes some of the key organizational features associated with adaptability. More recent work, by Bahrami, based on analysis of organization in Silicon Valley in the USA, furthers this work. The author is clear that new conditions require adaptability, and that adaptability is encouraged by organizational features:

> Many enterprises are in the midst of fundamental changes in organisational designs and management practices. Pioneering and traditional companies are experimenting with novel organisational structures and management processes in order to accommodate the fast pace of technological change, global competition, and the emergence of a knowledge-based economy. (Bahrami 1998: 184)

But what are these fundamental changes in organizational structures? They are familiar ones: 'These developments are collectively precipitating a move away from monolithic and rigid organisational designs which were geared for repetitive transactions and routine activities. The resulting impetus is toward flexible and agile organisational forms which can accommodate novelty, innovation and change' (Bahrami 1998: 185).

More specifically, Bahrami argues that organizations need to be flexible. Flexibility has three ingredients:

- *agility*, which means being quick to respond, to redefine, to refocus, and to take advantage of opportunities;
- *versatility*, or the ability to do different things and apply different methods and standards;
- *flexibility*, which means resilience or robustness – the ability to withstand setbacks, to come back from disasters.

Bahrami argues that flexibility (or, in our terms, adaptability) requires that the *enterprise* (note, not the senior management of the enterprise) should be able to respond quickly and intelligently. The traditional, mechanistic type of organization, with a clear hierarchical separation of thinking (strategy-making) and doing (strategy implementation), is inadequate:

> Separating the brain (the centre – which plans a response) from the muscles (the line units – which enact the response) can lead to slow response and result in information distortion through hierarchical filtering processes. The executives with the most up to date understanding of evolving market realities are typically in the trenches. They are thus best positioned to strategise and execute the necessary actions in real time as new imperatives unfold. (Bahrami 1998: 189)

Bahrami usefully identifies a number of recent developments which *could* contribute to organizational adaptability. Delayering could result in reduced time lags between decision and action, as well as widening individuals' workloads and thereby, potentially, increasing their understanding of a wider range of organizational processes and environmental developments. The increasing use of multi-functional or multi-disciplinary teams could increase flexibility of response (since they can be formed and disbanded as required) and increase extra-divisional relationships and knowledge. As well as internal structural developments, organizations are increasingly exploring ways of changing the position and permeability of organizational boundaries. Such initiatives as outsourcing or joint ventures could represent, argues Bahrami, 'a flexible mode of blending capabilities, sharing risks, and generating options' (1998: 186).

However, although Burns and Stalker, Bahrami and others have, with remarkable consistency, offered valuable descriptions of the type of organization that would encourage learning and adaptability, a problem remains: if carried too far the defining qualities of the organic type of organization would result in the disappearance of the organization itself. Some discipline, some control, some direction, some agreed processes and standards are fundamental to what we mean by organization and to organization itself. But these are qualities associated with the mechanistic form of organization. As we noted at the beginning of this analysis, some advocates of the adaptive organization, while praising its capabilities and behaviour, seem almost to be describing a phenomenon which has moved beyond the defining – and practical – boundaries of organization. This, as noted, is most extreme in the case of advocates of the learning organization.

But there may be a solution to this paradox: that the form of organization required for today's (and tomorrow's) circumstances would be an organization that was not an organization. The solution is through the notion of the *balance* or *coexistence* of elements of both types of organization. This means that organizations are both organic and mechanistic (or have elements of both) and that they are constantly aware of the tension between these two elements and are constantly monitoring the balance and correcting it.

A study of the management of innovation conducted by Salaman and Storey reports that in a number of organizations staff described themselves as happy with the firm's capacity for innovation, suggesting that the reason for the organization's success in this area was that it was aware of the need for both tight and loose control and of the problematic nature of maintaining the balance between the two. Balance was explicitly understood and valued. Loose control encouraged innovation but could also cause excessive differentiation, or even fragmentation; control was driven by the need for standards and accountability but could stifle enterprise. Each was problematic as single principle. The solution was to try to live with both; as one manager said:

> Innovation comes from the ability to spot the less obvious initiatives and back them and that I think you see in the culture of resistance to the sorts of things the larger bureaucracy inevitably gets into: planning, monitoring, evaluation and the whole works. These two inevitably tend to clash and one of the critical things is how you actually try to bring these two things together because the organisation as it gets larger and it's decentralising, is also in danger of fragmenting. (quoted in Storey and Salaman forthcoming)

Another senior manager commented:

> In recent years the organization's been over-managed and under-led and therefore good ideas have been inhibited . . . You have a clear vision and a clear sense of purpose – that binds people together. And once you are confident that people know exactly what your mission is and know exactly what our values are and know what your purpose is and know what needs to be done you can spend less time predetermining the detail of how they should go about it, and asking them and checking them and double-checking them . . . (Storey and Salaman forthcoming)

Academic commentators have noted the same tendency. Bahrami, in an analysis of high-tech firms where adaptability is at a premium, notes that these firms have to be well organized. They need discipline and focus, they must have stringent accountability, duplication of effort must be minimized, control and co-ordination are crucial. Yet at the same time, and somehow within these constraints,

> a loose hands-off management style is needed to manage expectant professionals, maintain a conducive environment for creative thinking and provide a capability for rapid response to competitive and market developments . . . They need flexible organisational systems which can balance dialectical forces – facilitating creativity, innovation, and speed while instilling co-ordination, focus and control . . . many firms we observed were both structured and chaotic; they had evolved dualistic organisational systems designed to strike a balance between stability on the one hand and flexibility on the other. (Bahrami 1998: 188–90)

But balance between two types or principles of structuring is not enough, because structures aren't enough. Being able to balance two opposing tendencies obviously requires an awareness of the need to achieve this balance and a willingness to do so. It requires leadership, and leadership of a certain sort. As Pettigrew and Whipp remark, when change is necessary, leadership should not be seen in terms of the cliché of the heroic individual leader but rather in terms of the importance of building a climate for leading change while also raising energy levels and indicating the general direction of change. This 'involves people at every level of the business'; it 'calls for the resolution of not so much great single issues but rather a pattern of interwoven problems. The skill in leading change therefore centres on coping with a series of dualities and dilemmas' (Pettigrew and Whipp 1991: 165–6). Burns and Stalker note this same feature of leadership in the 'organic' organization: 'it is an essential presumption of the organic system that the leader's "authority" is taken by whoever shows himself most informed and capable, i.e. the "best authority". The location of authority is settled by consensus' (Burns and Stalker 1961: 122).

As well as leadership, the organization that generates learning and adaptability will also require, the commentators insist, distinctive cultures which support the sorts of behaviours the structures require. As Pettigrew and Whipp note, structural *and* cultural factors are critical (1991: 28). Reference to the list of qualities associated by Burns and Stalker with the 'organic' type of organization will show that many are as much cultural as structural. For organizational learning to occur on the bases outlined earlier, employees have to be committed to the organization and its goals and not merely compliant with its rules: 'the area of commitment to the concern – the extent to which the individual yields himself as a resource to be used by the working organization – is far more extensive in organic than in mechanistic systems' (Burns and Stalker 1991 edn.: 122).

Finally, and many authorities have stressed this point, in organic adaptive organizations the loss of control by formal means is compensated for by the strength of individuals' commitment to shared beliefs, goals and values. One important consequence of this is that employees feel free to share information, discuss issues, ask for help, check their understanding. Communication is at the heart of learning and adaptability (which is one reason why knowledge management is becoming increasingly popular). Once again Burns and Stalker recognize the importance of communication in this respect:

> The operation of an organic system of management hinges on effective communication . . . What is essential is that nothing should inhibit individuals from applying to others for information and advice, or for additional effort. This in turn depends on the ability to suppress differences of status and technical prestige . . . and on the absence of barriers to communication founded on functional preserves, privilege or personal reserve. (Burns and Stalker 1991 edn.: 252)

And communication of course – of the type required to underpin organizational adaptiveness – is not simply a technical matter; it is not a function of communications systems and technologies, or even of management information. The necessary sort of communication is a result of the employee's sense of identification with the organization and its objectives and a shared understanding or knowledge of what the organization stands for and aspires to. These characteristics are hard to achieve and hard to sustain; they cannot be achieved by off-the-shelf HR packages. They can only occur when they are integral to the way the organization is and the way it works. As Nonaka has noted: 'the knowledge-creating company is as much about ideals as it is about ideas'. If an organization is to be adaptive it has to be adaptive about itself: capable of reinventing the organization, challenging the organization. 'To create new knowledge means quite literally to re-create the company and everyone in it in a non-stop process of personal and organizational self-renewal' (Nonaka 1991: 97).

Summary and Conclusion

We started this book by quoting Eliot's beautiful lines to the effect that we would offer an analysis that would help the reader 'arrive where we started | And know the place for the first time'. This is an ambitious claim. You must judge if we have succeeded. What we have tried to do is to show that, behind the noise and confusion of SHRM, the strident hucksters' cries proclaiming the virtues of their miraculous snake oils and the insistent shouts of the stall-holders demanding that we check their wonderful magical wares; behind the warning cries of the academics clutching at our sleeves, Ancient Mariner-like, or standing gloomily with sandwich boards telling us that we are doomed, and that all such promises are empty and transient; behind the busy excitement of the current fashions without which any organization is, it seems, ill dressed and hopelessly out of touch, and behind the demands of exacting external author-ities sternly insisting that we install this or that current device which is syn-onymous with modernity, good sense and efficiency – behind all these temptations and admonitions there lurks sense. Or some sense.

In fact we argue that there lurk five different types of sense – five ways in which recent writings known broadly as SHRM can be seen to offer distinctive and sensible approaches to the improvement of organizational performance. This book can be seen, therefore, as a form of sense-making. The complex and in some ways chaotic and confused world of SHRM can be ordered and made sensible. That is why we hope we will help the reader know the place – SHRM – clearly for the first time.

Of course our interpretation, the framework by which we hope to make sense of current writings on organizational performance, is both emergent and imposed. We are convinced that these writings can be seen in terms of these five approaches – that they do them justice – but we also recognize that to some degree we are imposing this discipline on an inchoate and unformed set of debates and admonitions. The terrain does not produce the map: the map is in our minds, and creates the terrain.

Let's just say that we believe SHRM can be seen in these terms and that it helps to see it in these terms.

In a sense of course it doesn't matter what the authors whose work we have discussed here really meant, and whether or not they would accept our framework, or agree with how we have classified their contribution; this is not our business. The test of our framework is not the extent to which it reflects the intentions of our authors but a more pragmatic test: does this attempt to make sense of the world of SHRM help you, the reader, understand what SHRM is about and how it offers distinctive and different approaches to improving organizational performance? The key test is a practical one: does this framework work for you? Does it at the same time clarify and order the diffuse and diverse writings we call SHRM and enable you to see how they offer five ways in which you can either understand what organizations are trying to do, or make suggestions for what they should do, or (if an initiative doesn't fall into any of the approaches) what they should stop trying to do?

So the expression 'making sense' can be seen in a number of ways. First we try to make sense of SHRM writings by saying that, at best, if they mean anything useful and sensible then they must be offering recommendations for the improvement of organizational performance in some way. This in essence is what SHRM is about. Secondly, we identify five different, distinctive, and in some cases even opposed ways in which organizational performance can be improved, all and each of which are apparent within SHRM writings. Thirdly, we discuss, develop and to some extent evaluate each of these approaches and offer some consideration of their practical implications. Fourthly, by helping to make sense of SHRM we, by implication at least, help the reader to identify the non-sense in SHRM. It's possible that this is our most useful contribution: to help the harassed manager distinguish sense from non-sense in the recommendations, nostrums and panaceas that are daily thrust at her or him, all of which proclaim their privileged access to truth and wisdom, all of which carry total conviction, all of which define their critics or challengers as 'wreckers', Luddites, hopelessly out of date and out of tune, unreformed advocates of discredited forms or principles of organization.

Yet such critics are to be valued; and such enthusiasts are to be feared. Gary Hamel, an academic writer and highly paid consultant, was, for example, a great admirer of the organizational principles and values of an enormously large and, for a while – at least in terms of share price – highly successful US energy company – Enron. He extolled its virtues and encouraged other businesses to follow Enron's lead. The leaders of companies such as Enron were, said Hamel, 'radicals, activists and guerrilla fighters who fashion bullets made of ideas', who were building a 'new industrial order where imagination counts for more than capital, and rule-busting insights are more important than mere knowledge' (Hamel, quoted in Guthey 2001: 1). Under these circumstances some healthy scepticism would have been useful. There is no doubt that Enron did develop rule-busting insights, although not probably of the sort

Hamel had in mind in his eulogy, as its CEO will no doubt soon testify in a US court.

Admonitions like this can be hard to resist. Note the language, typical of such advocacy: the metaphors from warfare and violence which can readily be turned against those who resist the proposal; the total conviction, the moral superiority, the labelling of resistance or questioning as ill-informed or worse. It can be dangerous to question. At times like these it helps to be sceptical; it helps to have some sort of yardstick whereby the value and contribution (and underlying assumptions) of the proposed approach can be assessed. And this is what we offer in this book.

Our framework is clear; our analyses of the five approaches are complete; our assessments are done; the chaos and confusion of the busy world of SHRM are hushed. The rest is not our business: it is your business.

References

Abrahamson, E. (1996) 'Management fashion', *Academy of Management Review*, 21:1, 254–85.

Akin, G. and Hopelain, D. (1986) 'Finding the culture of productivity', *Organizational Dynamics*, 7:2, 19–32.

Allbrow, M. (1994) 'Accounting for organisational feeling', in L. Ray and M. Reed (eds), *Organising Modernity*, London: Routledge.

Amit, R. and Schoemaker, P. (1993) 'Strategic assets and organisational rents', *Strategic Management Journal*, 14, 33–46.

Argyris, C. (1976) 'Single-loop and double-loop models in research on decision-making', *Administrative Science Quarterly*, 21, 363–75.

Argyris, C. (1990) *Overcoming Organisational Defences: Facilitating Organisational Learning*, Boston: Allyn Bacon.

Argyris, C. (1994) 'Good communication that blocks learning', *Harvard Business Review*, July–Aug., 77–85.

Argyris, C. and Schon, D. (1978) *Organisational Learning: A Theory of Action Perspective*, Reading, MA: Addison-Wesley.

Arthur, J. B. (1994) 'Effects of human resource systems on manufacturing performance and turnover', *Academy of Management Journal*, 37:3, 670–87.

Ashkenas, R., Ulrich, D., Jick, T. and Kerr, S. (1995) *The Boundaryless Organisation: Breaking the Chains of Organisational Structure*, San Francisco, CA: Jossey-Bass.

Baden-Fuller, C. and Stopford, J. (1999) *Rejuvenating the Mature Business* (2nd edn), London: Thompson International.

Bahrami, H. (1998) 'The emerging flexible organisation: perspectives from Silicon Valley', in C. Mabey, G. Salaman and J. Storey (eds), *Strategic Human Resource Management: A Reader*, London: Sage.

Banbury, C. M. and Mitchell, W. (1995) 'The effect of introducing important incremental innovations on market share and business survival', *Strategic Management Journal*, 16, 161–82.

Barney, J. B. (1986) 'Organisational culture: can it be a sustained source of competitive advantage?', *Academy of Management Review*, 11:3, 656–65.

Barney, J. B. (1991) 'Firm resources and sustained competitive advantage', *Journal of Management*, 17:1, 99–120.

Barr, P. S., Stimpert, J. L. and Huff, A. S. (1992) 'Cognitive change, strategic action and organisational renewal', *Strategic Management Journal*, special issue: Summer, 15–36.

Bartlett, C. A. and Ghoshal, S. (1993) 'Beyond the M-form: toward a managerial theory of the firm', *Strategic Management Journal*, 14, special issue: Winter, 23–46.

Bate, P. (1992) 'The impact of organisational culture on approaches to organisational problem-solving', in G. Salaman et al. (eds), *Human Resource Strategies*, London: Sage; 1st pub. in *Organisation Studies*, 5:1 (1984), 43–66.

Beaumont, P. B. (1992) 'The US human resource management literature', in G. Salaman et al. (eds), *Human Resource Strategies*, London: Sage.

Becker, B. and Huselid, M. (1998) 'High performance work systems and firm performance: a synthesis of research and managerial implications', *Research in Personnel and Human Resources*, 16:1, 53–101.

Beer, M. et al. (1985) *Human Resources Management: A General Manager's Perspective*, New York: Free Press.

Beer, M. and Spector, B. (eds) (1985) *Readings in Human Resource Management*, New York: Free Press.

Beer, M. and Spector, B. (1993) 'Organizational diagnosis: its role in organizational learning', *Journal of Counseling and Development*, 71, 642–50.

Berger, P. and Luckmann, T. (1966) *The Social Construction of Reality*, London: Allen Lane.

Bleicher, K. (1983) 'Organisationkulturen und führungsphilosophien', in Bettewerb, *Zeitschrift für Betriebswirtschaftliche Forschung*, 35, 135–46.

Blyton, P. and Turnbull, P. (eds) (1992) *Reassessing Human Resource Strategies*, London: Sage.

Bowman, C. and Asch, D. (1996) *Managing Strategy*, Basingstoke: Macmillan.

Brunsson, N. (1982) 'The irrationality of action and action rationality: decisions, ideologies and organizational actions', *Journal of Management Studies*, 19:1, 29–44.

Brunsson, N. and Olsen, J. P. (1993) *The Reforming Organisation*, London: Routledge.

Burns, T. and Stalker, G. M. (1961) *The Management of Innovation*, Oxford: Oxford University Press; 2nd edn. 1991; 3rd edn. 1994.

Calori, R., Johnson, G. and Sarnin, P. (1992) 'French and British top managers' understanding of the structure and dynamics of their industries: a cognitive analysis and comparison', *British Journal of Management*, 3:2, 61–78.

Chandler, A. D. (1962) *Strategy and Structure*, Cambridge, MA: MIT Press.

Child, J. (1972) 'Organisational structure, environment and performance: the role of strategic choice', *Sociology*, 6:1, 1–22.

Child, J. (1987) 'Information technology, organization and response to strategic challenges', *California Management Review*, 30:1, 33–50

Clark, T. and Salaman, G. (1996) 'The management guru as organizational witchdoctor', *Organization*, 3:1, 85–107.

Clark, T. and Salaman, G. (1998) 'Telling tales: management gurus' narratives and the construction of managerial identity', *Journal of Management Studies*, 32:2, 137–61.

Clegg, S. and Dunkerley, D. (1980) *Organizations, Class and Control*, London: Routledge and Kegan Paul.

Cohen, W. M. and Levinthal, D. A. (1989) 'Innovation and learning: the two faces of R&D – implications for the analysis of R&D investment', *The Economic Journal*, 99, 569–96.

Conrad, C. (1985) 'Review of *A Passion for Excellence*', *Administrative Science Quarterly*, 30:3, 426–8.

Crozier, M. (1964) *The Bureaucratic Phenomenon*, London: Tavistock.

Cyert, R. M. and March, J. G. (1965) *A Behavioural Theory of the Firm*, Oxford: Blackwell.

Cyert, R. M. and March, J. G. (2001) 'A summary of basic concepts in the behavioural theory of the firm', 1st pub. in *A Behavioural Theory of the Firm* (Blackwell, 1965); repr. in G. Salaman (ed.), *Decision Making for Business: A Reader*, London: Sage.

Daft, R. (1983) *Organisation Theory and Design*, New York: West.

Daniels, K. (1999) 'Affect and strategic decision making', *The Psychologist*, 12:1, 24–7.

Daniels, K., Johnson, G. and de Chernatony, L. (1994) 'Differences in managerial cognitions of competition', *British Journal of Management*, 5, 21–9.

Davenport, T. (1993) *Process Innovations: Reengineering Work through Information Technology*, Boston, MA: Harvard Business School Press.

De Geus, A. (1988) 'Planning as learning', *Harvard Business Review*, Mar.–Apr., 70–4.

Deal, T. E. and Kennedy, A. A. (1982) *Corporate Cultures: The Rites and Rituals of Corporate Life*, Reading, MA: Addison-Wesley.

Deal, T. E. and Kennedy, A. A. (1991) *Corporate Cultures*, Harmondsworth: Penguin.

Delamarter, R. T. (1988) *Big Blue: IBM's Use and Abuse of Power*, London: Pan Books.

Denison, D. R. (1984) 'Bringing corporate culture to the bottom line', *Organizational Dynamics*, 12, 5–22.

Dodgson, M. and Besant, J. (1996) *Effective Innovation Policy*, London: Thomson Business Press.

Dore, R. (1973) *British Factory–Japanese Factory*, London: Allen & Unwin.

Du Gay, P. (1991) 'Enterprise culture and the ideology of excellence', *New Formations*, 13, 45–62.

Du Gay, P. (1994) 'Colossal immodesties and hopeful monsters: pluralism and organizational conduct', *Organization*, 1:1, 125–48.

Du Gay, P. (1996) 'Making up managers: enterprise and the ethos of bureaucracy', in S. Clegg and G. Palmer (eds), *The Politics of Management Knowledge*, London: Sage.

Du Gay, P. and Salaman, G. (1992) 'The cult(ure) of the customer', *Journal of Management Studies*, 29, 615–33.

Du Gay, P., Salaman, G. and Rees, B. (1996) 'The conduct of management and the management of conduct', *Journal of Management Studies*, 33, 263–82.

Dyer, L. and Reeves, T. (1995) 'Human resource strategies and firm performance: what do we know and where do we need to go?', *International Journal of Human Resources Management*, 6:3, 656–70.

Fineman, S. (1996) 'Emotions and organising', in S. R. Clegg, C. Hardy and W. R. Nord (eds), *Handbook of Organisation Studies*, London: Sage.

Fleck, L. (1979) *Genesis and Development of a Scientific Fact* (1st edn 1935), Chicago: University of Chicago Press.

Fombrun, C. J. (1983) 'Strategic management: integrating the human resource systems into strategic planning', *Advances in Strategic Management*, no. 2, Greenwich, CT: JAI Press.

Fombrun, C. J., Tichy, N. M. and Devanna, M. A. (1984) *Strategic Human Resource Management*, New York: John Wiley.

Foucault, M. (1980) *Power/Knowledge*, Brighton: Harvester.

Fowler, A. (1987) 'When chief executives discover HRM', *Personnel Management*, Jan., 3.

Fox, S. and McLeay, S. (1992) 'An approach to researching managerial labour markets: HRM, corporate strategy and financial performance in UK manufacturing', *International Journal of Human Resource Management*, 3:3, 523–54.

Freeman, C. (1982) *The Economics of Industrial Innovation* (2nd edn), London: Frances Pinter.

Gill, J. and Whittle, S. (1993) 'Management by panacea: accounting for transience', *Journal of Management Studies*, 30, 281–95.

Gioia, D. A. (1986) 'Conclusion: the state of the art in organisational social cognition – a personal view', in H. P. Sims and D. A. Gioia (eds), *The Thinking Organisation: Dynamics of Organisational Social Cognition*, San Francisco: Jossey-Bass.

Gioia, D. A. and Poole, P. P. (1984) 'Scripts in organizational behaviour', *Academy of Management Review*, 10, 527–39.

Gospel, H. (1990) *Markets, Firms, and the Management of Labour in Modern Britain*, Cambridge: Cambridge University Press.

Gouldner, A. W. (1954) *Patterns of Industrial Bureaucracy*, New York: The Free Press.

Gouldner, A. W. (1959) 'Organizational analysis', in Robert K. Morton, Leonard Broom and Leonard Cottrell, Jr. (eds), *Sociology Today: Problems and Prospects*, New York: Basic Books.

Gowler, D. and Legge, K. (1986) 'Images of employees in company reports: do company chairmen view their most valuable asset as valuable?', *Personnel Review*, 15:5, 9–18.

Grant, R. M. (1991) 'The resource-based theory of competitive advantage: implications for strategy formulation', *California Management Review*, Spring, 114–35.

Grant, R. M. (1991) *Contemporary Strategy Analysis: Concepts, Techniques Applications*, Cambridge, MA: Basil Blackwell.

Grant, R. M. (1995) *Contemporary Strategy Analysis: Concepts, Techniques, Applications* (3rd edn), Oxford: Blackwell.

Grant, R. M. (1996) 'Towards a knowledge-based theory of the firm', *Strategic Management Journal*, 17, 109–22.

Grant, R., Jammine, A. and Thomas H. (1988) 'Diversity, diversification and profitability among British manufacturing companies 1972–1984', *Academy of Management Journal*, 14, 51–68.

Grint, K. (1994) 'Reengineering history: social resonances and business process re-engineering', *Organization*, 1:1, 179–201.

Grinyer, P. H., Mayes, D. G. and McKiernan, P. (1988) *Sharpbenders: The Secrets of Unleashing Corporate Potential*, Oxford: Blackwell.

Guest, D. E. (1987) 'Human resource management and industrial relations', *Journal of Management Studies*, 24:5, 503–21.

Guest, D. (1990) 'Human resource management and the American dream', *Journal of Management Studies*, 27, 377–97.

Guest, D. (1992) 'Right enough to be dangerously wrong', in G. Salaman (ed.), *Human Resource Strategies*, London: Sage.

Guthey, E. (2001), 'Ted Turner's corporate crossdressing and the shifting image of American business leadership, enterprise and society', *The International Journal of Business History*, 2:1, 111–42.

Hall, R. (1994) 'A framework for identifying the intangible sources of sustainable competitive advantage', in G. Hamel and A. Heene (eds), *Competence-Based Competition*, Chichester: John Wiley.

Hall, S. (1997) 'The work of representation', in S. Hall (ed.), *Representation: Cultural Representations and Signifying Practices*, London: Sage.

Hamel, G., Doz, Y. L. and Prahalad, C. K. (1989) 'Collaborate with your competitors – and win', *Harvard Business Review*, Jan.–Feb., 133–9.

Hamel, G. and Prahalad, C. K. (1993) 'Strategy as stretch and leverage', *Harvard Business Review*, Mar.–Apr., 75–83.

Hammer, M. (1990) *Reengineering Work: Don't Automate, Obliterate*, Cambridge, MA: Harvard University Press.

Hammer, M. (1996) *Beyond Reengineering*, London: HarperCollins.

Hammer, M. and Champy, J. (1993) *Reengineering the Corporation: A Manifesto for Business Revolution*, London: Nicholas Brealey.

Haspeslagh, P. C. (1982) 'Portfolio planning: uses and limits', *Harvard Business Review*, Jan./Feb.

Hedberg, B. (1981) 'How organisations learn and unlearn', in P. C. Nystrom and H. W. Starbuck (eds), *Handbook of Organisational Design*, Oxford: Oxford University Press.

Henderson, R. M. and Clark, K. B. (1990) 'Architecture innovation: the reconfiguration of existing product technologies and the failure of established firms', *Administrative Science Quarterly*, 35, 9–30.

Hendry, C. and Pettigrew, A. (1986) 'The practice of strategic human resource management', *Personnel Review*, 15:5, 3–8.

Hendry, C. and Pettigrew, A. (1990) 'Human resource management: an agenda for the 1990s', *International Journal of Human Resource Management*, 1:1, 17–43.

Hendry, C., Pettigrew, A. and Sparrow, P. (1988) 'Changing patterns of human resource management', *Personnel Management*, 20:11, 37–41.

Hinterhuber, H. H. (1986) 'Strategie, Innovation und Unternehmenskultur', *Blick durch die Wirtschaft*, 20:10.

Hodgkinson, Gerard P. and Paul Sparrow (2002) *The Competent Organisation: A Psychological Analysis of the Strategic Management Process*, Buckingham: Open University Press.

Hofer, C. W. and Schendel, D. (1978) *Strategy Formulation: Analytical Concepts*, St Paul, MN: West Publishing.

Hofstede, G. (1980) *Culture's Consequences: International Differences in Work-Related Values*, London: Sage.

Huczynski, A. (1993a) *Management Gurus: What Makes Them and How To Become One*, London: Routledge.

Huczynski, A. (1993b) 'Explaining the succession of management fads', *International Journal of Human Resource Management*, 4, 443–63.

Hughes, T. (1984) 'The inventive continuum', *Science*, 5, 9.

Hunt, Brian, Baden-Fuller, Charles and Calori, Roland (1995) *Novotel (395-113-1)*, London: City University Business School.

Huselid, M. (1995) 'The impact of human resource management practices on turnover, productivity, and corporate financial performance', *Academy of Management Journal*, 38:3, 635–72.

Huselid, M. (1998) 'The impact of human resource management practices on turnover, productivity, and corporate financial performance', in C. Mabey, G. Salaman and J. Storey (eds), *Strategic Human Resource Management: A Reader*, London: Sage.

Jackson, B. (1996) 'Re-engineering the sense of self: the manager and the management guru', *Journal of Management Studies*, 33, 571–90.

Jacques, R. (1996) *Manufacturing the Employee*, London: Sage.

Jaggi, D. (1985) 'Corporate Identity als Unternehmerische Erfolgsformel', Paper presented at the Second Wemar – Tagung.

Janis, Irving (1972) *Victims of Groupthink: Psychological Study of Foreign-Policy Decisions and Fiascos* (2nd edn), Boston: Houghton Mifflin.

Janis, I. (1982) *Groupthink: Psychological Studies of Policy Decisions and Fiascos*, Boston: Houghton Mifflin.

Jones, A. M. and Hendry, C. (1994) 'The learning organisation: adult learning and organisational transformation', *British Journal of Management*, 5:2, 153–62.

Kamoche, K. (1991) *Understanding Human Resource Management*, Buckingham: Open University Press.

Kamoche, K. (1996) 'Strategic human resource management within a resource-capability view of the firm', *Journal of Management Studies*, 213–31.

Kaplan, R., and Norton, D. (1992) 'The balanced scorecard – measures that drive performance', *Harvard Business Review*, Jan.–Feb., 71–9.

Kanter R. M. (1991) 'Transcending business boundaries: 12,000 world managers view change', *Harvard Business Review*, 69:3, 151–64.

Kay, J. (1993) *Foundations of Corporate Success*, Oxford: Oxford University Press.

Keiser, A. (1997) 'Rhetoric and myth in management fashion', *Organisation*, 4:1, 49–74.

Keisling, P. (1984) 'Economics without numbers: review of *In Search of Excellence*', *Washington Monthly*, Mar., 40–6.

Keynes, J. M. (1936) *The General Theory of Employment, Interest and Money*, London: Macmillan.

Kirton, M. (1976) 'Adaptors and innovators: a description and measure', *Journal of Applied Psychology*, 61, 622–9.

Klepper, S. (1997) 'Industry life-cycles', *Industrial and Corporate Change*, 6:1, 145–81.

Kluckholn, F. R. (1964) 'Dominant value orientations', in C. Kluckholn and H. A. Murray (eds), *Personality in Nature, Society and Culture*, New York: Knopf.

Kochan, T. A. and Barocci, T. A. (1985) *Human Resource Management and Industrial Relations*, Boston, MA: Little Brown.

KPMG (1999) *Unlocking Shareholder Value: The Keys to Success. Mergers and Acquisitions, a Global Research Report*, Fort Worth, TX: KPMG.

Kuhn, R. L. (1982) *Mid-Sized Firms' Success Strategies and Methodology*, New York: Praeger.

Lant, Theresa K., Milliken, Frances J. and Batra, Bipin (1992) 'The role of managerial learning and interpretation in strategic persistence and reorientation: an empirical exploration', *Strategic Management Journal*, 13, 585–608; repr. in G. Salaman (ed.), *Decision Making for Business: A Reader*, London: Sage (2002).

Laroche, H. (1995) 'From decision to action in organizations: decision-making as a social representation', *Organizational Science*, 6:1, 62–75.

Legge, K. (1988) *Personnel Management in Recession and Recovery: Personnel Review*, 17:2 (special issue).

Legge, K. (1989) 'Human resource management: a critical analysis', in J. Storey (ed.), *New Perspectives on Human Resource Management*, London: Routledge.

Legge, K. (1995) *Human Resource Management*, Basingstoke: Macmillan.

Liddell Hart, B. (1972) *History of the First World War*, London: Pan Books.

Lippman, A. and Rumelt, R. P. (1982) 'Uncertain imitability: an analysis of inter-firm differences in efficiency under competition', *The Bell Journal of Economics*, 13:2, 418–38.

Littler, C. and Salaman, G. (1984) *Class at Work*, London: Batsford.

Mabey, C., Salaman, G. and Storey, J. (1998) *Human Resource Management*, Oxford: Blackwell.

Maidique, M. A. (1983) 'Point of view: the new management thinkers', *California Management Review*, 26:1, 151–62.

March, James (1999) *The Pursuit of Organisational Intelligence*, Oxford: Blackwell.

March, J. G. and Simon, H. A. (1958) *Organizations*, New York: Wiley.

Marginson, P., Edwards, P. K., Martin, R., Purcell, J. and Sisson, K. (1988) *Beyond the Workplace: Managing Industrial Relations in Multi-Plant Enterprises*, Oxford: Blackwell.

Markides, C. (n.d.) *The Challenge of Strategic Innovation: Strategic Leadership Research Programme*, London: London Business School.

Markides, C. (2001) 'A dynamic view of strategy', in M. A. Cusumano and C. C. Markides (eds), *Strategic Thinking for the Next Economy*, San Francisco: Jossey-Bass.

McGrath, R. G., Macmillan, I. C. and Venkataraman, S. (1995) 'Defining and developing competence: a strategic process paradigm', *Strategic Management Journal*, 16, 251–75.

Meek, L. (1992) 'Organizational culture: origins and weaknesses', in G. Salaman (ed.), *Human Resource Strategies*, London: Sage.

Miles, R., and Snow, C. (1984) 'Designing strategic human resource systems', *Organisational Dynamics*, Summer, 36–53.

Miller, D. (1986) 'Configurations of strategy and structure: towards a synthesis', in D. Asch and C. Bowman (eds), *Readings in Strategic Management*, Basingstoke: Macmillan.

Miller, P. and Rose, N. (1993) 'Governing economic life', in M. Gane and T. Johnson (eds), *Foucault's New Domains*, London: Routledge.

Miller, S., Hickson, D. and Wilson, D. (1996) 'Decision-making in organisations', in S. Clegg et al. (eds), *Handbook of Organisation Studies*, London: Sage.

Mintzberg, H., Quinn, B. J. and Ghoshall, S. (1995) *The Strategy Process*, Hemel Hempstead: Prentice-Hall.

Mintzberg, H. and Waters, J. A. (1985) 'Of strategies deliberate and emergent', *Strategic Management Journal*, 6, 257–72.

Miyazaki, K. (1994) *Building Competences in the Firm: Lessons from Japanese and European Optoelectronics*, London: Macmillan.

Morgan, G. (1986) *Images of Organisation*, London: Sage.

Morgan, G. (1988a) *Images of Organization*, London: Sage.

Morgan, G. (1988b) *Riding the Waves of Change*, San Francisco, CA: Jossey-Bass.

Morgan, G. (1997) *Images of Organization*, London: Sage.

Mueller, F. (1996) 'Human resources as strategic assets: an evolutionary resource-based theory', *Journal of Management Studies*, 33:6, 757–85.

Mueller, F. (1998) 'Human resources as strategic assets: an evolutionary resource-based theory', in C. Mabey, G. Salaman and J. Storey (eds), *Strategic Human Resource Management: A Reader*, London: Sage.

Needle, D. (2001) 'Organizational aspects of business', in G. Salaman (ed.), *Understanding Business: Organisations*, London: Routledge.

Nelson, R. and Winter, S. G. (1982) *An Evolutionary Theory of Economic Change*, Cambridge, MA: Belknap Press.

Nonaka, I. (1988) 'Creating organisational order out of chaos: self-renewal in Japanese firms', *California Management Review*, Spring, 57–74.

Nonaka, I. (1991) 'The knowledge-creating company', *Harvard Business Review*, Nov.–Dec., 96–104.

Nonaka, I. and Takeuchi, H. (1995) *The Knowledge-Creating Company*, Oxford: Oxford University Press.

Nonaka, I., and Takeuchi, H. (1998) 'The knowledge-creating company', in C. Mabey, G. Salaman and J. Storey (eds), *Strategic Human Resource Management: A Reader*, London: Sage.

Ogbonna, E. (1992) 'Organizational culture and human resources management: dilemmas and contradictions', in P. Blyton and P. Turnbull (eds), *Reassessing Human Resource Management*, London: Sage.

Ohmae, K. (1982) *The Mind of the Strategist*, New York: McGraw Hill.

Ouchi, W. G. (1981) *Theory Z: How American Business Can Meet the Japanese Challenge*, Reading, MA: Addison-Wesley.

Pavitt, K. (1989) *What Do We Know about the Usefulness of Science? The Case for Diversity*, DRC Discussion Paper 65, Science Policy Research Unit: University of Sussex.

Pedlar, M., Burgoyne, J. and Boydell, T. (1991) *The Learning Company: A Strategy for Sustainable Development*, Maidenhead: McGraw Hill.

Penrose E. (1959) *The Theory of the Growth of the Firm*, Oxford: Oxford University Press.

Peteraf, M. (1993) 'The cornerstones of competitive advantage: a resource-based view', *Strategic Management Journal*, 14, 179–91.

Peters, T. (1978) 'Symbols, patterns and settings', *Organizational Dynamics*, 9:2, 3–23.

Peters, T. (1987) *Thriving on Chaos*, Basingstoke: Macmillan.

Peters, T. (1989) 'New products, new markets, new competition, new thinking', *The Economist*, 4 Mar.

Peters, T. J. and Waterman, R. H. (1982) *In Search of Excellence: Lessons from America's Best-Run Companies*, New York: Harper & Row.

Pettigrew, A. (1973) *The Politics of Organisational Decision-Making*, London: Tavistock.

Pettigrew, A. (1988) 'Introduction: researching strategic change', in A. Pettigrew (ed.), *The Management of Strategic Change*, Oxford: Blackwell.

Pettigrew, A. and Whipp, R. (1991) *Managing Change for Competitive Success*, Oxford: Blackwell.

Pfeffer, J. (1981) 'Management as symbolic action', in L. L. Cummings and B. M. Shaw (eds), *Research in Organisational Behaviour*, vol. 4, Greenwich, CT: JAI Press.

Pollard, S. (1965) *The Genesis of Modern Management*, London: Edward Arnold.

Polyani, M. (1966) *The Tacit Dimension*, New York: Doubleday.

Porter, M. E. (1985) *Competitive Advantage*, New York: The Free Press.

Porter, M. E. (1996) 'What is strategy?', *Harvard Business Review*, Nov.–Dec., 61–78.

Prahalad, C. K. and Bettis, R. A. (1986) 'The dominant logic: a new linkage between diversity and performance', *Scientific Management Journal*, 7:6, 485–501.

Prahalad, C. K. and Hamel, G. (1990) 'The core competences of the corporation', *Harvard Business Review*, May–June, 79–91.

Prahalad, C. K. and Hamel, G. (1994) 'Strategy as a field: why search for a new paradigm?', *Strategic Management Journal*, 15, 5–16.

Presthus R. (1979), *The Organisational Society*, London: Macmillan.

Prospect Centre (1988) *Strategies and People*, Kingston: Prospect Centre.

Pugh, D. and Hickson, D. (1976) *Organizational Structure in its Context: The Aston Programme 1*, Saxon House.

Purcell, J. (1989) 'The impact of corporate strategy on human resource management', in J. Storey (ed.), *New Perspectives on Human Resource Management*, London: Routledge.

Putnam, W. J. (1993) *Cooperative Learning and Strategies for Inclusion: Celebrating Diversity in the Classroom*, Baltimore: Paul H. Brookes.

Quinn, J. B. (1978) 'Strategic change: logical incrementalism', *Sloan Management Review*, 1, 20.

Quinn, J. B. (1985) 'Managing innovation: controlled chaos', *Harvard Business Review*, 53 (May–June), 73–84.

Quinn, J. B. (1992) *Intelligent Enterprise: A Knowledge and Service Based Paradigm for Industry*, New York: The Free Press.

Ramsay, H. (1996) 'Managing sceptically: a critique of organizational fashion', in S. Clegg and G. Palmer (eds), *The Politics of Management Knowledges*, London: Sage.

Roberts, P. (1992) 'Human resource strategies and the management of change', in *B884 Human Resource Strategies*, Supplementary Readings, Book 1, Milton Keynes: Open University Press, 18–38.

Rose, N. (1995) 'Identity, genealogy, history', in S. Hall and P. du Gay (eds), *Questions of Cultural Identity*, London: Sage.

Rowland, K., and Summers, S. (1981) 'Human resource planning: a second look', *Personnel Administration*, Dec., 73–80.

Rumelt R. (1976) *Strategy, Structure and Economic Performance*, Cambridge, MA: Harvard Business School Press.

Rumelt, R. (1984) 'Toward a strategic theory of the firm', in R. Lamb (ed.), *Competitive Strategic Management*, Englewood Cliffs, NJ: Prentice-Hall.

Rumelt, R. (1991) 'How much does industry matter?', *Strategic Management Journal*, 12:3, 167–85.

Rumelt, R. (1995) 'The evaluation of business strategy', in H. Mintzberg, B. J. Quinn and S. Ghoshal, *The Strategy Process*, Hemel Hempstead: Prentice-Hall.

Rumelt, R. (1998) 'Evaluating business strategy', in H. Mintzberg, B. J. Quinn and S. Ghoshal (eds), *The Strategy Process*, Hemel Hempstead: Prentice-Hall.

Rumelt, R., Schendel, D. and Teece, D. (1991) 'Strategic management and economics', *Strategic Management Journal*, 12 (Winter special issue), 5–29.

Sackmann, S. (1990) 'Managing organisation culture: dreams and possibilities', in J. Anderson (ed.), *Communication Yearbook*, vol. 13, Newbury Park, CA.

Sackmann, S. (1992) 'Culture and subcultures: an analysis of organisational knowledge', *Administrative Science Quarterly*, 37, 140–61.

Salaman, G., Cameron, S., Hamblin, H., Lies P., Mabey C. and Thompson K. (eds) (1992) *Human Resource Strategies*, London: Sage.

Salaman, J. G. and Storey, J. (2002) 'Managers' theories about the process of innovation', *Journal of Management Studies*, 39:2, 147–65.

Scarborough, H. (ed.) (1996) *The Management of Expertise*, Management, Work and Organisations series, Basingstoke: Macmillan.

Schafer, M. and Crichlow, S. (1996) 'Antecedents of groupthink: a quantitative study', *Journal of Conflict Resolution*, 40:3, 415–35.

Schuler, R. S. and Jackson S. E. (1987) 'Linking competitive strategies with human resource management practices', *Academy of Management Executive*, 1:3, 207–19.

Schumpeter, J. A. (1934) *The Theory of Economic Development*, Cambridge, MA: Harvard University Press.

Schumpeter, J. A. (1942) *Capitalism, Socialism and Democracy*, New York: Harper Bros.

Schwenk, C. (1988) 'The cognitive perspective on strategic decision-making', *Journal of Management Studies*, 25:1, 41–55.

Sebald, W. G. (2001) *Austerlitz*, trans. Anthea Bell, New York: Random House.

Segal-Horn, S. (1995) 'Core competence and international strategy in service multi-nationals', in C. Armistead and R. Teare (eds), *Services Management: New Directions and Perspectives*, London: Cassell.

Senge, P. (1990a) *The Fifth Discipline: The Art and Practice of the Learning Organisation*, London: Century Business.

Senge, P. (1990b) 'The leader's new work', *Sloan Management Review*, 32:1, 7–23.

Severance, D. G. and Passino, J. H. (1986) *Senior Management Attitudes toward Strategic Change in US Manufacturing Companies*, Ann Arbor, MI: University of Michigan Press.

Sharfman, M. and Dean, J. (1997) 'Flexibility in strategic decision-making: informational and ideological perspectives', *Journal of Management Studies*, 34:2, 191–217.

Silver, J. (1987) 'The ideology of excellence: management and neoconservatism', *Studies in Political Economy*, 24 (Autumn), 105–29.

Silverman, D. (1970) *The Theory of Organisations*, London: Heinemann.

Simon, H. A. (1952) 'Some further requirements of bureaucratic theory', in R. K. Merton, A. P. Grey, B. Hockey and H. C. Selvin (eds), *Reader in Bureaucracy*, New York: Free Press.

Simon, H. A. (1957) *Administrative Behaviour* (2nd edn), New York: Macmillan.

Slatter, S. (1984) *Corporate Recovery*, Harmondsworth: Penguin.

Smircich, L. (1983) 'Concepts of culture and organisational analysis', *Administrative Science Quarterly*, 28, 339–58.

Smircich, L. and Stubbart. C, (1985) 'Strategic management in an enacted world', *Academy of Management Review*, 10:4, 724–36.

Smith-Cook, D., and Ferris, G. R. (1986) 'Strategic human resource management and form effectiveness in industries experiencing decline', *Human Resource Management*, 25:3, 441–58.

Snell, R. S. (2001) 'Moral foundations and their connections with characteristics of learning organizations, *Human Relations*, 54:3, 321–44.

Sparrow, P. (1994) 'The psychology of strategic management', in C. L. Cooper and I. T. Robertson (eds), *International Review of Industrial and Organisational Psychology, 9*, Chichester: Wiley.

Stalk, G., Evans, P. and Shulman, L. E. (1992) 'Competing on capabilities: the new rules of corporate strategy', *Harvard Business Review*, Mar.–Apr., 57–69.

Stevenson, H. H. (1976) 'Defining corporate strengths and weaknesses', *Sloan Management Review*, Spring, 51–68.

Stopford, J. and Baden-Fuller, C. (1990) 'Corporate rejuvenation', *Journal of Management Studies*, 27:4, 399–415.

Storey, J. and Salaman, G. (forthcoming) *Managing Innovation*.

Storey, J. and Sisson, K. (1993) *Managing Human Resources and Industrial Relations*, Buckingham: Open University Press.

Strauss, A., Schatzman, I., Ehrlich, R. D., Bucher R. and Sabshin, M. (2001) 'The hospital and its negotiated order', in G. Salaman (ed.), *Decision-Making for Business*, London: Sage.

Stubbart, C. I. and Ramaprasad, A. (1990) 'Comments on the empirical articles and recommendations for future research', in A. S. Huff (ed.), *Mapping Strategic Thought*, London: Wiley.

Teare, R. and Armistead, C. (1995) *Services Management: New Directions, New Perspectives*, London: Cassell.

Teece, D. (1980) 'Economies of scope and the scope of the enterprise', *Journal of Economic Behaviour and Organisation*, 1:3, 223–47.

Teece, D. (1982) 'Towards an economic theory of the multiproduct firm', *Journal of Economic Behaviour and Organisation*, 3, 39–63.

Teece, D., Pisano, G. and Shuen, A. (1990) 'Firm capabilities, resources and the concept of strategy', University of California Working Paper EAP–38.

Teece, David J. and Pisano, Gary (1998) 'The dynamic capabilities of firms: an introduction', in Giovanni Dosi, David J. Teece and Josef Chytry (eds), *Technology, Organization and Competitiveness: Perspectives on Industrial and Corporate Change*, Oxford: Oxford University Press.

Thomason, G. F. (1972) 'Organizational analysis', mimeo, Department of Industrial Relations, University of Wales, Cardiff.

Thompson, P. and McHugh, D. (1995) *Work Organisations: A Critical Introduction* (1st pub. 1990), London: Macmillan.

Thompson, P. and McHugh, D. (2001) 'Studying organisations: an introduction' and 'Re-inventing organisation man?', in G. Salaman (ed.), *Understanding Business: Organisations*, London: Routledge.

Thompson, P. and Warhurst, C. (1998) *Workplaces of the Future*, Basingstoke: Macmillan.

Tichy, N., Fombrun, C. and Devanna, M. A. (1982) 'Strategic human resource management', *Sloan Management Review*, Winter, 47–61.

Ulrich, P. (1984) 'Systemsteuerung und Kulturentwicklung', *Die Unternehmung*, 38, 303–25.

Valentin, E. (1994) 'Anatomy of a fatal business strategy', *Journal of Management Studies*, 31:3, 359–82.

Van de Ven, A. (1986) 'Central problems in the management of innovation', *Management Science*, 32:5, 590–607.

Walton, R. E. (1985) 'Towards a strategy for eliciting employee commitment based on policies of mutuality', in R. E. Walton and P. R. Lawrence (eds), *Human Resource Management: Trends and Challenges*, Boston, MA: Harvard Business School Press.

Walton, R. E. and Lawrence, P. R. (eds) (1985) *HRM Trends and Challenges*, Boston, MA: Harvard Business School Press.

Weber, M. (1964) *The Theory of Social and Economic Organisation*, edited and with a foreword by Talcott Parsons, London: The Free Press.

Weick, K. (1979) *The Social Psychology of Organising*, Reading, MA: Addison-Wesley.

Weick, K. (1995) *Sensemaking in Organisations*, Thousand Oaks, CA: Sage.

Weick, K. and Westley, F. (1996) 'Organisational learning: affirming an oxymoron', in S. Clegg, C. Hardy and W. Nord (eds), *Handbook of Organisation Studies*, London: Sage.

Whipp, R. (1991) 'Change and competition: the role of learning', *International Journal of Human Resource Management*, 2:2, 165–92.

Whittington, R. (1993) *What is Strategy and Does it Matter?*, London: Routledge.

Whittington, R. (2000) *What is Strategy and Does it Matter?* (2nd edn), London: Thompson International.

Wilde, G. J. S. (1982) 'The theory of risk homeostasis', *Risk Analysis*, 2:4, 209–25.

Williamson, O. E. (1975) *Markets and Hierarchies*, New York: The Free Press.

Winterscheid, B. (1994) 'Building capability from within: the insider's view of core competence', in G. Hamel and A. Heene (eds), *Competence-Based Competition*, Chichester: Wiley & Sons.

Wood, S. (1989) 'New wave management', *Work, Employment and Society*, 3, 379–402.

Zimmerman, D. (1971) 'The practicalities of rule use', in J. Douglas (ed.), *Understanding Everyday Life*, London: Routledge and Kegan Paul; repr. in G. Salaman (ed.), *Decision Making for Business: A Reader*, London: Sage.

Index

Aalborg group of economists, 166
Abrahamson, E., 121
Accenture, 76
advantage
    analysing sources of, 73–4
    cost advantage, 134
    see also competitive advantage
airlines, 79, 138
    reservation systems, 79
Akin, G., 63
alignment, 19, 28
Allbrow, M., 165
Amit, R., 72–3
architecture, 89, 130
Argyris, C., 154, 157, 161, 172–4
Arthur, J. B., 64
Asch, D., 137
Ashkenas, R., 31
Aston studies, 42–3, 175
Austerlitz, 150
autonomy, 12

Baden-Fuller, C., 128
Bahrami, H., 178–80
Banbury, C. M., 140
Barney, J. B., 63, 70
Barr, P. S., 163
Bartlett, C. A., 28
Bate, P., 118, 173
Beaumont, P. B., 37, 62, 63
Beer, M., 28, 37, 170
benchmarking, 6, 83, 129

Berger, P., 163
Besant, J., 172
best practice, 119
Bettis, R. A., 162
Bleicher, K., 63
Boston Consulting Group (BCG), 142–4
boundaries, 7, 9
Bowman, C., 137
Boydell, T., 156–9, 166
BPR, *see* business process re-engineering
Brunsson, N., 16, 57, 112, 122
bureaucracy, 4–8, 39–41
    advantages of, 4
    critique of, 7, 11
    dysfunctions, 6, 41
Burgoyne, J., 156–9, 166
Burns, T., 41, 46, 154, 174, 176–8, 181
business planning process, 56
business process re-engineering (BPR),
    9–11
Business Week, 13

Calori, R., 164
capability, 25, 27–33, 36, 70, 83–5, 90
    building, 88–9
    and change, 87–8
    complexity of, 80–1
    core, 70, 71, 145
    distinctive, 72–3, 130–1
    innovative, 86
    link with strategy, 25
causal ambiguities, 74, 76

Champy, J., 9, 17
Chandler, A. D., 5, 28, 76, 86
change, 3, 8, 9, 14, 15, 27–33, 44–5, 123, 157
    academic commentators, 15, 22
    common issues, 44–5
    literature, 13–17, 23
    strategy-based, 32
    structural, 3, 8
    theories of, 24
Child, J., 43
Clark, K. B., 96, 114, 168, 175
Clark, T., 16, 58, 121
Clegg, S., 41
Cohen, W. M., 87
competencies, 39, 68
    core competencies, 75, 85, 145
    distinguishing features, 69
competitive advantage, 72, 80, 83–5, 130–3, 166
    innovation as source of, 139–42
    Porter's generic strategies, 131–3, 137–8
Conrad, C., 14
consultants, 14–16, 22, 44, 57
    commentators on, 121
contingency approach, see fit
core skills, 7
cost competitiveness, 3
Crichlow, S., 106
Crozier, M., 161
culture, 11–14, 36, 55, 112–19, 162–3, 173
Cyert, R. M., 108, 111, 115

Daft, R., 72
Daniels, K., 164
Davenport, T., 9, 10
De Geus, A., 153
Deal, T. E., 63
decision-making, 119
    see also strategy
Delamarter, R. T., 14
Denison, D. R., 63
Devanna, M., 18, 28
Direct Line, 140
Dodgson, M., 172
Dore, R., 120–1

downsizing, 19, 20
Du Gay, P., 123–4, 157
Dunkerley, D., 41
durability, 83
Dyer, L., 64

electronic data systems, 78
employees
    attitude, 11
    behaviour, 35–7
    commitment, 8, 18–20, 32, 62, 181
    values and beliefs, 14
Enron, 184
enterprise, 124, 157, 178
environment, 26, 164, 168
environmental mapping, 28
E–S–C, 25–7, 34–5, 57, 152
Ethiopia, 37–8
    Ethiopian People's Revolutionary Democratic Front (EPRDF), 38
'Excellence' approach, 58
exploitation, 57
exploration, 57

Ferris, G. R., 59
Fineman, S., 164
firm, the, 127
    resource-based theory of, 127
    unitary view of, 10
fit, 21, 28, 34–64
    conscious agency, 43
    core ingredients, 44
    as a diagnostic tool, 61
    literature, 59
    potential difficulties, 56
    strategic, 129–30
    strategy and capability, 21
    structure and strategy, 28, 34–64, 154
    value of, 60
flexibility, 178
Fombrun, C. J., 18, 28
Foucault, M., 120, 122–3
Fox, S., 59
Freeman, C., 140

Ghoshal, S., 28
Gill, J., 16, 121–2
Gioia, D. A., 162

Gospel, H., 121
Gouldner, A., 42
Grant, R., 67, 69, 71, 72, 73, 75, 80–1, 83,
    134, 144
Grint, K., 58
Grinyer, P. H., 145
group processes, 98, 104–7
groupthink, 105–7, 161
growth share matrix, 142–4
Guest, D. E., 15, 29, 58, 62, 63, 156

Hall, S., 120, 123
Hamel, G., 70, 71, 73, 75, 87, 152, 170,
    184
Hammer, M., 5, 7, 9–11, 17
Haspeslagh, P. C., 144
Hedberg, B., 157
Henderson, R. M., 96, 114, 168, 175
Hendry, C., 18, 21, 157, 174
Hickson, D., 42
hierarchy, 78–9, 108
Hinterhuber, H. H., 63
Hodgkinson, G. P., 150
Hofer, C. W., 25
Hofstede, G., 173
Honda, 135
Hopelain, D., 63
Huczynski, A., 16, 122
Hughes, T., 169
human resource management, 45
human resource systems, high-
    commitment, 64
Huselid, M., 64
Hyundai, 134

ICI, 74
information systems, 78, 80
innovation, 47, 49, 52–5, 86–7, 131,
    139–42, 153–5, 170
    complementary, 140
    new technological systems, 141
    radical, 168
    typology of innovations, 141

Jackson, S. E., 47–8
Jaggi, D., 63
Janis, I., 105, 161
Jones, A. M., 157, 174

Kamoche, K., 67
Kanter, R. M., 2
Kaplan, R., 61
Kay, J., 73, 89
Keiser, A., 121
Keisling, P., 13
Keynes, J. M., 24
Kirton, M., 157
Klepper, S., 128
Kluckholn, F. R., 173
knowledge
    development, 8
    management, 75
    sharing, 8
    tacit, 75–6, 80, 86
Kosovo, 65
KPMG, 101
Kuhn, R. L., 59

Lada, 134
Lant, T. K., 115, 117, 163
Lawrence, P. R., 62
leadership, 106, 181
learning, 74, 90, 117, 153–7, 162
    barriers to, 161
    double-/single-loop, 172–4
    interconnected, 169
    organizational, 165–73
    radical, 172
    types of, 171–3
    see also organization: learning
Legge, K., 18, 21, 58–9
Levinthal, D. A., 87
Liddell Hart, B., 102–4, 117
Lippman, S. A., 74
Littler, C., 11, 13
Luckmann, T., 163

Mabey, C., 3, 8, 10, 18, 63
Maidique, M. A., 13
managers, 12, 17, 26, 32, 44, 52–3, 82, 156,
    161, 163–5
    information systems, 80
    learning framework, 117
    senior, 54–5, 59, 75, 168, 174
March, J. G., 57, 95, 98, 108, 111, 115
markets, 123–4, 136, 139
Marginson, P., 59

market
    application of principles of, 6, 7
    free-market system, 5
    moralized notion of, 6
Markides, C., 97, 115, 172
McHugh, D., 12, 13
McLeay, S., 59
Meek, L., 14
Mengistu regime, 37–8
mergers and acquisitions, 101–2
Miles, R., 50–1
Miller, D., 34, 138
Miller, P., 157
Miller, S., 98
Mintzberg, H., 129, 138–9
Mitchell, W., 140
Miyazaki, K., 87, 90
Morgan, G., 55, 118, 166
Mueller, F., 37, 69, 75

Nelson, R., 76
Nike, 7
Nonaka, I., 75, 76, 151–2, 169, 171, 182

Ogbonna, E., 14
Ohmae, K., 147–8
Olsen, J., 16, 57, 122
organization
    adaptive, 150–82
    amnesiac, 75
    boundaryless, 31
    knowledge-based, 32
    learning (LO), 32, 155–65
    mechanistic, 176, 179; features of, 176
    organic, 41–2, 45, 173–82; features of,
        177–8
organizational analysis, 120–1
organizational politics, 107–9

Pavitt, K., 87
Pedlar, M., 156–9, 166
Penrose, E., 70, 127, 154
performance, 24, 25, 92–3, 129–30
    closed approach, 61–3
    improving, 23–33
Peteraf, M., 70, 74
Peters, T., 5–7, 12, 13, 17

Pettigrew, A., 18, 21, 108, 109, 157, 169,
    171, 181
Pfeffer, J., 13
Pisano, G., 167–8, 171
Poole, P. P., 162
Porter, M. E., 71, 127, 129, 131–3, 137
Prahalad, C. K., 70, 71, 73, 75, 85, 162
Presthus, R., 161
processes, 9–11, 36, 109–12
    cognitive, 164
    group, 98, 104–7
Procter & Gamble, 89
Pugh, D., 42
Purcell, J., 60
Putnam, W. J., 166

Quinn, J. B., 75, 97, 147, 156, 170

Ramaprasad, A., 163
Ramsay, H., 121
Reeves, T., 64
Reich, Stephen, 20
replicability, 85
resources, 127
    and capabilities, 73–4, 83–5
    imitability of key resources, 74
risk and uncertainty, 146–7
Roberts, P., 161
Rose, N., 157
routines, 90, 96
Rowland, K., 59
Rumelt, R., 2, 65, 74, 127, 144–6

Sackmann, S., 63, 162
Salaman, G., 11, 13, 16, 58, 116, 121,
    123–4, 151, 157, 179–80
SBU, see strategic business unit
Schafer, M., 106
schema, 163, 165
Schendel, D., 2, 25
Schoemaker, P., 72, 73
Schon, D., 173
Schuler, R. S., 47–8
Schumpeter, J., 140
Schwenk, C., 113
Sebald, W. G., 149
Senge, P., 157, 164, 172

SHRM, *see* strategic human resource
    management
Shuen, A., 70
Silver, J., 13
Silverman, D., 110
Simon, H. A., 110, 113–14
skills, marketability of, 65–6
Slatter, S., 145
Smircich, L., 14, 116, 165
Smith-Cook, D., 59
Snell, R. S., 161–3, 165
Snow, C., 50–1
Somme offensive, 102–4, 106–7, 117
Sparrow, P., 164
Spector, B., 28, 37, 170
Stalk, G., 85, 151
Stalker, G. M., 41, 46, 154, 174, 176–8,
    181
Stevenson, H. H., 81–2
Stopford, J., 128
Storey, J., 47, 116, 151, 179–80
strategic business unit (SBU), 3, 7, 8, 71,
    142–4
strategic human resource management
    (SHRM), 15, 17–21, 28
strategic thinking, 66, 95–124
    rational approach, critique of, 111–12
    rationality, 97–101, 119–20, 124
strategy, 24–33, 93–4
    business, 26–7
    classifications, 45–7, 56
    competition, 127, 129–30
    cost-focused, 134
    cost leadership, 132, 134
    development, 21, 67, 128–47
    differentiation-based, 132, 135–6
    perspectives on, 128–9
    Porter's strategy types, 59
    resource-based, 29, 65–91
    tests, 145–6
    understanding, 24, 25
strengths and weaknesses, defining
    criteria, 82–3

structure, 35–6
Stubbart, C., 116, 163, 165
Summers, S., 59
Swatch, 135
systems theory, 42

Takeuchi, H., 152, 156, 169, 171
teamworking, 6
Teece, D., 2, 167–8, 171
Telco, 47, 49, 52–4
Thomason, G. F., 42
Thompson, P., 2, 9, 12, 13
Tichy, N., 18, 28
transaction cost approach, 77–8
transferability, 84
transparency, 84

Ulrich, P., 63
UK health trust, example of, 39
UK insurance company, typical, 55
UN campaign, 65

Valentin, E., 114, 161
Van de Ven, A., 97

Walton, R. E., 18
Warhurst, C., 2, 9
Waterman, R. H., 7, 12, 17
Waters J. A., 129
Weber, M., 40, 41, 99–100, 120, 124, 151
Weick, K., 162, 164
Whipp, R., 152–3, 157, 169, 171, 181
Whittington, R., 21, 67, 128
Whittle, S., 16, 121–2
Wilde, G. J. S., 147
Williamson, O. E., 77
Winter, S. G., 76
Wood, S., 156
work practices, high-performance, 64

YMCA, 134

Zimmerman, D., 110